P9-DDD-957

cut here

To bypass the Start menu, double-click the program's shortcut icon.

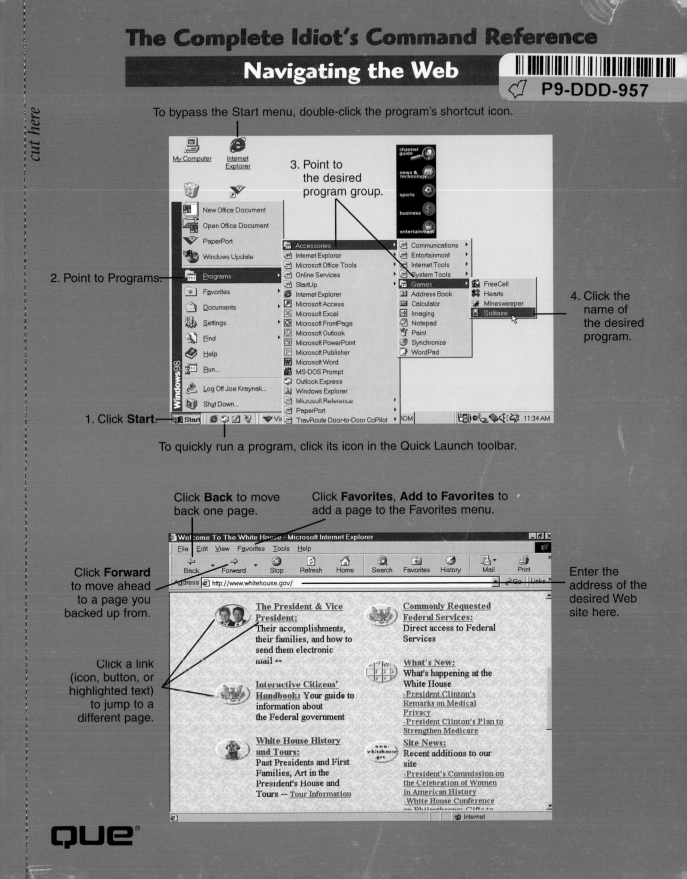

3. Point to the desired program group.

2. Point to Programs.

4. Click the name of the desired program.

1. Click **Start**.

To quickly run a program, click its icon in the Quick Launch toolbar.

Click **Back** to move back one page.

Click **Favorites**, **Add to Favorites** to add a page to the Favorites menu.

Click **Forward** to move ahead to a page you backed up from.

Enter the address of the desired Web site here.

Click a link (icon, button, or highlighted text) to jump to a different page.

que®

Savvy Software Shopper's Form

Copy this form and take it with you whenever you go shopping for software. Read the minimum requirements printed on the software package and complete this form to ensure that your computer can run the software.

Software Requirements

Program Name: _____

Price: _____

Operating System:	Windows 98	Windows 2000	DOS
	Windows 95	Windows NT	OS/2
	Windows 3.1		

Processor Type: Pentium III or comparable
Pentium II or comparable
Pentium MMX or comparable
Pentium Pro or comparable

Processor Speed: _____ MHz

Minimum Memory (RAM): _____ MB

Desired Memory (RAM): _____ MB

Hard Drive Space: _____ GB

CD-ROM Speed: _____

DVD Required?   Yes   No

Display/Graphics: SVGA   VGA
Colors: _____
Resolution: _____
Video Memory: _____ MB

Audio Output: 32-bit   16-bit   Other: _____

Modem: 56Kbps   33.6Kbps
28.8Kbps   14.4Kbps

Special Printer?   No   Yes, type: _____

Additional Equipment:	Scanner	MIDI input	Joystick
	Digital camera	Microphone	Speakers

_____

_____

_____

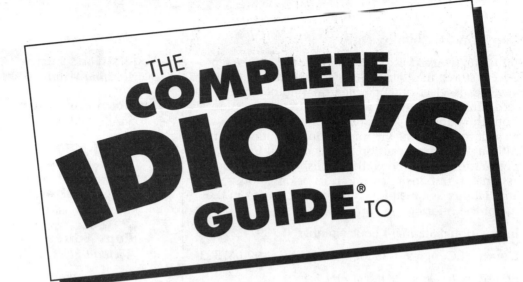

THE COMPLETE IDIOT'S GUIDE® TO

Computer Basics

by Joe Kraynak

A Division of Macmillan Computer Publishing
201 W. 103rd Street, Indianapolis, IN 46290

The Complete Idiot's Guide to Computer Basics

Copyright © 2000 by Que

International Standard Book Number: 0-7897-2299-2

Library of Congress Catalog Card Number: 99-067323

Printed in the United States of America

First Printing: March, 2000

01   00

Trademarks

Warning and Disclaimer

Associate Publisher
Greg Wiegand

Acquisitions Editor
Angelina Ward

Development Editor
Sarah Robbins

Managing Editor
Thomas F. Hayes

Project Editor
Karen S. Shields

Copy Editor
Victoria Elzey

Indexer
Kelly Castell

Proofreaders
Maribeth Echard
Harvey Stanbrough

Technical Editor
Harrison Neal

Illustrator
Judd Winick

Team Coordinator
Sharry Lee Gregory

Interior Designer
Nathan Clement

Cover Designer
Michael Freeland

Copywriter
Eric Borgert

Production
Cyndi Davis-Hubler

Contents at a Glance

Contents

12 Editing and Printing Your Letter 105

13 Designing Personalized Greeting Cards, Banners, and Other Publications 115

14 Creating an Address Book and Other Listy Stuff 125

xiv

Dedication

To my son, Nick, for his perseverance and courage.

Acknowledgments

Several people had to don hard hats and get their hands dirty to build a better book. I owe special thanks to Angelina Ward for choosing me to author this book and for handling the assorted details to get this book in gear. Thanks to Sarah Robbins for guiding the content of this book and keeping it focused on new users. And thanks to Harrison C. Neal for making sure the information in this book is accurate and timely. Karen Shields deserves a free trip to Aruba for shepherding the manuscript (and art) through production. Special thanks also goes to Victoria Elzey for ferreting out all my typos and fine-tuning my sentences. The Macmillan production team merits a round of applause for transforming a collection of electronic files into such an attractive, bound book.

Tell Us What You Think!

As the reader of this book, you are our most important critic and commentator. We value your opinion and want to know what we're doing right, what we could do better, what areas you'd like to see us publish in, and any other words of wisdom you're willing to pass our way.

As an Associate Publisher for Que, I welcome your comments. You can fax, email, or write me directly to let me know what you did or didn't like about this book—as well as what we can do to make our books stronger.

Please note that I cannot help you with technical problems related to the topic of this book, and that due to the high volume of mail I receive, I might not be able to reply to every message.

When you write, please be sure to include this book's title and author as well as your name and phone or fax number. I will carefully review your comments and share them with the author and editors who worked on the book.

Fax: 317-581-4666

Email: consumer@mcp.com

Mail: Greg Wiegand
         Associate Publisher
         Que
         201 West 103rd Street
         Indianapolis, IN 46290 USA

Introduction: Bringing Computers Down to Earth

Computers are the most excessively hyped tool of the 20th Century. Every newspaper and magazine has at least one article about computers or some computer-related industry. News programs and morning shows commonly have a 2-minute piece on some popular, new computer gadget. Entire movie plots are based on digitized virtual worlds, computer scams, or stories about Bill Gates. And we live under the constant implication that without computers, our lives would somehow be incomplete, our children would be dumber, and our institutions would crumble.

This is nonsense. The only way we can become less human, less intelligent is to buy into the hype, to trust computers more than our own human ingenuity, to believe that a computer can teach us more than a good book, and to position the computer above ourselves in the evolutionary chain. To overcome the hype, we need to bring computers down to earth. We must understand that the computer is *our* tool, *our* servant, and not the other way around.

Welcome to *The Complete Idiot's Guide to Computer Basics*

Most computer documentation is based on the assumption that you, the user, are the computer's servant. The documentation lists the parts of the computer and explains how each part works, as if you had purchased a computer to impress your friends and neighbors rather than to perform a particular job.

The Complete Idiot's Guide to Computer Basics is different. Instead of setting up the computer as your master, this book places *you* in charge of the computer. *The Complete Idiot's Guide to Computer Basics* assumes that you want to do something practical with your computer and it shows you how to use your computer as you would use any tool to perform practical, hands-on tasks, such as

- ➤ Typing and printing letters.
- ➤ Designing your own custom greeting cards.
- ➤ Making a personal address book.
- ➤ Automating mass mailings.
- ➤ Sending and receiving email messages.
- ➤ Shopping, investing, and planning vacations on the Internet.
- ➤ Managing your finances.
- ➤ Using your computer as your own personal library.

How Do You Use This Book?

You don't have to read this book from cover to cover (although you might miss some savvy tidbits if you skip around). If you just purchased a new computer, start with Chapter 1, "Setting It Up and Turning It On," to learn how to get it up and running. If you need a quick lesson on using Windows, skip ahead to Chapter 2, "Meeting Windows: Up Close and Personal." If you need to get wired to the Internet, check out Chapter 16, "Connecting to the Outside World with a Modem." To provide some structure for this hodgepodge of computer skills and techniques, I divided the book into the following seven parts:

➤ Part 1, "Firing Up Your Computer: Bare-Boned Basics," deals with the bare minimum: setting up and turning on your computer, dealing with Microsoft Windows, running programs, and warming up with a few games.

➤ Part 2, "Personalizing Your Work Space," shows you how to take control of the Windows desktop (a virtual desktop on which you create documents and play games). Here, you learn how to pick a theme for your desktop, change the background, turn on a screen saver, configure the audio clips, install programs, and give yourself more room to work.

➤ Part 3, "Creating Letters and Greeting Cards," teaches you everything you need to know to type a letter, change the type size and style, center text, and print your letter. Here, you also learn how to use a desktop publishing program to design and print custom greeting cards, flyers, and banners.

➤ Part 4, "Getting Wired on the Internet," launches you into the world of telecommunications. In this part, find out how to select and install a modem, connect to an online service, surf the Internet, send and receive electronic mail, and much more.

➤ Part 5, "Managing Your Finances," shows you how to use your computer to manage your checking account, pay bills online, create your own budget, and even track your investments.

➤ Part 6, "Kids and Other Family Stuff," helps you successfully and safely introduce your computer to your family. Here, you learn where to find the best games and educational software, safely introduce kids to the Internet, make your own digital photo album, and even trace your family's roots.

➤ Part 7, "Maintaining Your Investment," acts as your computer maintenance guide. Here, you learn how and when to clean your computer and how to give your computer regular tune-ups to keep it running like new.

How We Do Things in This Part of the Country

I used several conventions in this book to make the book easier to use. For example, when you need to type something, here's how it will appear:

type this

Just type what it says. It's as simple as that.

Likewise, if I tell you to select or click a command, the command appears **bold**. This enables you to quickly scan a series of steps without having to reread all the text.

If you want to understand more about the command you're typing, you can find some background information in boxes. There are five kinds of boxes in this book. They're distinguished by special icons that help you learn just what you need:

Panic Attack

You did everything right, but the same error message keeps popping up on your screen or, worse yet, nothing happens. When your computer or program does the unexpected, look to the panic attack sidebar for an explanation and a fix.

Inside Tip

When you've been in the computer business for as long as I have, you learn better ways to perform the same tasks and pick up information that helps you avoid common pitfalls. To share in this wealth of knowledge, check out the Inside Tips.

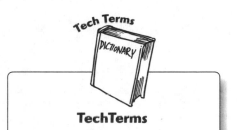

Whoa!

Before you press that button, check out the Whoa! sidebar for precautionary notes. Chances are that I've made the same mistake myself. Let me tell you how to avoid the same blunder.

TechTerms

In the computer industry, jargon and cryptic acronyms rule. When a computer term baffles you or an acronym annoys you, look to the TechTerms sidebar for a plain English definition.

Computer Cheats

Do the steps required to perform a simple computer task seem convoluted? Then, they probably are. Software programs commonly have hidden shortcuts that help you perform a task more efficiently. Look for the Computer Cheats sidebar for tips from the masters.

Part 1

Firing Up Your Computer: Bare-Boned Basics

Right after you purchase a car, the salesperson sits you down behind the wheel and shows you how to work the controls. You learn the essentials, such as how to tune the radio, activate cruise control, adjust the seat, and work the headlights and windshield wipers.

When you purchase a computer—a much more complicated piece of machinery—you're on your own. You get several boxes containing various gadgets and cables, and it's up to you to figure out how to connect everything, turn it on, and start using it.

To make up for this lack of guidance, this part acts as your personal tutor, leading you step-by-step through the process of setting up and starting your computer and using the controls (the keyboard and mouse) to run programs and enter commands.

Chapter 1

Setting It Up and Turning It On

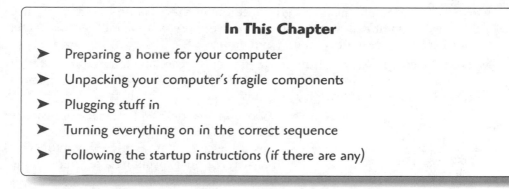

In This Chapter

➤ Preparing a home for your computer

➤ Unpacking your computer's fragile components

➤ Plugging stuff in

➤ Turning everything on in the correct sequence

➤ Following the startup instructions (if there are any)

Bringing home your first computer is nearly as exhilarating and worrisome as adopting a puppy. You're excited, but you really don't know what to expect or how to get started. Where should you set up your computer? How do you connect everything? What's the proper sequence for turning on the parts? How do you respond to the questions that appear onscreen the first time you start the computer?

This chapter shows you what to expect. Here, you learn how to prepare a space for your computer, set it up, and turn on everything in the correct sequence. This chapter also provides plenty of tips and tricks to help you make sure you received everything you ordered, to test your computer, and to answer any questions the computer asks you the first time you start it.

Finding a Comfortable Home for Your Computer

Your home seems spacious until you take delivery of a new sofa or entertainment center. Then you just can't figure out how you're going to wedge that new piece into your existing collection. Likewise, few people think of where they're going to place their computer until they bring it into their home or office. In their haste to get the computer up and running, they may place the computer on a rickety card table in a dank room, where it sits until they get the time and money to set it up properly.

This is a risky strategy. Perching your computer on unstable furniture in a damp or dusty room can significantly reduce its life expectancy—not to mention your enjoyment of the computer. Think ahead and prepare your computer area *before* you start connecting components:

➤ Think about how you're going to use the computer. If you intend to use the computer as a tool for the family, don't stick it in the basement next to that treadmill you never use. Place it in a room that's convenient for everyone and where you can supervise your kids.

➤ House the computer next to a grounded outlet that's *not* on the same circuit as a clothes dryer, air conditioner, or other power-hungry appliance. Power fluctuations can damage your computer and destroy files.

➤ Keep the computer away from magnetic fields created by fans, radios, large speakers, air conditioners, microwave ovens, and other appliances. Magnetic fields can mess up the display and erase data from your disks.

➤ Choose an area near a phone jack or install an additional jack for your modem. (If you purchased the computer mainly for working on the Internet, consider installing a separate phone line for your modem.)

➤ Place your computer in an environment that is clean, dry, cool, and out of direct sunlight. If you have no choice, cover the computer after turning it off to keep it clean. (Don't cover it when the power's on; it needs to breathe.)

➤ To reduce glare from the monitor, make sure it doesn't directly face a window or other source of bright light. Otherwise, the glare will make it difficult for you to see the screen.

➤ Give the computer room to breathe. The computer has fans and vents to keep it cool. If you block the vents, the computer might overheat.

Inside Tip

Test the Outlet

If you're in an old house and you're not sure whether the outlet is grounded, go to the hardware store and buy an outlet tester; it has indicator lights that show when the outlet is properly grounded.

Get a Surge Suppressor

To prevent lightning damage to your computer (which is usually excluded from manufacturer warranties), plug all your computer components into a high-quality surge suppressor. The surge suppressor should have a UL rating of 400 or less, an energy-absorption rating of 400 or more, and a warranty that covers damage to the surge suppressor *and* to your computer.

Unpacking Your New Toys

When you bring your computer home (or when it's delivered), you will be tempted to tear into the boxes and unpack everything. Before you do, read the following list of precautions for unpacking and connecting your equipment:

➤ Take your time. It's easy to get flustered and make mistakes when you're in a hurry.

➤ Clear all drinks from the work area. You don't want to spill anything on your new computer.

➤ Don't force anything. Plugs should slide easily into outlets. If you have to force something, the prongs are probably not aligned with the holes they're supposed to go into. Forcing the plug will break the prongs.

➤ Don't turn on *anything* until *everything* is connected. On some computers, you can safely plug in devices while the power is on, but check the manual to make sure.

➤ When unpacking your equipment, keep the boxes on the floor to avoid dropping any equipment.

➤ If your computer arrives on a cold day, give the components time (two to three hours) to adjust to the temperature and humidity in the room. Any condensation needs to dissipate before you turn on the power.

➤ Don't cut the boxes. Carefully peel off the packing tape. This serves two purposes: It reduces the risk of hacking through a cable or scratching a device, and it keeps the boxes in good condition in case you have to return a device to the manufacturer.

➤ If you have trouble pulling a device, such as a monitor, out of the box, turn the box on its side and slide the device out onto the floor. Don't flip the box over and pull the box off the device.

➤ Save all the packing material, including the Styrofoam and bubble wrap. Many manufacturers accept returns only if you return the device as it was originally packed. The packing material is also useful if you need to move your computer to a different home or office later.

➤ Read the packing list(s) thoroughly to make sure you received everything you ordered. If something is missing, contact the manufacturer or dealer *immediately*.

➤ Find all the cables. The cables are often stored in a separate compartment at the bottom of the box. They're easy to overlook. (Some cables, including the all-important printer cable, may not be included.)

➤ Inspect the cables. Look for cuts in the cables and check for bent pins on the connectors. Although you can straighten the pins using tweezers or needle-nose pliers, you can easily snap off a pin, voiding the warranty. If you find a bent or damaged pin, call the manufacturer.

➤ Remove any spacers or packing materials from the disk drives and printer. Cardboard or plastic spacers are commonly used to keep parts from shifting during shipping. To avoid damaging your new equipment, remove these spacers before you turn on your computer.

Inside Tip

Don't Forget the Warranties

As you dig through the boxes, find the warranty forms, fill them out, and mail them in. This ensures that if a device goes belly up within the warranty period, the company will fix or replace the device. Taking time now to complete the forms could save you hundreds of dollars down the road.

Making the Right Connections

When everything is unpacked, arrange all the devices on your desk. If you connect the devices before arranging them, you'll tangle the cables. If you have a standard desktop unit, you can place the monitor on top of it. If you have a mini-tower or full tower system unit, you can set it on the floor. (If the floor is carpeted, set the unit on an antistatic pad to prevent static build-up that could damage the sensitive components inside the unit.)

After everything is properly positioned, you can connect the devices. This is where life gets a bit complicated. Connections differ depending on the computer's design and the types of components you're connecting. For example, although most computers include a central system unit into which you plug the monitor, keyboard, mouse, and printer, some newer computers combine the system unit, monitor, and speakers as a single device into which you plug other devices. In addition, newer computers make greater use of USB (Universal Serial Bus) ports, special receptacles that enable you to connect a string of up to 127 devices to a single receptacle. If your computer comes with a USB mouse and keyboard, you need to plug them into the USB ports instead of into the standard PS/2 mouse or keyboard ports.

To figure out where to plug things in, look for words or pictures on the back (and front) of the central unit (the system unit or combination system unit/monitor). Most receptacles (a k a ports) are marked, and some newer systems even have color-coded cables. If you don't see any pictures next to the receptacles, try to match the plugs with their outlets, as shown in Figure 1.1. Look at the overall shape of the outlet to see if it has pins or holes. Count the pins and holes and make sure there are at least as many holes as there are pins. As a last resort, look for the documentation that came with your computer.

Figure 1.1

Look for clues on the system unit to figure out where to plug in devices.

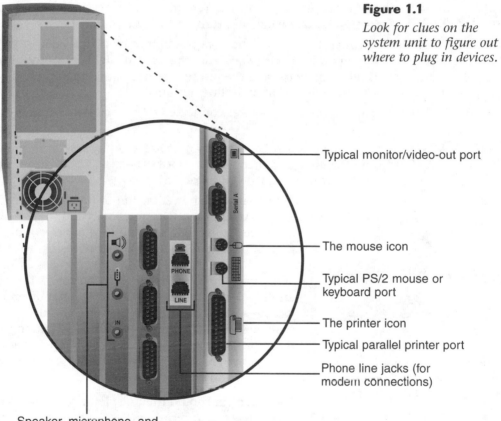

Typical monitor/video-out port

The mouse icon

Typical PS/2 mouse or keyboard port

The printer icon

Typical parallel printer port

Phone line jacks (for modem connections)

Speaker, microphone, and other audio ports

Bringing the Beast to Life

Dr. Frankenstein must have had a real rush just before he flipped the switch and sent that mega-volts jolt through his monster's patchworked body. You get a similar thrill just before you turn on your new computer. What's the screen going to look like? What sounds will it make? How fast will things pop up on the monitor?

Well, you're about to have all your questions answered as you perform the following steps to start your computer:

1. Press the button on the monitor or flip its switch to turn it on. Computer manufacturers recommend that you turn on the monitor *first*. This allows you to see the startup messages, and it prevents the monitor's power surge from passing through the system unit's components. (On many newer computers, the monitor turns on automatically when you turn on the system unit.)

2. Turn on the printer if the printer has a power button or switch (many new printers have no power switch). Make sure the On Line light is lit (not blinking). If the light is blinking, make sure the printer has paper, and then press the **On Line** button (if the printer has an online button).

3. If you have speakers or other devices connected to your computer, turn them on.

4. Make sure your floppy disk drive is empty. If it has a floppy disk in it, press the eject button on the drive and then gently remove the disk. (Don't worry about removing any CDs from the CD-ROM drive.)

5. Press the power button or flip the switch on the system unit. (On notebooks and some newer desktop models, you must hold the button for one or two seconds before releasing it.)

Panic Attack

Install the Ink Cartridges

If this is the first time you're turning on your printer, you must install the ink or toner cartridge. Check the printer manual for instructions.

What happens next varies from one computer to another. Most computers perform a series of startup tests, load a set of basic instructions, and display text messages (white text on a black background) on the monitor. These messages typically disappear before you have time to read them, so don't worry if things seem to rush by too quickly.

Your monitor should then display a colorful screen with a message indicating that the computer is starting Windows. You should then see the Windows desktop, which is shown in Figure 1.2. However, some computers come with their own software that runs a tutorial or displays a special menu on startup.

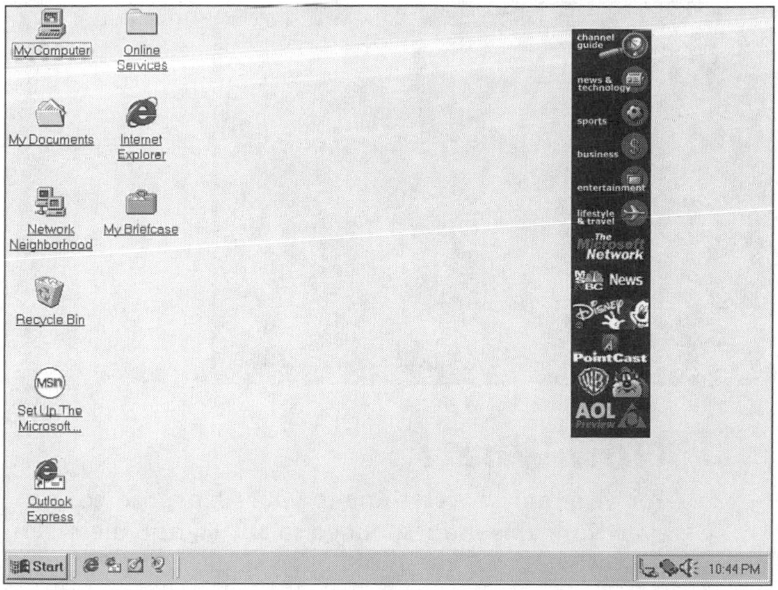

Figure 1.2
When your computer finally settles down, it should display the Windows desktop.

Installing the Software That Runs Your Hardware

You're not the first person to have turned on your computer. The manufacturer or dealer turned it on right after it came off the assembly line to test the computer before shipping it. However, the manufacturer typically tests the computer without the printer and other accessories connected, so the first time you run your computer with everything connected, Windows runs the Add New Hardware Wizard. (A *wizard* is a series of screens that lead you step by step through the process of performing a task.)

The Add New Hardware Wizard steps you through the process of installing the software (called a *device driver*) that tells Windows how to communicate with a particular device. If a device came with its own device driver (on a floppy disk or CD), use that driver instead of the driver included with Windows. The Add New Hardware driver displays a **Have Disk** button, which you can click to install a driver from a disk. Otherwise, you must install the driver from the Windows CD, which should be included with your system. Follow the onscreen instructions, as shown in Figure 1.3, and use your mouse as described here:

➤ To point to an option or button, slide your mouse across the desktop until the arrow points to the desired button or option.

➤ To select an option or "press" a button, position the tip of the mouse pointer over the option or button and then press and release the left mouse button without moving the mouse. (This is called a "click.")

13

Figure 1.3

The Add New Hardware Wizard or Add Printer Wizard leads you through the process of installing a device driver.

Add New Hardware Wizard

This wizard installs the software for a new hardware device.

Before continuing, close any open programs.

To begin installing the software for your new device, click Next.

< Back | Next > | Cancel

Panic Attack

Installation Woes

If you have trouble installing a device, read through the installation and troubleshooting sections in the device's manual. If all else fails, look for a technical support telephone number in the manual. The manufacturer's technical support department may be able to help. However, be prepared to pay long distance charges and to be placed on hold for several minutes.

Now What?

You've arranged everything to your liking, turned everything on, and responded to any startup messages. Now what?

At this point, you're ready to start working (or playing). If the Windows desktop is displayed, as shown in Figure 1.2, you can click the Start button to check out which games and programs are installed on your computer. When you're ready to start running programs and performing basic tasks in Windows, move on to Chapter 2, "Meeting Windows: Up Close and Personal."

Shutting It Down or Leaving It On?

You may be wondering whether it's better to leave your computer on or turn it off when you're not using it. In most cases, leaving the computer on is a good idea. Newer system units and monitors have built-in power-saving features that automatically shut down the devices that use the most power (disk drives and monitors) or place them in standby mode.

Turning your computer on and off places additional strain on the power switches and sensitive electrical components. Each time you turn the computer off and back on, the components cool down and heat up, which, over a long period of time, can cause components or solder joints to crack.

When your computer goes into power-saving mode, the screen may go blank. Don't panic. Your computer is just taking a snooze. The best way to wake it up is to press and release the **Shift** key. Sometimes, you can wake your computer by rolling the mouse around, but the Shift key is more reliable—and because the Shift key doesn't type any characters or enter any commands, it's a safe way to snap your computer out of hibernation.

If you decide to leave your computer on, make sure you save any documents you're working on before you step away. (You'll learn how to save documents in Chapter 11, "I Just Want to Type a Letter!") Saving a document records the document to the hard drive so that if the power goes out, you don't lose your work.

Get an Uninterruptible Power Supply (UPS)

If you decide to leave your computer on all the time, consider purchasing an uninterruptible power supply to keep a steady flow of current running to your computer during short power outages or "brownouts" (those fluctuations that cause your lights to flicker and may force your computer to restart).

The Least You Need to Know

You don't need a degree in computer science to set up a computer and turn it on, but to set up and turn on your computer *properly*, you should know at least the following:

➤ Place your computer in an environment that is clean, dry, and cool.

➤ Plug all your computer components into a high-quality surge suppressor or uninterruptible power supply to prevent damage from lightning and power fluctuations.

➤ When inserting a connector into a port, make sure the pins align with the holes, and never force the connection.

➤ Turn on all the components that are connected to the central unit before you turn on the central unit so your computer can identify the components during startup and you can view the startup messages.

➤ The first time you run your computer, you might need to install hardware drivers (software that tells Windows how to use specific devices).

➤ It's okay to leave your computer on when you're not using it, but make sure you save your work before you step away from the computer.

Chapter 2

Meeting Windows: Up Close and Personal

In This Chapter

➤ First encounters with your new electronic desktop

➤ Mastering your mouse and keyboard

➤ Conversing with menus and dialog boxes

➤ Moving, resizing, and hiding windows on your desktop

➤ Deleting files and folders (and getting them back)

When you start your computer, it automatically runs some version of Windows: Windows 98, Windows 95, or Windows 2000 (or Windows NT for networked computers). But what is Windows?

If you pry off the top of your desk and hang it on the wall, you have Windows...well, sort of. Though its initial appearance may be deceiving, Windows is little more than an electronic desktop that's displayed on a two-dimensional vertical surface—your computer's monitor. It even comes complete with its own *desktop utilities*, including a calculator, a notepad, and a blank canvas you can doodle on during your breaks. This chapter teaches you the basics of how to work on your new, computerized desktop.

Inside Tip

Which Windows Version Do You Have?

This book assumes you are using a relatively new computer that is running Windows 95, 98, NT, or 2000. For performing basic tasks, these versions of Windows are nearly identical. To find out which version of Windows you're running, hold down the **Alt** key and double-click (click the left mouse button twice real fast) on the **My Computer** icon.

Windows Nickel Tour

When you first start your computer, your new desktop appears, very neat and tidy. Several *icons* (small pictures) dot the surface of the Windows desktop, and a gray strip called the *taskbar* appears at the bottom of the screen, as shown in Figure 2.1. On the left end of the taskbar is the all-important Start button, which opens a menu containing the names of all the programs installed on your computer.

If the icon names are underlined, you have a version of Windows that's more recent than the original Windows 95, and Web Style is turned on; you click once on an icon to run its corresponding program. If the icon names are not underlined, you must double-click the icon to run the program. To turn Web Style on, take the following steps:

1. Double-click the **My Computer** icon.
2. Click **View** in the menu bar near the top of the window, and then click **Folder Options**.

Figure 2.1

Initially, the Windows desktop is sparsely populated.

Icons (also called shortcuts)

The Windows desktop

Start button

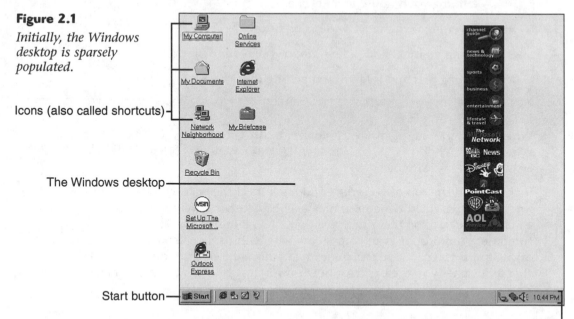

Taskbar

3. Click **Web Style**, and then click the OK button.

4. Click **File** in the menu bar, and then click **Close**.

With Web Style on, you simply point to icons to select them and single-click icons to activate them. With Web Style off, you click to select and double-click to activate.

The Land Where Mouse Is King

Windows was designed to make it possible for managers and politicians to use computers. Instead of having to press special key combinations to enter commands, the person can point to what he or she wants and then click a button to select or activate it. Fortunately, smart people can also take advantage of the mouse by mastering the following basic mouse moves:

➤ **Point.** Roll the mouse around till the tip of the onscreen arrow is over the item you want.

➤ **Click.** Point to something (usually an icon or menu command), and then press and release the left mouse button. Be careful not to move the mouse when you click, or you might click the wrong thing or move an object unintentionally.

➤ **Right-click.** This is the same as clicking, but you use the right mouse button. A couple years ago, the right mouse button was pretty useless. Now it is mainly used to display *context menus,* which contain commands that apply only to the currently selected object.

➤ **Double-click.** This is also the same as clicking, but you press and release the mouse button twice real fast without moving the mouse.

➤ **Drag.** Point to an object and then hold down the left mouse button while you move the mouse. You typically drag to move an object, to draw (in a drawing or paint program), or to select text (in a word-processing program). In some cases, you can drag with the right mouse button; when you release the mouse button, a context menu typically appears, asking what you want to do.

Panic Attack

Hey, My Windows Desktop Looks Different!

The icons you see on your desktop might differ depending on how you or the manufacturer installed Windows and on whether you have additional programs.

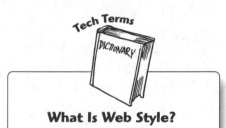

Tech Terms

What Is Web Style?

Web Style makes your Windows desktop look and act like an Internet Web page. On a Web page, you click icons, buttons, or under-lined text (called *links*) to jump from one page to another. See Chapter 20, "Poking Around on the Web," for more information. Web Style is a key feature of Windows 98's "Active Desktop," a design that integrates Windows with the Web.

Similar in shape to the standard two-button mouse, Microsoft's IntelliMouse has a small gray wheel between the left and right buttons, as shown in Figure 2.2. In applications that support the IntelliMouse (including most new Microsoft applications), you can do two things with the wheel: spin it and click it. What spinning and clicking do depend on the application. For example, in Microsoft Word, you can use the wheel to scroll more accurately, as outlined here:

➤ Rotate the wheel forward to scroll text up; rotate backward to scroll down.

➤ To pan up or down, click and hold the wheel while moving the mouse pointer in the direction of the text you want to bring into view. (Panning is sort of like scrolling, but it's smoother.)

➤ To autoscroll up or down, click the wheel, and then move the mouse pointer up (to scroll up) or down (to scroll down). Autoscrolling remains turned on until you click the wheel again.

➤ To zoom in or out, hold down the **Ctrl** key and rotate the wheel. Rotate forward to zoom in or backward to zoom out.

Figure 2.2

The IntelliMouse sports a wheel to simplify scrolling.

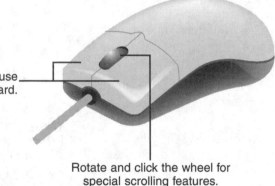

The left and right mouse buttons are standard.

Rotate and click the wheel for special scrolling features.

The Keyboard Is Special, Too

Although the keyboard has lost some of its glory to the mouse, it still retains its importance as the primary tool for inserting text and bypassing clunky menu systems. To master the computer keyboard, you must be familiar with not only the typing keys, but also some of the more unique keys described below:

➤ **Function keys.**   The 10 or 12 F keys at the top or left side of the keyboard (F1, F2, F3, and so on) were frequently used in old DOS programs to quickly enter commands. F1 is still used to display help in Windows and in most Windows programs, and you can assign some function keys to perform specialized tasks in most programs.

➤ **Arrow keys, Page Up, Page Down, Home, and End.**   Also known as *cursor-movement* keys, these keys move the cursor (the blinking line or box) around on the screen.

➤ **Numeric keypad.**   A group of number keys positioned like the keys on an adding machine. You use these keys to type numbers or to move around on-screen. Press the **NumLock** key to use the keys for entering numbers. When NumLock is turned off, the keys act as arrow or cursor-movement keys. Most computers automatically turn on NumLock on startup.

➤ **Ctrl and Alt keys.**   The Ctrl (Control) and Alt (Alternate) keys give the other keys magical powers. For example, in Windows, you can press **Ctrl+S** (hold down the **Ctrl** key and press **S**) to quickly save a document.

➤ **Esc key.**   You can use the Esc (Escape) key in most programs to back out of or quit what you are currently doing.

➤ **Print Screen/SysRq.**   This key sends a copy of your screen to your printer or to the Windows Clipboard, which is pretty useless unless you're a nerd who writes computer books and is hard up for some illustrations

➤ **Scroll Lock.**   Another fairly useless key, Scroll Lock (in some programs) makes the arrow keys push text up and down on the screen one line at a time instead of moving the cursor up and down.

➤ **Pause/Break.**   The king of all useless keys, Pause/Break used to stop your computer from performing the same task over and over again, something that older programs liked to do.

A Special Key, Just for Windows

Many newer keyboards have an extra key that has the Windows logo on it. You can use this Windows key to quickly enter certain commands, as outlined in Table 2.1.

Table 2.1   Windows Key Shortcuts

Press	To
▣	Open the Start menu.
▣+**Tab**	Cycle through running programs.
▣+**F**	Find a file.
Ctrl+▣+**F**	Find a computer on a network.
▣+**F1**	Display the Windows Help window.
▣+**R**	Display the Run dialog box (for running programs).
▣+**Break**	Display the System Properties dialog box.
▣+**E**	Run Windows Explorer for managing folders and files.
▣+**D**	Minimize or restore all program windows.

Turbo-Surfing the Web with an Internet Keyboard

The latest craze in the keyboard market is the *Internet keyboard*, a keyboard that contains additional, programmable keys you can assign to specific Web pages or to your favorite programs (see Figure 2.3). Instead of typing the address of the Web page you want or poking around on menus to find the desired Web page, program, or document, you simply press one of the programmable keys.

Figure 2.3

An Internet keyboard contains keys you can assign to your favorite Web pages and programs. (Photo courtesy of Logitech, Inc.)

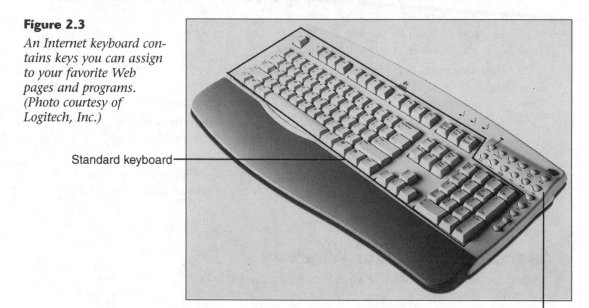

Standard keyboard

Programmable keys

Ordering from Menus and Dialog Boxes

Computer technology hasn't quite reached the point of *2001: A Space Odyssey* (you know, that 1968 Stanley Kubrick flick in which the astronauts actually converse with Hal, the computer that runs the spaceship). However, Windows provides several ways for you to "talk" to your computer by clicking buttons, selecting menu commands, and responding to dialog boxes (onscreen fill-in-the-blank forms).

Clicking Menu Options

Windows' interactive tool of preference is the menu. You'll find menus everywhere: on the left end of the taskbar, in menu bars near the top of most program windows, in toolbars, and even hidden inside objects. To open a menu, you simply click its name, and it drops down or pops up on the screen. Then you click the desired menu option. (To display a hidden—*context*—menu, right-click the desired object or the selected text or image.)

As you flip through any menu system, you may notice that some of the menu options look a little strange. One option might appear pale. Another might be followed by a series of dots. And still others have arrows next to them. Their appearance tells all:

Quick Keyboard Menus

To quickly open a menu without moving your fingers away from the keyboard, hold down the **Alt** key and press the key that corresponds to the underlined letter in the menu's name. For example, press **Alt+F** to open the File menu.

➤ Light gray options are unavailable for what you are currently doing. For example, if you want to copy a chunk of text but you have not yet selected the text, the Copy command is not available; it appears light gray.

➤ An option with an arrow next to it opens a submenu that requires you to select another option. Point to the option to open the submenu.

➤ An option with a check mark indicates that an option is currently active. To turn the option off, click it. This removes the check mark; however, you won't know it, because selecting the option also closes the menu.

➤ An option followed by a series of dots (...) opens a dialog box that requests additional information. You learn how to talk to dialog boxes in the next section.

Whoa!

"Smart" Menus

To further confuse new users, Microsoft has come up with something called the "smart" menu, which lists only the most commonly selected options. To view additional options, you must point to a double-headed arrow at the bottom of the menu. In addition, the menu is designed to customize itself, so options automatically move up on the menu the more often you use them. In other words, you never know where they'll be. In case you can't tell, I hate smart menus.

Talking with a Dialog Box

If you choose a menu command that's followed by a series of dots (...), the program displays a dialog box requesting additional information. You must then navigate the dialog box, select the desired options, type any required text entries, and give your okay—all using the following controls:

Tabs—If a dialog box has two or more "pages" of options, tabs appear near the top of the pages. Click the tab for the desired options.

Text boxes—A text box is "fill in the blank"; it allows you to type text, such as the name of a file.

Option buttons—Option buttons (also known as *radio buttons*) allow you to select only one option in a group. Click the desired option to turn it on and turn any other selected option in the group off.

Check boxes—Check boxes allow you to turn an option on or off. Click in a check box to turn it on if it's off or off if it's on. You can select more than one check box in a group.

List box—A list box presents two or more options. Click the option you want. If the list is long, you'll see a scrollbar. Click the scrollbar arrows to move up or down in the list.

Drop-down list box—This list box has only one item in it. It hides the rest of the items. Click the arrow to the right of the box to display the rest of the list, and then click the item you want.

Spin box—A spin box is a text box with controls. You can usually type a setting in the text box or click the up or down arrow to change the setting in predetermined increments. For example, you might click the up arrow to increase a margin setting by .1 inch.

Slider—A slider is a control you can drag up, down, or from side to side to increase or decrease a setting. Sliders are commonly used to adjust speaker volume, hardware performance, and similar settings.

Command buttons—Most dialog boxes have at least three buttons: OK to confirm your selections, Cancel to quit, and Help to get help.

Get Help Within a Dialog Box

In the upper-right corner of most dialog boxes is a button with a question mark on it. Click the button, and a question mark attaches itself to the mouse pointer. Then you can click an option in the dialog box to display information about it. You can also right-click the option and choose **What's This?**

Bypassing Menus by Using Toolbar Buttons

Although menus contain a comprehensive list of available options, they are a bit clunky. To enter a command, you must click the menu name, hunt for the desired command, and then select it. To help you bypass the menu system, most programs include toolbars that contain buttons for the most frequently entered commands. To enter a command, you can simply click the desired button.

What's This Button For?

Some of the pictures used to iden-tify buttons are no more helpful than Egyptian hieroglyphics. To view the name of a button, rest the mouse pointer on it. (You don't need to click.)

Rearranging the Windows Inside Windows

Each time you run a program or open a document in Windows, a new window opens on your desktop. After several hours of work, it can become as cluttered as a real desktop, making it difficult to locate desktop utilities and documents. To switch to a window or reorganize the windows on the desktop, use any of the following tricks:

➤ To quickly change to a window, click its button in the taskbar. (To hide the window later, click its button again.)

➤ If you can see any part of the window, click it to move it to the front of the stack.

➤ To quickly arrange the windows, right-click a blank area of the taskbar and, from the shortcut menu that appears, choose one of the following options: **Tile Horizontally**, **Tile Vertically**, or **Cascade**.

➤ To close a window (and exit the program), click the **Close** button (the one with the X on it) that's located in the upper-right corner of the window.

➤ To increase the size of a window so it takes up the whole screen, click the **Maximize** button (just to the left of the Close button). The Maximize button then turns into a Restore button, which you can click to return the window to its previous size.

➤ To shrink a window, click the **Minimize** button (two buttons to the left of the Close button). The minimized window appears as a button on the taskbar. Click the button on the taskbar to reopen the window.

➤ To resize or reshape a window, place your mouse pointer in the lower-right cor-ner of the window and, when the pointer turns to a double-headed arrow, drag the corner of the window.

➤ To move a window, drag its title bar. (You can't move a maximized window because it takes up the whole screen.)

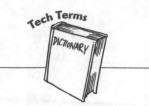

Tech Terms

DICTIONARY

Seeing More with Scrollbars

If a window cannot display everything it contains, a scrollbar appears along the right side or bottom of the window. Click the arrow at either end of the scrollbar to scroll in the direction the arrow is pointing. To scroll faster, drag the scroll box inside the scrollbar in the desired direction.

What's on Your Computer?

Windows gives you two ways to poke around on your computer and find out what's on your disks. You can double-click the **My Computer** icon (located on the desktop), or you can choose **Start**, **Programs**, **Windows Explorer**. If you double-click **My Computer**, Windows displays icons for all the disk drives on your computer, plus three folder icons: Control Panel (which allows you to change system settings), Printers (for setting up a printer), and Dial-Up Networking (for Internet access). To find out what's on a disk or in a folder, double-click its icon. (Remember, if your icons are underlined, click once; double-clicking these icons might perform the action twice.)

Windows Explorer is My Computer's older, more capable sibling. It allows you to perform the same basic tasks you can perform in My Computer, but it provides a two-pane window that displays a folder list on the left and a file list on the right. This two-paned layout enables you to easily copy and move files and folders from one disk or folder to another by dragging them from one pane to the other, as shown in Figure 2.4.

Figure 2.4

Windows Explorer is a useful tool for copying and moving files.

Drag a file from its current location to the desired folder.

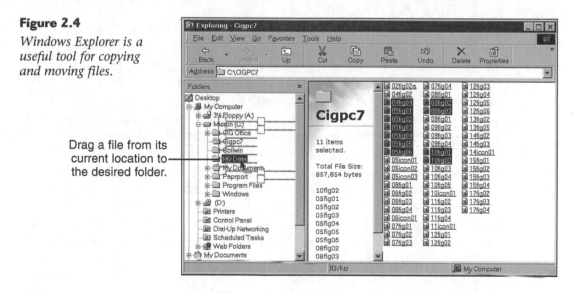

Trashing Files in the Recycle Bin

Windows comes complete with its own trash compactor. Whenever a file or icon has outlived its usefulness, either drag it over the trash can icon (the Recycle Bin) and release the mouse button, or select the file in My Computer or Windows Explorer and click the **Delete** button. This moves the file to the Recycle Bin without permanently deleting it, so you can recover it later if the need should arise.

Recycle Bin Properties

To change the properties of the Recycle Bin, including the maximum amount of disk space it can use, right-click the **Recycle Bin** icon and click **Properties**.

Pulling things out of the Recycle Bin is as easy as dragging them into it. Double-click the **Recycle Bin** icon to display its contents. Click the item you want to restore (**Ctrl+click** to select additional items). Open the **File** menu and click **Restore**.

Help Is on Its Way

If you plan to thrive in the world of computers, learn how to use the help system in Windows and your Windows programs. These online help systems might not provide the detailed hand-holding instructions you find in books, but they usually provide the basic information you need to get started.

If you get stuck in Windows, click the **Start** button and click **Help**. The Help window appears, offering a table of contents and an index. Click the **Contents** tab if you're searching for general information about how to perform a task or use Windows. Double-click a book icon to view additional subtopics, and then double-click the desired topic.

For specific help, click the **Index** tab. Click inside the text box at the top, and then start typing the name of the feature, command, or procedure for which you need help. As you type, the list scrolls to show the name of the topic that matches your entry. Double-click the desired topic. (For a more thorough search, click the **Search** tab and perform your search.)

The Least You Need to Know

Before you begin to run programs, fiddle around with computer games, type documents, or start surfing the Internet, you should master the following Windows concepts and tasks:

➤ When you start your computer, Windows presents you with an electronic *desktop* on which you will do all your work.

➤ With a mouse, you click an object or command by resting the tip of the mouse pointer on the item and then pressing and releasing the left mouse button.

➤ A keyboard is used mainly for typing text, but it can be used to quickly enter commands.

➤ When you choose an option that's followed by three dots, Windows displays a dialog box asking for additional information.

➤ Three buttons appear in the upper-right corner of every window. Use these buttons to open, close, or quickly hide or restore the window.

➤ To manually resize a window, drag its lower-right corner.

➤ To see what's on your computer, click or double-click the **My Computer** icon.

➤ To delete a file or icon, drag it over the Recycle Bin icon and release the mouse button.

➤ For more information about Windows, click the **Start** button and click **Help**.

Chapter 3

Launching Your First Program

In This Chapter

➤ Picking a program from the Start, Programs menu

➤ Running programs right from the Windows desktop

➤ Quickly launching programs from the taskbar

➤ Rearranging programs on the Start menu

An empty desktop may be a rare and beautiful sight, but it's useless. To get something done, have some fun, or at least make your boss think you're productive, you need a little clutter. You need to run a program or two.

The standard (albeit slow) method of running a program is to open the Start menu and click the name of the desired program. (The next section shows you just what to do.) However, Windows provides several more creative and much faster ways to run programs with a single click of the mouse. In this chapter, you get to try various techniques for running programs, so you can settle on the method that's best for you.

Picking a Program from the Start Menu

Whenever you install a program, the installation utility places the program's name on the Start, Programs menu or one of its submenus. To run the program, you simply click the **Start** button, point to **Programs**, point to the desired program group (the name of the program's submenu), and click the program's name, as shown in Figure 3.1.

3. Point to the desired program
group (and subgroup, if necessary).

Figure 3.1

*You can find all installed
programs on the Start,
Programs menu.*

2. Point to **Programs**.

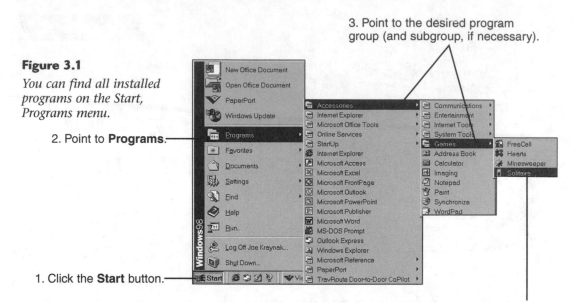

1. Click the **Start** button.

4. Click the program's name.

More Creative Ways to Run Programs

Where Else Is the Program?

For some programs, the installation utility places a shortcut icon on the Windows desktop or at the top of the Start menu so you don't have to poke around on the Start menu to find the program.

Think of the Start menu as a storage cabinet in your basement. If you need something, you can always find it in the storage cabinet, but it's not the most convenient location. You might store your heavy-duty party-size cookware in the cellar, but you store the pots and pans you use daily right next to your stove.

The same is true in Windows. It's fine to run the programs you rarely use from the Start menu or one of its submenus, but if you use a program frequently, you need to place it in a more convenient location and use the techniques described in the following sections to run the program.

Make Your Own Program Shortcut

As you saw in the previous chapter, the Windows desktop displays a few icons, called *shortcuts*, that enable you to run commonly used programs. Unlike bona fide icons that represent files, these "dummy" icons merely point to the original file. Windows displays a small arrow in the lower-left corner of each shortcut icon to indicate that it is not an actual file icon.

If you frequently run a program, you can create your own shortcut for that program and place it on the Windows desktop by performing the following steps:

1. Open the **Start** menu, point to **Programs**, and open the submenu that contains the desired program.

2. Point to the program you want to add to the desktop.

3. Hold down the **Ctrl** and **Shift** keys and, using the right mouse button, drag the program to a blank area on the desktop.

4. Release the mouse button and the Ctrl and Shift keys. A context menu pops up, asking if you want to copy or move the program or create a shortcut.

5. Click **Create Shortcut(s) Here**. Windows places a shortcut icon for the program on the desktop.

Inside Tip

Safely Deleting Shortcuts

Deleting a shortcut does not delete the original file it points to. However, deleting an actual file or program icon does delete the corresponding document or program file.

To quickly arrange icons on the desktop, right-click a blank area of the desktop, point to **Arrange Icons**, and click **Auto Arrange**. (If you turn the Auto Arrange feature off, you can drag icons anywhere on the desktop.)

Run Programs from Your Keyboard

You don't need a fancy programmable keyboard to have quick keyboard access to your programs. Windows lets you program any standard keyboard to run programs with a single key press. But first, you must assign a keystroke to the desired program. To do so, follow these steps:

1. Right-click the program's icon and choose **Properties**. (The icon might be on the Start, Programs menu, on the Windows desktop, or in My Computer or Windows Explorer.)

2. Click in the **Shortcut Key** text box.

3. Press the key you want to use to run this program. You can use any key except Esc, Enter, Tab, Spacebar, Backspace, Print Screen, or any function key or key combination used by Windows. If you press a number or character key, Windows automatically adds Ctrl+Alt+ to create a *key combination*. For example, if you press **A**, Windows will create the Ctrl+Alt+A key combination, and you will use **Ctrl+Alt+A** to run the program.

4. Click **OK**.

31

Make Your Own Program Folder

Did you get a little carried away making your own program shortcuts? If you did, consider storing your shortcuts in a separate folder. It's easy. Just right-click a blank area on the desktop, point to **New**, and click **Folder**. Windows places a new folder on the desktop. Type a name for the folder and press **Enter**. Drag the desired program icons from the desktop over your new folder icon and release the mouse button; this moves the shortcuts to the folder, removing them from the desktop. You can click or double-click your folder icon to view its contents.

Run Programs When Windows Starts

Here's one last trick. If you always run a particular program right after starting your computer, you can make Windows run the program for you on startup.

Here's how:

1. Right-click a blank area of the taskbar and click **Properties**.
2. Click the **Start Menu Programs** tab.
3. Click the **Advanced** button. This displays the entire Start menu and its submenus in Windows Explorer.
4. Click the plus sign next to **Programs**.
5. Change to the folder that contains the program you want Windows to run on startup, and then select the program icon by pointing at it (if its name is underlined) or clicking it (if the name is not underlined).
6. Scroll down the folder list on the left until you can see the StartUp folder.
7. Drag the highlighted program icon from the file list on the right over the **StartUp** folder on the left and release the mouse button.

The next time you start your computer, Windows will start and then automatically run the program you just placed in the StartUp folder.

Moving a Program to a More Convenient Location

If Windows buries your favorite program five levels down on the Start menu, you don't have to live with it. You can move your programs to place them right at your fingertips. Simply open the menu on which the program appears, and then drag the program to the desired location—to the Programs submenu, the top of the Start menu, another submenu, a blank area on the desktop, or the programs folder you created in the previous section. If you drag the program to a different location on the Start menu, a horizontal bar appears as you drag the program, showing where it will be placed (see Figure 3.2). When the bar shows the desired location, release the mouse button.

This bar shows where the program will be placed.

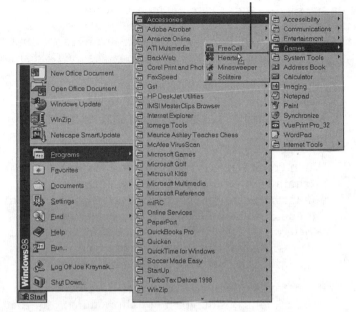

Figure 3.2

You can rearrange items on the Start menu and its submenus.

Running Programs with a Single Click

In late versions of Windows 95, Microsoft introduced a nifty little program launch pad called the Quick Launch toolbar. This toolbar roosts just to the right of the Start button and provides single-click access to commonly used programs. Initially, the Quick Launch toolbar contains the following four buttons:

Launch Internet Explorer Browser runs Microsoft's Internet Explorer, a program for navigating the World Wide Web.

Launch Outlook Express runs Microsoft's email program to enable you to send and receive electronic mail over an Internet connection.

Show Desktop minimizes all open program windows to take you immediately to the Windows desktop.

View Channels displays a list of Web sites you can click to immediately "tune into" the most commercialized sites on the Web.

Not-So-Stupid Taskbar Tricks

Trick 1: Drag the top edge of the taskbar up to make the taskbar taller. Trick 2: Drag the taskbar to the top, left, or right side of the desktop and see what happens. Trick 3: Right-click a blank area of the taskbar and click **Properties** to view additional options.

To add your own buttons to the Quick Launch toolbar, simply drag the desired program icon to a blank spot on the toolbar and release the mouse button. If the button does not immediately appear, drag the vertical bar just to the right of the Quick Launch toolbar to the right to make the toolbar bigger. You can also turn on other similar toolbars or create your own toolbar; right-click a blank area of the taskbar and point to **Toolbars** to check out your options.

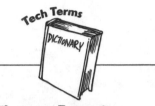

Filename Extensions

Filenames consist of two parts: the main filename and its extension (the last 1–3 characters that follow the period). Windows typically hides the filename extensions in My Computer and Windows Explorer. To view extensions, open **My Computer**, open the **View** menu, and click **Folder Options**. Click the **View** tab and click **Hide File Extensions for Known File Types** to remove the check mark. Click **OK**.

Opening Documents with a Single Click

When you install a program, Windows associates that program with certain document types. For example, if you install Microsoft Word, Windows associates Word with all document files whose names end in .doc. Whenever you click or double-click a document icon that's associated with Word, Windows automatically runs Word and opens the document in Word.

If you frequently open a particular document to edit it or refer to it, consider placing a shortcut icon for that document on the Windows desktop or in the Quick Launch toolbar. Use My Computer or Windows Explorer to change to the folder in which the document is stored, and then, using the right mouse button, drag the document's icon to the desired location. Release the mouse button and click **Create Shortcut(s) Here**.

The Least You Need to Know

All you really need to know to successfully run programs in Windows is how to open the Start menu and poke around till you find the desired program. However, to run programs more efficiently, you should know the following:

➤ You can right-drag a program icon to a blank area on the desktop to create your own program shortcut.

➤ You can right-click an icon and click **Properties** to assign a key combination to a program.

➤ You can drag a program icon from a submenu to a more convenient location on the Start menu.

➤ For one-click access to a program or document, drag its icon to the Quick Launch toolbar.

➤ You can reconfigure the taskbar by dragging its top edge up to make it taller or by dragging it to a different location on the desktop.

Chapter 4

Warming Up with Some Computer Games

In This Chapter

➤ Honing your mouse skills with Solitaire

➤ Feeding your addiction for FreeCell

➤ Playing Hearts against some virtual friends

➤ Finding mines without blowing yourself up

Before you drive your first golf ball or try to ace your first serve in tennis, you take a few practice swings to warm up. This prevents you from completely missing the ball or throwing out your back.

Similarly, before you get into the thick of the battle with your computer, you should warm up with a few games. Windows comes with several games (Solitaire, FreeCell, Hearts, and Minesweeper), which are very helpful for honing your mouse skills and having a little fun in the process. This chapter teaches you the basics of playing these games and throws in a few tips to help you win.

Installing and Running the Windows Games

The first step in playing the Windows games is to find the games. When you or the computer manufacturer installed Windows, the installation utility may not have installed the games. To determine whether the games are installed, click the **Start** button, point to **Programs** and then **Accessories**, and look for **Games**. If you have a Games menu, you're in luck. Point to it, and then click the name of the game you want to play.

If the Games menu is nowhere to be found, the games are not installed. To install the games, take the following steps:

1. Insert the Windows CD into your computer's CD-ROM drive.

2. Click the **Start** button, point to **Settings**, and click **Control Panel**. The Windows Control panel appears.

3. Double-click the **Add/Remove Programs** icon. The Add/Remove Programs Properties dialog box appears.

4. Click the **Windows Setup** tab, as shown in Figure 4.1. Windows Setup checks to determine which components are installed on your computer. The Components list displays groups of related components; for example, Accessories includes Paint, WordPad, and Games. The check boxes indicate the following:

   Clear box (no gray, no check mark) indicates that none of the components in this group are installed.

   Clear box with check (check mark but no gray) indicates that all the components in this group are installed.

   Gray box with check (gray and check mark) indicates that some of the components in this group are installed.

Figure 4.1

You can easily determine which Windows components are installed.

All components in the group are installed.

Some components are installed.

No components are installed.

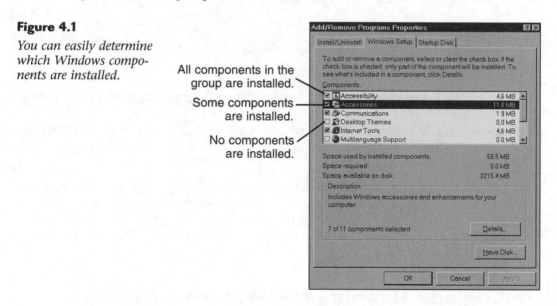

5. Double-click **Accessories**, or click **Accessories** and click the **Details** button.

6. Click the check box next to **Games** to place a check mark in the box.

7. Click **OK**. This returns you to the original list of component groups.

8. Click **OK**. Windows Setup copies the necessary files from the Windows CD.

If Windows displays a message telling you to restart your computer, save all open documents, exit all open programs, and click the option to restart your computer. When your computer starts, the Windows Start, Programs, Accessories menu will have a Games submenu listing the four Windows games.

Using Your $1000 Computer As a $1 Deck of Cards

Whenever I walk into a school or business, I invariably see three or four computers with Solitaire up and running. Workers and managers alike seem to love honing their mouse skills on a daily basis, and Solitaire is definitely the game of choice.

Because the rules of Solitaire are common knowledge, I won't go into boring detail about how to play the game. However, dealing and moving the cards around onscreen requires a knowledge of the basic moves:

➤ When you start the game, Windows automatically deals the cards. To start a new game, open the **Game** menu and click **Deal**.

➤ To move a card, drag it to the desired stack. To move a string of cards from one stack to another, drag the topmost card in the stack to the desired stack, as shown in Figure 4.2.

➤ To flip through the cards in the deck, click the deck.

➤ To move an ace or other card up to a suit stack (in the upper-right corner of the window), double-click the card.

➤ To undo a move, open the **Game** menu and click **Undo**.

➤ To set scoring options, open the **Game** menu, click **Options**, enter your preferences, and click **OK**.

Click the deck to flip through it.

Use the Game menu to redeal and to set scoring options.

Drag a card from the deck to the desired stack.

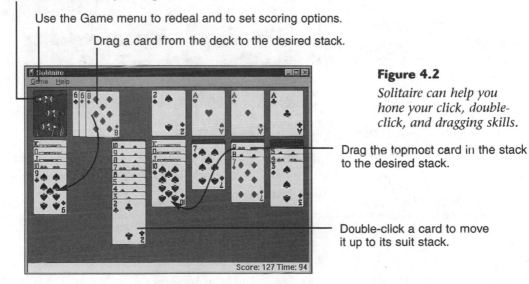

Figure 4.2

Solitaire can help you hone your click, double-click, and dragging skills.

Drag the topmost card in the stack to the desired stack.

Double-click a card to move it up to its suit stack.

Becoming a FreeCell Junkie

FreeCell is reverse Solitaire. You start with eight stacks of cards, all face up, four free cells, and four home cells. To win, you must create a stack of cards for each suit in the home cells, and the cards of each stack must be arranged from lowest to highest, starting with the ace. The free cells act as temporary storage areas for cards, so you can move cards around from stack to stack. If you fill the free cells and have no other move available, you lose.

Win Every Game!

FreeCell is the most addictive Windows game because it is possible to win *every* game you play. As you start playing, you may find this difficult to believe because the game is challenging. But if you play it right, you can't lose.

To play FreeCell, follow these steps:

1. Click the **Start** button, point to **Programs**, **Accessories**, **Games**, and then click **FreeCell**. A blank FreeCell window appears.

2. Open the **Game** menu and click **New Game**. FreeCell deals eight stacks of cards, all face up.

3. Look at the bottom of each stack to determine whether you can move a black or red card onto a card of the opposite color that is one level higher (for example, a red 5 onto a black 6). Click the card you want to move.

4. Move the mouse pointer over the card onto which you want to move the selected card and click. (When you move the mouse pointer over the card, a down arrow appears, indicating that the move is legal, as shown in Figure 4.3. If no arrow appears, you can't move the card.)

Use the free cells
to move cards.

FreeCell places exposed
aces in the home cells.

Figure 4.3

With FreeCell, every game is winnable.

The down arrow indicates
that this move is legal.

You can move one or
more cards from one
stack to another.

40

5. If the card on which you want to play is buried under a stack, you can uncover the card by dragging cards off it and onto the free cells, but be careful not to use up all your free cells.

6. If you have a blank stack, you can start a new stack in its place by dragging one or more cards to the empty stack.

7. When you uncover an ace, FreeCell automatically adds it to one of the four home spaces in the upper-right corner. FreeCell also moves any exposed cards that can be placed on the aces (2, 3, 4, and so on) up to their corresponding aces.

8. If you complete all four home stacks (from ace up to king), FreeCell displays a dialog box congratulating you and asking if you want to play again. If you're a true addict or addict wannabe, click **Yes** and keep playing!

Moving Multiple Cards

You can move a stack of cards to another card. For example, you can move a stack consisting of a red jack, black 10, and red 9 onto a black queen. However, there must be enough open free cells to make the move.

Playing Hearts with Virtual Players

Hearts is a multiplayer game designed to be played on a network; however, you can play against three computer players. In Hearts, low score wins. You try to give your hearts (each worth one point) and the Queen of Spades (worth 13 points) to the other players, or you try to win all the hearts and the Queen of Spades to score zero and penalize your opponents 26 points each.

Personally, I've found this to be the most aggravating game of the bunch; the computer players are ruthless! However, in case you like the thrill of stiff competition, here's how you play:

1. Click the **Start** button, point to **Programs**, **Accessories**, and then **Games**, and click **Hearts**. The Microsoft Hearts Network dialog box asks for your name.

2. Type your name in the **What's Your Name?** text box.

3. To play against the computer players, click **I Want to Be the Dealer** and click **OK**. (If you're connected to a network, you can click **I Want to Connect to Another Game** to play against real people on the network. Hearts will then ask you to enter the name of the dealer's computer.)

Cheating at FreeCell

If you're obsessed about winning every game, and you get in a jam, you can still win. Press **Ctrl+Shift+F10**, click **Abort**, and play any card. FreeCell automatically moves all cards to the home stacks and chalks up another win.

4. Click the three cards you want to pass to the player to your left, as shown in Figure 4.4. In most cases, you want to get rid of the Queen of Spades and any high hearts you're holding. (For every fourth deal, no cards are passed.)

Figure 4.4

Typically, you want to dump your hearts and the Queen of Spades.

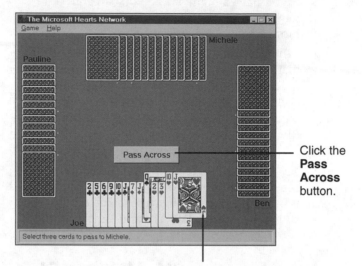

Click the **Pass Across** button.

Select three cards to pass to another player.

5. Click the **Pass** button (labeled Pass Left, Pass Right, or Pass Across, depending on the hand). Each player passes three cards to the left, so you end up with three new cards.

6. Click **OK** to accept the new cards (you have no choice).

7. If one of the other players has the 2 of Clubs, he or she plays it. If you have the 2 of Clubs, click it to play the card. (The 2 of Clubs always starts the game.)

8. Moving clockwise, each player plays a card of the same suit (a club in the first round). If you don't have a club, you can play any card except the Queen of Spades or a heart. The player who plays the highest card of the same suit as the first card played takes the cards and leads the next round. (You cannot lead with a heart unless someone played a heart in a previous round.)

9. Continue playing until you and the other players have played all your cards. When you're done, Hearts displays the score. Click **OK** to start a new hand. (The first person to reach 100 loses.)

Taking a Virtual Risk with Minesweeper

Minesweeper is a game of strategy in which several mines are hidden under a grid of tiles. Your job is to turn over the tiles in an attempt to find out where the mines are located—without getting blown up. Turn over the wrong tile, and you're history!

This may sound a little confusing at first. After all, you're supposed to uncover the mines, right? Well, not exactly. Your goal is to flip over all the tiles *surrounding* the tile that hides the bomb. When you flip a tile, a number appears in the square to indicate the number of neighboring squares that contain bombs. These numbers help you determine which tiles are hiding bombs.

Let's start a game, and you'll see how this works:

1. Click the **Start** button, point to **Programs**, **Accessories**, and then **Games**, and click **Minesweeper**. The Minesweeper grid appears, displaying 64 tiles hiding 10 mines.

2. The first move is the most risky. Cross your fingers and click a tile. May the force be with you. If you're lucky, the tile and any neighboring tiles that are not hiding mines flip over, and numbers appear next to some tiles.

3. Analyze the numbers to predict where a mine is hidden. For example, in Figure 4.5, you know there are mines under the first two tiles from the left in the third row because the number 2 in the fourth row is only touching two tiles. Therefore, those two files in the third row must be mines.

Figure 4.5

Analyze the numbers and use them as clues to determine where the mines are hidden.

You know that this tile is hiding a mine because it is the only tile that's next to a tile containing the number 1.

This tile has one mine next to it.

This tile has two mines next to it.

4. Continue flipping tiles until you blow yourself up, or flip all the tiles except the 10 that are hiding mines. When you successfully locate all 10 mines, Minesweeper displays a message congratulating you. If you mess up, the smiley face turns into a sad face; click the sad face to start over.

Minesweeper offers several options for making the game more interesting and challenging. You can even create your own custom games by specifying the number of tiles and mines to use. You can find these options on the Game menu.

Mark Suspicious Tiles

As you flip tiles, you can right-click a tile that you suspect is hiding a mine. Right-click once to place a question mark on the tile, right-click again to flag the tile, or right-click a third time to remove the flag.

The Least You Need to Know

Do you really *need* anything we covered in this chapter? Well, no, but if you're going to retain your sanity in the world of computers, you had better learn to have some fun. Here's the least you should know about the Windows computer games:

➤ The Windows games may not be installed on your computer. Display the Windows Control Panel (**Start**, **Settings**, **Control Panel**), double-click the **Add/Remove Programs** icon, and click the **Windows Setup** tab to install missing components.

➤ To run a game, select the desired game from the **Start**, **Programs**, **Accessories**, **Games** menu.

➤ Each game has its own Help menu to bring you up to speed.

➤ You play Solitaire in Windows just as you play the game with a real deck of cards, except you need to know how to click and drag.

➤ When playing FreeCell, don't stick a card in a free cell unless you know you'll be able to play it in the near future.

➤ When playing Hearts, dump your hearts and the Queen of Spades on unsuspecting players, unless you're pretty sure you can win all the hearts and the Queen of Spades.

➤ To win at Minesweeper, analyze those numbers carefully. Those who guess lose.

➤ To become more productive in Windows, uninstall the computer games and get to work!

Part 2
Personalizing Your Work Space

If you're like most people, you enjoy decorating your home or office to add your own personal touch. You might paint the walls a different color, hang a few photos of friends or family members, or populate your shelves with knickknacks or beanie babies.

In similar ways, you can decorate your computer desktop. Windows provides the tools you need to change the color of your desktop, pick a theme for icons and mouse pointers, turn on an animated screen saver, create your own icons and menus, and install additional games and other programs. This part shows you how to renovate your computerized desktop.

Chapter 5

Using a Cool Desktop Background

In This Chapter

➤ Jazzing up the appearance of your desktop with themes

➤ Picking your own color scheme

➤ Hanging some self-adhesive wallpaper

➤ Making your desktop look like a Web page

➤ Transforming your desktop into a custom newsroom

Are you tired of that avocado green Windows desktop? Do your shortcut icons look dumpy next to those of your friends and colleagues? Do you want to jazz up your work area? Put it in motion with some animated graphics? Make your Windows desktop the envy of your department? Of course, you do.

In this chapter, you make your personal computer more personal. Here you learn how to take control of the Windows desktop to make it look and act the way you want it to.

Animating Your Desktop with Themes

Spreading your work out on the standard Windows desktop is about as exciting as spending an eight-hour day in a gray cubicle—the surroundings are anything but inspiring. Fortunately, Windows provides a selection of *desktop themes* to revitalize your working environment. Each desktop theme contains a graphical desktop background and specialized icons, mouse pointers, and sounds. For example, the Jungle

Conserve Disk Space

The desktop themes consume more than 30 megabytes of disk space. If you're running low on disk space, install only one or two themes. To install selected themes, double-click **Desktop Themes** instead of clicking the check box next to it. Then, click the check box next to each theme you want to install.

theme places a jungle scene on the Windows background and plays animal sounds when certain events occur, such as Windows startup.

Installing Desktop Themes

To use a desktop theme, first make sure the desktop themes are installed on your computer. Open the **Start** menu, point to **Settings**, and click **Control Panel**. Double-click the **Add/Remove Programs** icon, and then click the **Windows Setup** tab. If the **Desktop Themes** check box is blank, click the box to place a check mark in it. Then insert the Windows CD into your computer's CD-ROM drive, click **OK**, and follow the onscreen instructions. When the installation is complete, you're ready to pick a theme that suits your tastes.

Picking Your Favorite Desktop Theme

Let the fun begin! Take the following steps to check out the available desktop themes and pick your favorite theme:

1. Click the **Start** button, point to **Settings**, and click **Control Panel**.

2. In the Control Panel, double-click the **Desktop Themes** icon. The Desktop Themes dialog box appears, as shown in Figure 5.1.

3. Open the **Theme** drop-down list and choose the desired desktop theme.

4. The selected theme appears in the preview area. To preview the screen saver, click the **Screen Saver** button. (For details about screen savers, skip ahead to Chapter 6, "Turning On an Animated Screen Saver.")

5. Windows plays the screen saver. Move the mouse pointer or press the **Shift** key to turn it off.

6. To preview mouse pointers, sounds, and icons, click the **Pointers**, **Sounds**, **etc...** button.

7. The Preview window appears. Click the tab for the type of object you want to preview: **Pointers**, **Sounds**, or **Visuals**. Double-click an item in the list to display it in the preview area or play a sound. When you're done, click the **Close** button.

8. You can disable individual components of the desktop theme by clicking the name of each component to remove the check mark from its box. Click **OK** to save your settings.

Preview area   Select a theme.

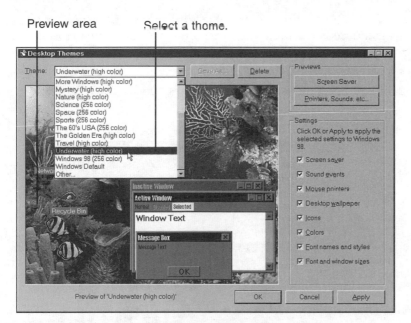

Figure 5.1

Select the desired desktop theme.

Messing with the Screen Colors

A desktop theme makes a nice novelty item, but the color combinations and fonts used in some of the themes can make it almost impossible to decipher the text and get any work done. If you're looking for a more subtle change in the desktop appearance, try tweaking the color scheme yourself.

To try out various color combinations, right-click a blank area of the desktop and click **Properties**. The Display Properties dialog box appears. Click the **Appearance** tab to access the color schemes and options shown in Figure 5.2.

To change the colors and/or fonts used for the desktop, for windows, and for dialog boxes, here's what you do:

1. Open the **Scheme** drop-down list and click the name of a theme that piques your interest. (You may have to try several themes to find one that's close to the ideal.)

2. To change the properties of an object (the desktop, a window's title bar, a button, or other item), click the object in the preview area or open the **Item** drop-down list and click its name.

What a Drag!

If your computer seems a bit sluggish after you turn on a desktop theme, you might want to disable it. Desktop themes require disk space and memory that some computers just can't spare.

3. Set the desired size and color for the selected object using the **Size** spin box and **Color** drop-down list. (Size is specified in points; there are 72 points per inch.)

4. If the object contains text, use the **Font**, **Size**, and **Color** controls to specify your preferences for the text style, size, and color.

5. Repeat steps 2–4 for any other objects whose properties you want to change.

6. Click **OK**.

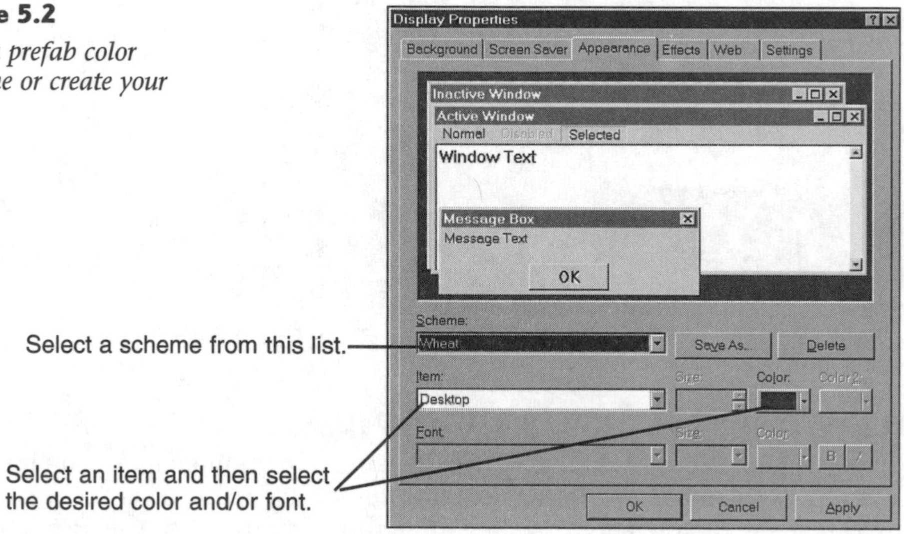

Figure 5.2

Pick a prefab color scheme or create your own.

Select a scheme from this list.

Select an item and then select the desired color and/or font.

Hanging Wallpaper in the Background

Have you ever decorated your desk with wallpaper? Of course not! Maybe a new coat of varnish, some paint, or even contact paper, but never wallpaper. Well that's about to change. In Windows, you can use wallpaper to add a more graphic background to your desktop.

To hang wallpaper in Windows, first right-click a blank area of the desktop and click **Properties**. Click the **Background** tab, if necessary, to bring it to the front. In the **Select an HTML Document or a Picture** list, click the name of the desired wallpaper. If the preview area shows a dinky icon in the middle of the screen, open the **Display** drop-down list and click **Tile** (to use the image as a pattern to fill the screen) or **Stretch** (to make the image as big as the desktop). Click **OK**.

You can use a favorite Web page, your own digitized photos, or computer graphics as wallpaper. Windows can use any Web page (whose filename ends in .html) and any common image file types (.bmp, .gif, and .jpg) as backgrounds. You can draw an image using the Paint program, included with Windows, scan the image (if you have a scanner), use a digitized photo, or even copy a picture from the Internet. Just make sure you save the image in the proper format (.bmp, .gif, or .jpg).

The Select an HTML Document or a Picture list displays the names of all Web pages and bitmapped (.bmp) files stored in the Windows folder. To use a file stored in a different folder or to use a .gif or .jpg file as the background, click the **Browse** button, change to the disk and folder that contains the Web page or image, and double-click its name. To learn how to change to a disk and folder, see "Save It or Lose It" in Chapter 11, "I Just Want to Type a Letter!"

Snatch an Image off the Web

To copy an image from the Web, right-click the image and choose the command for saving the picture. Use the **Save As** dialog box to save the file to the Windows folder on drive C. To save a Web page, open the page in Internet Explorer, and then open the **File** menu and click **Save As**.

Controlling the Desktop Icons and Visual Effects

A quick glance at the desktop icons might give the impression that they're immutable. However, Windows does provide a set of options for controlling the appearance and behavior of these icons and other visual elements that make up the desktop.

To change the appearance of the icons, right-click a blank area of the Windows desktop and click **Properties**. In the Display Properties dialog box, click the **Effects** tab (see Figure 5.3) and take any of the following steps:

➤ To change the appearance of one of the desktop icons, left click the icon, and then click the **Change Icon** button. Click the desired icon and click **OK**.

➤ To display only the icons' names when you choose to view the desktop as a Web page, turn on **Hide Icons When the Desktop Is Viewed As a Web Page**.

➤ To display larger icons, turn on **Use Large Icons**.

➤ To make the icons look a little fancier, turn on **Show Icons Using All Possible Colors**. (This consumes slightly more memory.)

➤ To make windows, menus, and lists appear to spread out onto the desktop (instead of just popping up on screen), turn on **Animate Windows**, **Menus**, **and Lists**.

➤ To make the onscreen type appear less blocky, turn on **Smooth Edges of Screen Fonts**.

➤ To display the contents of a window while you're dragging it across the screen, turn on **Show Window Contents While Dragging**. (By default, Windows displays only an outline of the window you're dragging.)

When you're done entering your preferences, click **OK** to save your settings and return to the desktop.

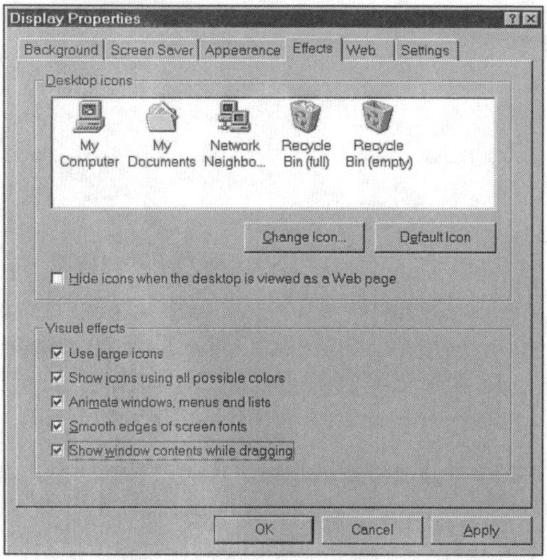

Figure 5.3

The Effects tab lets you change the appearance of icons and other desktop effects.

What's This Web Tab For?

Microsoft was a little subtle about unveiling its plot for global domination. There were no great speeches, no press releases, not even the standard printed manifesto. Instead, Microsoft released a new version of Windows 95 that included a deceptively revamped Windows desktop, called the "active desktop," which it then included in the new Windows 98.

Though nearly identical in appearance to the old desktop, this new desktop includes several features designed to make it more customizable and to integrate it with the Internet (specifically, the Web) and with any of your network connections. Here's a list of what the active desktop has to offer:

➤ **Web Style**   You met Web Style in Chapter 2, "Meeting Windows: Up Close and Personal." With Web Style on, Windows gives you one-click access to your files, folders, and programs.

➤ **Quick Launch Toolbar**   You met the Quick Launch toolbar in Chapter 3, "Launching Your First Program." This toolbar and the whole taskbar–toolbar approach gives you easy access to the programs you run most often.

➤ **Channel Bar**   When you choose to view the desktop as a Web page, the channel bar pops up on the right side of the screen. This bar contains buttons for sites that supposedly have the best content on the Web... in Microsoft's judgment. If you're connected to the Internet, you can click one of the channel bar buttons to quickly access a site.

➤ **Active Desktop Components**   Active desktop components are windows to the Internet. These objects can pull data from the Internet and display it on your desktop to provide you with up-to-the-minute news, stock prices, sports scores, weather reports, and much more. As you will see in this section, you can snatch active desktop components right off the Web.

The Web tab (in the Display Properties dialog box) is your key to mastering the active desktop and turning on active desktop components. If you don't have an Internet connection, or if you're not sure whether you do, work through Part 4, "Getting Wired on the Internet," first. You can then add active components to your desktop by taking the following steps:

1. Right-click a blank area of the Windows Desktop, point to **Active Desktop**, and click **Customize My Desktop**. The Display Properties dialog box appears.

2. Click the **Web** tab. The Web options allow you to view the desktop as a Web page and add components.

3. Click **New**. The New Active Desktop Item dialog box appears, asking if you want to go to the Active Desktop Gallery.

My New Button Doesn't Work!

If your "New" button is ghosted (appears light gray) and doesn't do anything, Web Style is not on. Click the check mark next to **View My Active Desktop As a Web Page** to activate the New button. To make the most of your active desktop, click the **Folder Options** button, click **Yes** to confirm, and make sure Web Style is on.

4. Click **Yes**. This runs Internet Explorer and connects you to the Internet if you are not already connected. Internet Explorer loads the Active Desktop Gallery Web page.

5. Follow the trail of links to the desktop component you want. A page appears, as shown in Figure 5.4, describing the component and displaying a link or button for downloading it. (A *link* is an icon, graphic, or highlighted text that points to another Web page or file.)

Figure 5.4

Active desktop components are readily available on the Web.

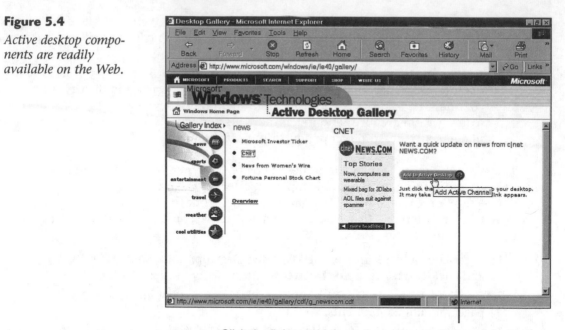

Click the link to add the active component to your desktop.

6. Click the link or button to download (copy) it and place it on your desktop. Internet Explorer displays a dialog box, asking for your confirmation.

7. Click **Yes**.

8. A second dialog box appears, indicating that Windows will set up a subscription for this component. Click **OK**. Internet Explorer downloads the component and places it on the desktop.

Locking Your Desktop Settings

If you share your computer with a colleague at work or with other family members at home, you don't want other people reconfiguring Windows after you have painstakingly entered your preferences. To prevent others from messing up your desktop, you can set up Windows for multiple users. To do so, take the following steps:

1. Click the **Start** button, point to **Settings**, and click **Control Panel**.

2. Double-click the **Passwords** icon.

3. Click the **User Profiles** tab.

4. Make sure the option **Users Can Customize Their Preferences and Desktop Settings** is selected.

5. Make sure both options under **User Profile Settings** are checked.

6. Click **OK**.

When you start Windows, a dialog box prompts you to enter your name and password. Instruct each person who uses your computer to enter a unique name and (optional) password when prompted to log on. Any preferences or desktop settings the user enters are then stored under that person's name, and they do not affect settings that the other users enter.

When a user is done using the computer, he or she should log off. To log off, click the **Start** button and choose **Log Off [***yourname***]** (*[yourname]* varies depending on who's logged on). When the confirmation dialog box appears, click **Yes**. (In earlier versions of Windows, you must choose **Start**, **Shut Down** to display the option for logging off.) Windows restarts without restarting your computer and displays a dialog box prompting the next user for his or her name and password.

Panic Attack

Don't Forget Your Password

If you forget your password, you can still use Windows, but you'll lose your customized settings. Write down your password and keep it in a safe place.

The Least You Need to Know

Although decorating your desktop may not be the most productive endeavor, it does provide some mild entertainment, and it teaches you an important lesson: You're in control of your computer and Windows. To control your desktop, make sure you know the following:

➤ To install or remove Windows features, run **Add/Remove Programs** from the Control Panel and click the **Windows Setup** tab.

➤ To preview and select from available desktop themes, click the **Desktop Themes** icon in the Windows Control Panel.

➤ To access most customization options for the desktop, right-click a blank area of the desktop and click **Properties**.

➤ To change the size, color, and font used for a feature of the Windows desktop, click the **Appearance** tab in the Display Properties dialog box and use the settings available there.

➤ To give your desktop a graphic background, select the desired wallpaper on the Background tab in the Display Properties dialog box.

➤ To prevent other users from changing your desktop settings, use the Passwords icon in the Control Panel to set up your computer for multiple users.

Chapter 6

Turning On an Animated Screen Saver

In This Chapter

➤ Understanding the purpose of screen savers

➤ Turning on a screen saver included with Windows

➤ Using a screen saver to deter corporate spies

➤ Conserving energy with power savers

Have you ever seen a school of fish swimming across a computer screen? How 'bout a flock of flying toasters? A shower of meteors? A pack of creepy crawling cockroaches?

If you've seen any of these animated patterns scurrying about a monitor, you have already witnessed screen savers in action. This chapter provides additional details about screen savers. Here, you learn the real purpose of screen savers and how to turn on a Windows screen saver.

Screen Savers Do Serve a Purpose

On older monitors, if the same image was displayed on the screen for a day or so, the image would become permanently burned into the screen, leaving a faint "ghost" image. To prevent ghost images, programmers developed screen savers designed to blank the screen or display a moving picture when the computer is not used for a specified period of time. When you're ready to use the computer again, you simply roll the mouse or press the **Shift** key to deactivate the screen saver.

Newer monitors are not as susceptible to this problem (commonly called *burn-in*), but screen savers still manage to grow in popularity. After all, a screen saver can make a pretty cool decoration and a fantastic conversation piece.

Screen savers serve another purpose: They deter passersby from snooping at your screen while you're away from your desk. For example, if you play Solitaire all day at work and you don't want your boss to know about it, you can activate a screen saver whenever you step away from your desk. You can even set up the screen saver with password protection, so one must use a password to deactivate it.

More Screen Savers

The best screen savers included with Windows are part of the desktop themes. If you selected a theme in the previous chapter, you have already selected a screen saver. Follow the instructions in this chapter to change the screen saver's properties.

Checking Out the Windows Screen Savers

Windows comes with several of its own screen savers. To check out the selection, right-click a blank area of the Windows desktop, click **Properties**, and click the **Screen Saver** tab. Open the **Screen Saver** drop-down list and click the name of a screen saver that appeals to you, as shown in Figure 6.1. To view the screen saver in action, click the **Preview** button. To deactivate the screen saver (and return to the Display Properties dialog box), roll the mouse or press the **Shift** key.

Figure 6.1

Check out the screen savers included with Windows.

A picture of the screen saver appears here.

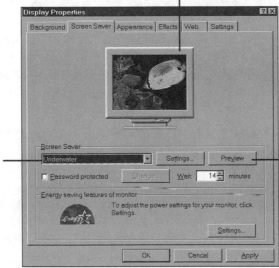

Click the screen saver's name.

Click the **Preview** button to see the screen saver in action.

Even if you installed the desktop themes, your list of screen savers may come up a little short. Some Windows screen savers, including the popular Scrolling Marquee, are not installed during a typical Windows installation. Run Windows Setup again (**Start**, **Control Panel**, **Add/Remove Programs**, **Windows Setup** tab), double-click **Accessories**, and make sure the **Screen Savers** check box is clear (not gray) and is checked. Click **OK** twice to save your changes and exit Windows Setup.

More Screen Savers

When you hit the Internet in Part 4, use a search tool on the Web to search for "screen saver." You'll find scads of cool free screen savers. Save the screen saver to your hard disk (C:) in the Windows\System folder. It will then appear in the list of available screen savers.

The Scrolling Marquee is great for keeping family members and co-workers informed when you're away from your desk. Open the **Screen Saver** list, and click **Scrolling Marquee**. Click the **Settings** button. Drag over the text in the **Text** box, type the desired message, and click **OK**. Click **OK** to save your changes and close the Display Properties dialog box. When the Scrolling Marquee screen saver clicks in, it displays your message scrolling across the screen.

Turning a Screen Saver On and Off

To turn on a screen saver, first select the desired screen saver, as explained in the previous section. Click the arrows to the right of the **Wait ___ Minutes** spin box to specify how long your system must remain inactive (no typing and no mouse movement) before the screen saver kicks in. To specify how the screen saver operates (for example, the number of flying windows), click the **Settings** button, enter your preferences, and click **OK** to return to the Display Properties dialog box. To save your settings, click **OK**.

When your computer remains inactive for the specified period of time, the screen saver kicks in. To turn off the screen saver, simply move your mouse or press the **Shift** key.

Using a Password for Weak Security

Don't let that Password Protected option next to the screen saver lull you into a false sense of security. The screen saver password is designed only to prevent someone from taking a quick peek at your screen. As a deterrent against computer hackers, it's about as effective as locking your bike with a paper clip chain. If someone wants to use your computer, all the person has to do is turn it off, turn it back on, and then disable the screen saver before it kicks in.

However, if you're looking for some free security, the screen saver password is better than nothing. To make the screen saver require a password, click the **Password Protected** check box, and then click the **Change** button. Type the desired password in the **New Password** and **Confirm New Password** text boxes and click **OK**. Whenever you return to your computer and move the mouse or press a key to turn off the screen saver, it will prompt you to enter your password.

Conserving Energy

Computers are not energy hogs, but if you leave your computer on even when you're not using it, it can consume a good deal of electricity over a long period of time. To trim your energy costs and conserve power, consider taking advantage of your computer's built-in energy-saving features. You can activate these features in Windows by performing the following steps:

1. Right-click a blank area of the Windows desktop and click **Properties**. The Display Properties dialog box appears.

2. Click the **Screen Saver** tab.

3. Under Energy Savings Features of Monitor, click **Settings**. The Power Management Properties dialog box appears, as shown in Figure 6.2. (You can also access the power-saving settings by double-clicking the **Power Management** icon in the Windows Control Panel.)

Conservation Catastrophes

Some computers are not very energy-conscious and may not cooperate with Windows' power-saving settings. If your computer locks up when you try to wake it from Standby mode, you might need to restart your computer and disable the power-saving settings.

4. Open the **Power Schemes** drop-down list and select **Home/Office Desk** (if you have a desktop computer) or **Portable/Laptop** (if you're using a notebook computer).

5. Open the **System Standby** list and choose the period of inactivity you want to pass before Windows places your computer on standby. (In standby mode, Windows places the monitor and hard disk drive(s) in low-power mode and activates other power-saving features that your computer supports.)

6. Open the **Turn Off Monitor** list and choose the period of inactivity you want to pass before Windows shuts down your monitor.

7. Open the **Turn Off Hard Disk(s)** list and choose the period of inactivity you want to pass before Windows shuts down your computer's hard disk drive(s).

8. Click **OK**.

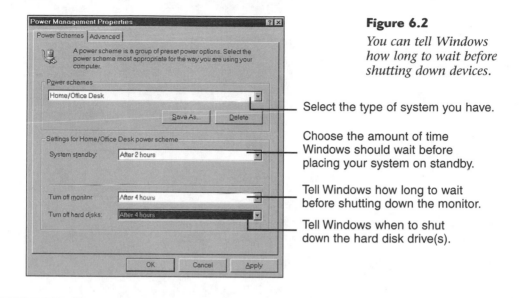

Figure 6.2
*You can tell Windows
how long to wait before
shutting down devices.*

— Select the type of system you have.

— Choose the amount of time
Windows should wait before
placing your system on standby.

— Tell Windows how long to wait
before shutting down the monitor.

— Tell Windows when to shut
down the hard disk drive(s).

The Least You Need to Know

Although screen savers are no longer the essential tools they once were, they're still fun, and they do provide a low level of security. When working with the Windows screen savers, keep the following information in mind:

➤ The primary purpose of a screen saver is to keep passersby from sneaking a peek at your screen when you're getting a cup of coffee.

➤ Each desktop themecomes with its own screen saver, so if you chose a theme, you already turned on a screen saver.

➤ To view the screen saver options, right-click a blank area of the desktop, click **Properties**, and click the **Screen Saver** tab.

➤ To change the properties of the selected screen saver, click the **Screen Saver Settings** button on the Screen Saver tab.

➤ To have the screen saver ask for a password before releasing control of the computer, click the **Password Protected** option, click the **Change** button, and enter the desired password.

➤ Don't rely on the screen saver password to prevent unauthorized use of your computer.

➤ To activate the Windows power management utilities, click the **Screen Saver** tab in the Display Properties dialog box, and then click the **Settings** button under **Energy Savings Features of Monitor**.

Chapter 7

Making Your Computer Play Cool Sounds

> ### In This Chapter
>
> ➤ Testing your sound card and speakers
>
> ➤ Adjusting the volume and balance
>
> ➤ Making Windows play some different tunes
>
> ➤ Playing audio CDs while you work
>
> ➤ Turning your computer into a recording studio

In addition to the beeps and grunts your computer emits at startup, it's capable of producing more refined tunes. When you start Windows, for instance, it ushers itself in with heavenly harp music or some other short audio clip. When you open a menu, close a window, or exit a program, Windows plays a unique audio clip for each of these actions or *events*. If you listen closely as you work in Windows, you'll be able to link each sound with its event.

If you keep listening closely (over several weeks), the sounds may start to annoy you and inspire an overwhelming desire to smash your speakers. Before you take such drastic action, read through this chapter. Here, you'll learn how to pick a different sound scheme, assign different sounds to various Windows events, and even mute your system altogether. As an added bonus, this chapter shows you how to play audio CDs in your computer's CD-ROM drive.

Checking Your Audio Equipment

If you've ever prepared for a speech or presentation, you know how important it is to test your equipment before show time. After setting up and turning on the microphone, you hold it a few inches from your mouth and do the standard "Testing... one... two... testing..." thing. Well, before you start messing with audio clips in Windows, you should test your sound card and speakers to make sure they are operating properly. Here's what you do:

1. Open the **Start** menu, point to **Settings**, and click **Control Panel**.
2. Double-click the **Sounds** icon. The Sounds Properties dialog box appears, as shown in Figure 7.1.
3. Click the name of a Windows event that has a speaker icon next to it, and then click the **Play** button next to Preview.

At this point, Windows should play the audio clip that's assigned to the selected event. If you can't hear the clip, try adjusting the volume (as explained in the next section) or skip ahead to the troubleshooting section to track down less obvious causes.

Figure 7.1

Use the Sounds Properties dialog box to test your computer's audio output.

Click a Windows event that has a speaker icon next to it.

Click the **Play** button.

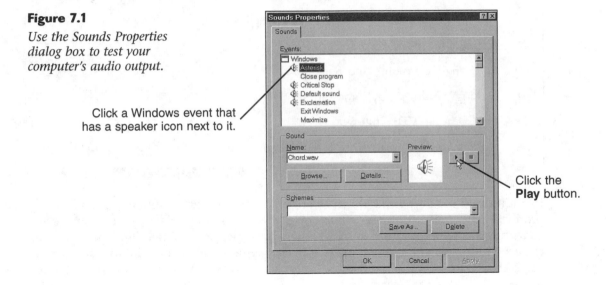

Adjusting the Volume

The big problem with computer audio is that there are too many volume controls. You may find a volume control on the sound card (where the speakers plug in), on the speakers, and in Windows. In addition, if you're playing a computer game that has audio clips (most do), it may have its own volume control!

The trick to adjusting the volume is to start with the obvious controls first: the volume dials on the sound card and speakers. Set these controls to the desired level. If you're not sure which way to turn them, set them at the halfway point.

Next, check the volume control in Windows. Right-click the speaker icon in the lower-right corner of your screen and click **Open Volume Controls** to display the Volume Controls window. Open the **Options** menu and click **Properties**. In the **Show the Following Volume Controls** list, make sure each check box (except PC Speaker) is marked, and then click **OK**. This gives you access to all the available volume controls, as shown in Figure 7.2.

Make sure the Mute option below each control is *not* checked (Mute disables a device). The Mute All option, below the leftmost control, is labeled "Mute All" and can mute all the controls; make absolutely sure Mute All is *not* checked. Drag the slider for each volume control to the desired position. Repeat the steps from the previous section to test the volume settings and readjust the settings as desired.

Drag a Volume slider up to increase volume or down to decrease it.

Drag a Balance slider to the left or right to change the balance.

Figure 7.2

The Volume Controls window lets you set the volume and balance.

Make sure the Mute and Mute All options are not checked.

Tech Terms

System Tray

On the right end of the taskbar is a reserved area that displays the current time, the speaker icon, and icons for other programs that Windows is running in the background. (When Windows is printing a document, a little printer icon appears.) This area is known as the *system tray*.

Troubleshooting Audio Problems

So you've adjusted all the volume controls, and you still can't get a peep out of your computer. What's the problem? Read through the following list to check for the most common causes of computer audio problems:

➤ Are the speakers plugged into the right jack on the sound card? (It's easy to plug the speakers into the microphone or input jack by mistake.)

➤ If you have amplified speakers, are they plugged into a power source? If the speakers have a power switch or button, are the speakers turned on?

➤ Are the audio features enabled for the sound card? In the Windows Control Panel, double-click the **Multimedia** icon. On the **Audio** tab, under **Playback**, open the **Preferred Device** list and choose your sound card. Click the **Devices** tab and click the plus sign (+) next to **Audio Devices**. Right-click the name of your sound card and click **Properties**. Make sure **Use Audio Features on This Device** is selected and click **OK**. Click **OK** to save your changes.

If Windows still doesn't play the audio clips, you may need to dig a little deeper to find the cause of the problem. Perhaps you need to reinstall the sound card's driver, or maybe the sound card is conflicting with another device on your computer. (A conflict occurs when two devices try to use the same settings and/or resources at the same time.)

Fortunately, Windows has a collection of troubleshooters that can help you track down the causes of common hardware problems and fix them. To run the Sound troubleshooter, display the Windows Help screen (choose **Start**, **Help**). Click the **Contents** tab, click **Troubleshooting** (at the bottom of the list), and click **Windows 98 Troubleshooters**. Click **Sound** and follow the onscreen instructions; the troubleshooter displays a series of questions to lead you through the process of fixing the problem.

Choosing a Different Sound Scheme

When you're certain your audio system is working properly, you can try out various sound schemes included with Windows. A sound scheme is a collection of audio clips assigned to various Windows events (such as opening or exiting a program).

To check out different sound schemes, double-click the **Sounds** icon in the Windows Control Panel, as explained in "Checking Your Audio Equipment." Open the **Schemes** list and click the name of the sound scheme you want to try (refer to Figure 7.1). Click the **OK** button.

No Sound Schemes?

If the Schemes list provides only the "Windows Default" and "No Sounds" options, the schemes are not installed. Run **Add/Remove Programs** from the Control Panel, click the **Windows Setup** tab, double-click **Multimedia**, and make sure **Multimedia Sound Schemes** is selected. Pop in the Windows CD, click **OK** to close the Multimedia dialog box, and click **OK** again to start the installation.

Assigning Specific Sounds to Events

Picking a sound scheme is like choosing a vacation package. Each scheme provides all the settings you need for a consistent, thematic sound. If you want more control over which sounds Windows plays for the various events, you can assign a specific audio clip to each event.

To assign audio clips to events, display the Sounds dialog box as explained earlier in this chapter. In the **Events** list, click the event whose sound you want to change. Open the **Sound** list and click the name of the desired audio clip, as shown in Figure 7.3. To preview the sound, click the **Play** button, as explained earlier. To save your settings, click **OK**.

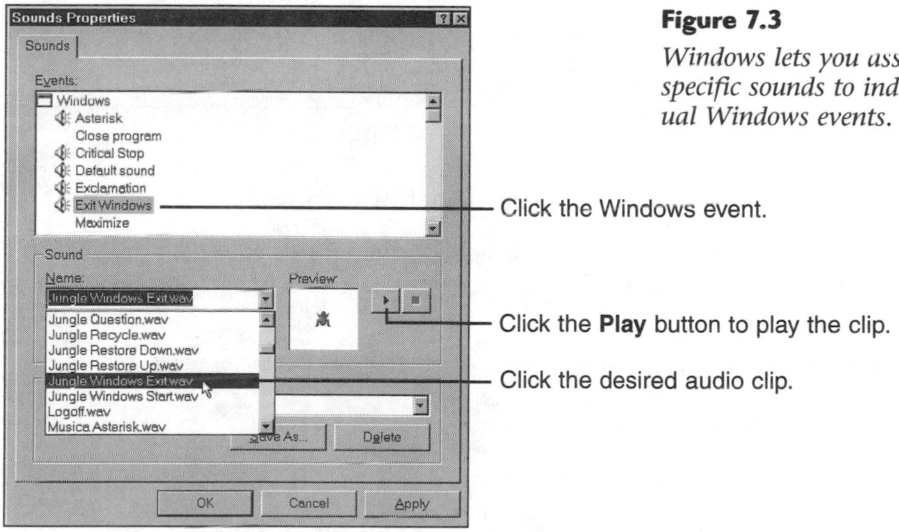

Figure 7.3

Windows lets you assign specific sounds to individual Windows events.

Click the Windows event.

Click the **Play** button to play the clip.

Click the desired audio clip.

Listening to CDs While You Work

Do you like to listen to a little background music while you work? Maybe some Red Hot Chili Peppers or Nine Inch Nails? Well, just pop your favorite CD into the CD-ROM drive and start jammin'! If your computer has a sound card, the audio will play through the speakers. If not, plug a set of headphones into the headphone jack on the CD-ROM drive. (If you plug in headphones, control the volume by using the volume control on the CD-ROM drive.)

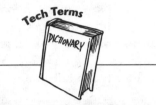

More Cool Audio Clips

In Part 4, when you start poking around on the Internet, you may stumble upon some cool audio files. If the filename ends in .wav, you can assign the audio file to a Windows event. Save the file to the Windows/Media folder on your hard drive, and it will appear in the Sound list.

Windows should start to play the audio CD as soon as you insert it. If Windows does not start to play the CD, click the Windows **Start** button (lower-left corner of the screen), point to **Settings**, and click **Control Panel**. Double-click the icon labeled **System**, and then click the **Device Manager** tab. Click the plus sign (+) next to **CDROM**, and then double-click the name of your CD-ROM. Click the **Settings** tab and make sure there is a check mark in the **Auto Insert Notification** box. Click **OK** to save your changes, and then click **OK** again to close the System Settings dialog box. With Auto Insert Notification turned on, Windows should start playing your audio CD as soon as you insert it.

Windows uses a utility called CD Player to play the CD (see Figure 7.4). If the CD Player window does not appear immediately, click the **CD Player** button in the taskbar. You can use the CD Player's buttons just as you would the buttons on any standard audio CD player.

No Headphone Jack?

If your CD-ROM drive has no headphone jack or volume control, don't worry. Manufacturers are finally beginning to realize that the additional jack and volume control are superfluous.

Click **Play** to start playing the CD.

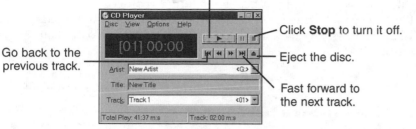

Go back to the previous track.

Click **Stop** to turn it off.

Eject the disc.

Fast forward to the next track.

Figure 7.4

CD Player lets you use your computer as a standard audio CD player.

Recording Your Own Audio Clips

Now that you know how to assign sounds to Windows events and play audio CDs, you're ready to completely customize the Windows sound machine. Using the Windows Sound Recorder, you can record your own voice (if you have a microphone) or snippets from audio CDs, save your recordings as files, and then attach them to specific Windows events! Sounds pretty cool, eh? But first, you need to run Sound Recorder and use it to "tape" audio clips.

To run Sound Recorder, open the **Start** menu, point to **Programs**, **Accessories**, **Entertainment**, and click **Sound Recorder**. The Sound Recorder appears, as shown in Figure 7.5. Recording your voice is easy: Click the **Record** button, speak into the microphone, and then click the **Stop** button. Recording bits of music from CDs is a little tougher because you must flip back and forth between Sound Recorder and CD Player—you have to be pretty fast with the mouse.

Multimedia Audio CDs

Many musical groups now put out CDs that include music videos, digitized photos, and other multimedia offerings. Don't be surprised if a menu or program pops up on your screen when you insert an audio CD.

Open the File menu and click **Save** to save the recording as a file.

Click the **Record** button.

To stop recording, click the **Stop** button.

Figure 7.5

You can use Sound Recorder to record your voice or audio CD clips.

When you're done recording, open Sound Recorder's **File** menu and select **Save**. Type a name for the file. Unless you specify otherwise, Sound Recorder saves the recording as a WAV file and tacks on the .wav extension to the filename. If you plan to attach the sound to a Windows event, change to the Windows/Media folder before you click the **Save** button.

The Least You Need to Know

The audio features in Windows give your computer another dimension and can make your computing experience much more enjoyable. To control these audio features, you must master the basics:

➤ To access the volume controls, double-click the speaker icon on the right end of the taskbar.

➤ To check out the Windows sound schemes, double-click the **Sound** icon in the Windows Control Panel.

➤ To pick a different sound scheme, open the **Schemes** list in the Sounds Properties dialog box and click the desired sound scheme.

➤ To assign a different sound to a Windows event, click the event in the Sounds Properties dialog box, and then choose the desired sound from the Sound list.

➤ To play an audio CD, just pop it into your computer's CD-ROM drive.

➤ You can use Sound Recorder to record your voice, sound effects, or clips from audio CDs, and then you can attach those sounds to Windows events.

Chapter 8

Taking Control of Your Menus and Programs

In This Chapter

➤ Rearranging your Start menu with Windows Explorer

➤ Transforming the Windows desktop into a toolbar

➤ Transforming a folder into a toolbar

➤ Scheduling programs to run automatically

If you've ever spent a few hours cleaning and reorganizing your office, you know that with a little effort, you can transform it from a disorganized mess into a model of neatness and efficiency. The same is true of the Windows desktop.

By putting in a little time up front, you can redesign your desktop to conform to the way you work. You can place commands in more convenient locations on the Start menu, make your own desktop icons, transform folders into toolbars, and use Task Scheduler to automatically run programs for you. By the end of this chapter, you'll have the Windows desktop of your dreams!

Rearranging the Start Menu with Explorer

In Chapter 3, you learned how to drag program groups and individual programs to different locations on the Start menu. In the process, you probably noticed that dragging and dropping items on the Start menu is not the smoothest operation around. As you drag an object, menus open and close, making it difficult for you to drop the object in a precise location.

An easier way to rearrange items is to display the Start menu as a folder in Windows Explorer and then drag icons from one of the Start menu's folders to another. Try it yourself:

1. Right-click the **Start** button and click **Explore**. This starts Windows Explorer, which opens the Start Menu folder.

2. Click the plus sign next to **Programs**, and then click the plus sign next to any subfolders that appear below the Programs folder.

3. To move a submenu, drag its icon to the desired location in the folder list. For example, to move the Accessories menu to the top of the Start menu, drag the **Accessories** folder over the **Start** folder. (To move it back to its original location, drag the **Accessories** folder over the **Programs** folder.)

4. To move a program, first change to the folder that currently contains the program (in the folder list, on the left).

5. In the folder list, make sure you can see the destination folder (the folder to which you want to move the program).

6. Drag the program's icon from the file list (on the right) over the destination folder and release the mouse button (see Figure 8.1).

Figure 8.1

Windows Explorer is a great tool for restructuring your Start menu.

2. Drag the program icon over the desired destination folder.

1. Change to the folder that contains the program you want to move.

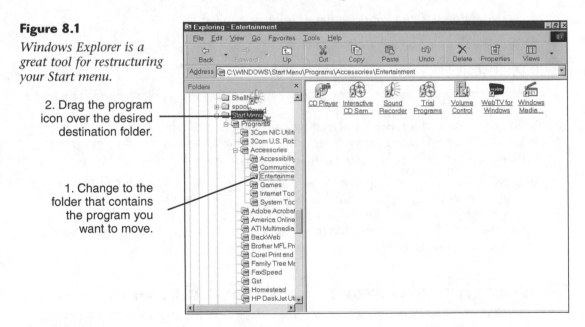

Making Your Own Toolbars

Chapter 3, "Launching Your First Program," showed you how to use the Windows Quick Launch toolbar to run programs with a single click. You even learned how to create your own Quick Launch buttons for your favorite programs.

However, the Quick Launch toolbar is much more powerful and versatile than Chapter 3 revealed. The following sections take you behind the scenes to show you how to turn on additional "Quick Launch" toolbars and create your own custom toolbars.

Turning On the Desktop Toolbar

If you think the Quick Launch toolbar is cool, you'll be happy to know that Windows has several more toolbars just like it:

➤ **Address** displays a text box into which you type a Web page address to open a specific Web page on the Internet. (You'll learn more about Web pages and addresses in Part 4, "Getting Wired on the Internet.")

➤ **Links** is another toolbar you can ignore for the time being. It contains buttons for connecting to popular Web sites.

➤ **Desktop** contains buttons for all the icons on the Windows desktop. Instead of double-clicking a desktop icon, you can simply click its button in the Desktop toolbar.

Let's check out the Desktop toolbar. Right-click a blank area on the taskbar, point to **Toolbars**, and click **Desktop**. Voilà! The Desktop toolbar appears. Because the taskbar is limited on space, you won't see many buttons. To see a complete collection of the Desktop toolbar's buttons, click the double-headed arrow (>>) at the right end of the Desktop toolbar, as shown in Figure 8.2.

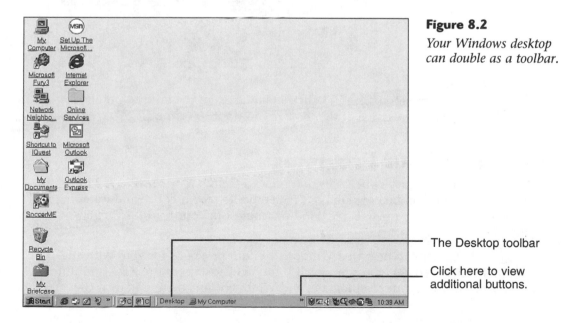

Figure 8.2

Your Windows desktop can double as a toolbar.

The Desktop toolbar

Click here to view additional buttons.

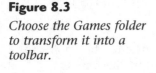

Stretch That Taskbar

You can make the taskbar larger and then make it tuck itself out of the way when you're not using it. See Chapter 9, "Giving Yourself More Room to Work," for details.

Transforming a Folder into a Toolbar

Gee, that was fun. But the Desktop, Address, and Links toolbars don't seem very useful, do they? I know I never use them. But wouldn't it be cool to have a Games toolbar with buttons for running Solitaire, FreeCell, Minesweeper, and Hearts? Let's make that toolbar right now:

1. Right-click a blank area of the taskbar, point to **Toolbars**, and click **New Toolbar**.

2. Click the plus signs (+) next to **C**, **Windows**, **Start Menu**, **Programs**, and **Accessories**.

3. Click **Games**, as shown in Figure 8.3.

4. Click **OK**. Windows creates the Games toolbar and nests it inside the taskbar.

Figure 8.3

Choose the Games folder to transform it into a toolbar.

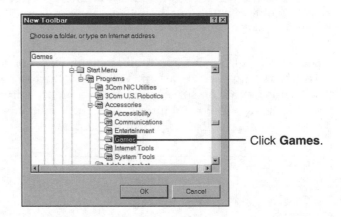

Click **Games**.

To turn off any of the toolbars, right-click a blank area of the taskbar, point to **Toolbars**, and click the name of the toolbar you want to turn off.

Automating Your Programs

I have one of those fancy coffee pots that brews a fresh pot of coffee every morning just before I roll out of bed—assuming I remember to feed it coffee and water before I hit the sack. Wouldn't it be great if Windows could run your favorite programs for you?

Well, you'll be happy to hear that Windows *can* run programs for you. With the Windows Task Scheduler, you simply tell Windows the days of the week and time of day you want it to run the program, and Windows runs the program at the scheduled time(s). Not only is Task Scheduler useful for running the programs you use most often, but it's great for running disk cleanup and maintenance utilities on a regular basis.

To schedule a program to run, take the following steps:

1. Open the **Start** menu.

2. Point to **Programs**, **Accessories**, **System Tools**, **Scheduled Tasks**, and then click **Add Scheduled Task**. This runs the Scheduled Task Wizard.

3. Read the Task Scheduler overview, and then click **Next**.

4. Click the program you want the Scheduled Task Wizard to run, as shown in Figure 8.4, and click **Next**.

Computer Cheats

Quick Toolbars

Instead of taking the standard steps for creating a toolbar, you can simply drag any folder from My Computer or Windows Explorer over a blank area of the taskbar and release the mouse button. Windows automatically converts the folder into a toolbar.

Click the program's name.

Figure 8.4

Pick the program you want the Scheduled Task Wizard to run for you.

Click **Next**.

5. Click the frequency you want Task Scheduler to run the program and click **Next**. (For example, you can have Task Scheduler run the program daily, weekly, one time only, or whenever you start your computer.)

6. Specify the time of day and the days of the week on which you want Task Scheduler to run the program.

7. (Optional) Click **Open Advanced Properties...** and enter additional preferences for running the program. (The available options vary from one program to another, so you'll have to improvise here.)

8. Click **Finish**.

Computer Cheats

Run Programs on Startup

To have a program automatically run at startup, make a shortcut icon for the program and move it to the **Start**, **Programs**, **StartUp** folder.

When Task Scheduler is running, its icon appears in the system tray (at the right end of the taskbar). To disable Task Scheduler (prevent it from running programs), double-click its icon, open the **Advanced** menu, and click **Stop Using Task Scheduler**.

The Least You Need to Know

Many Windows users continue to dig around in time-consuming menus and submenus to run their programs. By mastering a few basic Windows configuration features, you can streamline operations and save yourself loads of time. Keep the following information at your fingertips:

➤ To display the contents of the Start menu in Windows Explorer, right-click the **Start** button and click **Explore**.

➤ To turn on the Desktop toolbar, right-click a blank area on the taskbar, point to **Toolbars**, and click **Desktop**.

➤ To transform any folder into a toolbar, drag the folder icon over a blank area of the taskbar and release the mouse button.

➤ Use the Task Scheduler to automatically run a favorite program on specified days and times.

➤ When Task Scheduler is running, an icon for it appears in the taskbar.

Chapter 9

Giving Yourself More Room to Work

In This Chapter

➤ Shrinking your desktop icons down to size

➤ Messing with your display's color settings

➤ Trashing icons you don't use

➤ Hiding the taskbar when you don't need it

➤ Reorganizing your desktop with folders

When you start working, you notice that your Windows desktop can become every bit as cluttered and unmanageable as a real-life desktop. Fortunately, your Windows desktop is much easier to tidy up. You can shrink everything on your desktop to give yourself more room, rearrange the icons, dump icons you don't use, hide the taskbar, and even tuck icons into separate folders to keep them out of the way.

Sound like fun? Heck no, but by learning to organize your desktop, you can work more efficiently and give yourself more time to do the fun stuff. This chapter shows you just what to do.

Clearing Desk Space by Making Everything Smaller

Wouldn't it be great if you could grab the edges of your monitor and stretch it? Maybe turn your 15-inch monitor into a big-screen, 21-inch version? Well, you can't, but you can do the next best thing—shrink everything on the desktop to give yourself a little more real estate. Here's what you do:

1. Right-click a blank area of the desktop and click **Properties**.

2. Click the **Settings** tab.

3. Drag the **Screen Area** slider to the right one or more notches, as shown in Figure 9.1. As you drag, watch the preview area to see how the new setting affects the display.

4. When the preview area shows the desired desktop appearance (or the slider won't budge), click **Apply**.

5. Click **OK** to save your settings.

Figure 9.1

You can't make your display bigger, but you can make everything on it smaller.

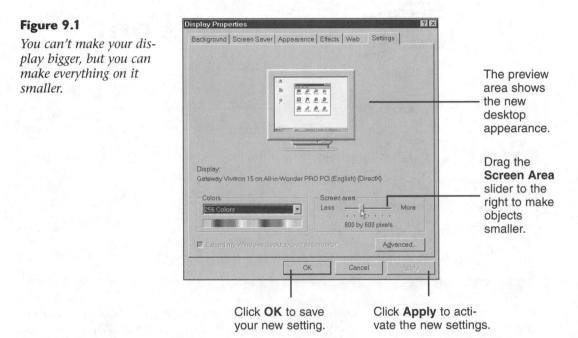

The preview area shows the new desktop appearance.

Drag the **Screen Area** slider to the right to make objects smaller.

Click **OK** to save your new setting.

Click **Apply** to activate the new settings.

The Icon Won't Stay Put!

If you try to move an icon and it jumps to a different location, Auto Arrange is on. To turn it off, right-click the desktop, point to **Arrange Icons**, and click **Auto Arrange**.

What About the Color Settings?

As you were fiddling around with the screen area setting, you might have noticed the Colors drop-down list off to the left (refer to Figure 9.1). This list provides options for increasing or decreasing the number of colors used to display everything from icons to digitized photos. With more colors at its disposal, the monitor can display high-quality images more realistically.

So you want the highest setting possible, right? Well, not exactly. To display additional colors, your computer's display card and processor must work a little harder. Additional colors also consume more memory. The basic approach here is to choose the lowest setting that provides satisfactory quality. I set my display to 256 colors, which does a fairly good job of displaying photos and other detailed graphics. If you do any photo or video editing, you might want to bump up the setting.

Keep It Simple

A fancy desktop packed with animated shortcuts and fancy wallpaper is cool, but all that fancy stuff consumes precious resources. To keep your computer running at top speed, opt for a clean, simple desktop.

Rearranging Your Desktop Icons

Although the icons on the desktop provide convenient access to all of your programs and files, you can get a little carried away with them. In about 15 minutes, you can completely cover the surface of the desktop with shortcuts, making it nearly impossible to find anything. Fortunately, Windows has several tools to help you reorganize the icons on your desktop. Try the following techniques:

➤ To move an icon, drag it to the desired location.

➤ To have Windows rearrange the icons for you, right-click the desktop, point to **Arrange Icons**, and click **By Name**, **By Size**, **By Type**, or **By Date**.

➤ To have Windows line up the icons without rearranging them by name, size, type, or date, right-click the desktop and click **Line Up Icons**.

➤ To have Windows automatically line up icons when you move them, right-click the desktop, point to **Arrange Icons**, and click **Auto Arrange**.

I Can't Read the Icon Names

Don't worry. You can make some adjustments. Open the Display Properties dialog box again. To make the text bigger, click the **Settings** tab; click the **Advanced** button, and choose **Large Fonts**. If icons overlap, click the **Appearance** tab, choose one of the **Icon Spacing** options (Vertical or Horizontal) from the **Item** list, and increase the spacing.

Computer Cheats

Right-Click & Delete

To quickly delete icons, files, or folders, right-click any one of the selected items and click **Delete**.

Computer Cheats

Make Your Taskbar Huge

To make your taskbar larger, move the mouse pointer over its top edge so the pointer appears as a two-headed arrow, and then drag up. With Auto Hide on, you don't have to worry about the taskbar taking up too much screen space.

Getting Rid of Icons You Don't Use

The best way to clean up your desktop is to delete the icons you never use. First, select the icon you want to delete. If Web Style is on, point to the icon; if Web Style is off, click the icon. **Ctrl+point** or **Ctrl+click** to select additional icons. Then, drag any one of the selected icons over the **Recycle Bin** icon and release the mouse button. Windows displays a dialog box asking for your confirmation. Click **Yes**.

Remember, if you delete an icon or other object by mistake, you can get it back. Double-click the **Recycle Bin** icon, click the icon you accidentally deleted, and then open the **File** menu and click **Restore**.

Hiding the Taskbar

The taskbar is a great tool to have around, but when you're working on a document, playing a game, or viewing a Web page, you need that extra half-inch of screen space where the taskbar resides. To reclaim the space, make the taskbar hide itself when you're doing other stuff:

1. Right-click a blank area of the taskbar and click **Properties**.
2. Click **Auto Hide**, as shown in Figure 9.2.
3. Click **OK**.

Figure 9.2
Give yourself some elbowroom.

Turn on **Auto Hide**. ———

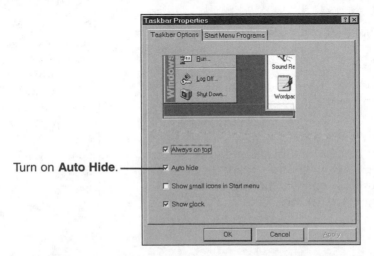

As you work, the taskbar hides below the bottom of the screen (unless you moved the taskbar to a different edge of the screen). To bring the taskbar back into view, simply move the mouse pointer to the edge of the screen where the taskbar hangs out.

Tucking Stuff into Folders

Another trick for cleaning up your desktop is to stuff icons into folders. For example, you might have one folder for your business programs, another for games, and a separate folder for documents you commonly work on. To make a new folder, right-click the desktop, point to **New**, and click **Folder**. Type a name for the folder and then click outside the icon to save the name.

After you have a folder in place, you can move icons from the desktop simply by dragging and dropping them onto the new folder icon.

Computer Cheats

Make Your Folder a Toolbar

After moving the shortcut icons to your new folder, drag and drop the folder icon onto a blank area of the taskbar to create a toolbar containing buttons for the shortcuts in the folder.

The Least You Need to Know

A well-organized desktop can make everything on your computer more accessible. To take control of your desktop, keep the following information in mind:

➤ Use the Display Properties dialog box to shrink everything on the desktop and increase your work area.

➤ If you mess with your display's Color Palette settings, choose a setting of 256 colors or more.

➤ To have Windows automatically arrange the icons on the desktop, right-click the desktop, point to **Arrange**, and click **Auto Arrange**.

➤ If you don't use a particular shortcut icon, drag it to the Recycle Bin.

➤ To hide the taskbar, right-click it, choose **Properties**, and turn on **Auto Hide**.

➤ To create a folder, right-click the desktop, point to **New**, and click **Folder**.

Chapter 10

Installing and Removing Programs

In This Chapter

➤ Picking programs your computer can run

➤ Finding out whether your computer has room for a new program

➤ Installing a program in 10 minutes or less

➤ Running CD-ROM programs

➤ Getting rid of programs you don't use

For me, the term "install" triggers flashbacks to the weekend I spent installing our new water heater. I envision misplaced tools, lost parts, leaking pipes, and a badly bruised ego.

Although installing a program is typically less traumatic, the process can have similar, unforeseen problems. For instance, you might pick up the wrong version of the program—the Macintosh version rather than the Windows version. Or the program might have a quirky installation routine that doesn't install all of the components you need.

This chapter is designed to help you avoid the most common pitfalls, deal with unexpected problems, and successfully install your new programs.

Buying Software That Your Hardware Can Run

Even the most experienced computer user occasionally slips up and buys a program that his or her computer can't run. The person might own a PC running Windows and pick up the Macintosh version of the program by mistake. Or maybe the program requires special audio or video equipment that the person doesn't have.

Before you purchase any program, read the minimum hardware requirements that are printed on the outside of every software package to determine whether your computer has what it takes to run the program:

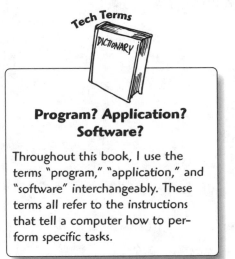

Program? Application? Software?

Throughout this book, I use the terms "program," "application," and "software" interchangeably. These terms all refer to the instructions that tell a computer how to perform specific tasks.

Computer type   Typically, you can't run a Macintosh program on an IBM-compatible computer (a *PC* or *personal computer* that runs Windows). If you have a PC, make sure the program is for an IBM PC or compatible computer. (Some programs include both the Macintosh and PC versions.)

Operating system   Try to find programs that are designed specifically for the operating system you use. If your computer is running Windows 98, don't buy a program developed for Windows 95. (Although Windows 98 can run most applications designed for Windows 95, Windows 98 might have problems running some Windows 95 programs.)

Free hard disk space   When you install a program, the installation routinely copies files from the installation disks or CDs to the hard disk. Make sure your hard disk has enough free disk space, as explained in the next section.

CPU requirements   CPU stands for *central processing unit*. This is the brain of the computer. If the program requires at least a Pentium processor and you have a 486 processor, your computer won't be able to run the application effectively.

Type of monitor   All newer monitors are SVGA (Super Video Graphics Array) or better, and most programs don't require anything better than SVGA. Some games and graphics programs require a specific type of display card, such as a 3D card or an advanced video card.

Mouse   If you use Windows, you need a mouse or some other pointing device. A standard Microsoft two-button mouse is sufficient. Some programs have special features you can use only with an IntelliMouse.

Joystick   Although most computer games let you use your keyboard, games usually are more fun if you have a joystick. Digital joysticks are the current trend.

CD-ROM drive   If you have a CD-ROM drive, it usually pays to get the CD-ROM version of the application. This simplifies the program installation, and the CD-ROM version might come with a few extras. Check for the required speed of the drive, as well.

Sound card   Most new applications require sound cards. If you plan to run any cool games, use a multimedia encyclopedia, or even explore the Internet, you'll need a sound card. Some applications can use the old 8-bit sound card, but newer applications require a 16-bit or better sound card, which enables stereo output.

Amount of memory (RAM)   If your computer does not have the required memory, it might not be able to run the program or the program might cause the computer to crash (freeze up).

Use the Tearout Card

Before you go shopping for programs, tear out the Savvy Software Shopper's Form at the front of this book and make some copies of it. Use the forms to record each program's minimum hardware requirements.

You can find out most of what you need to know from the System Properties dialog box. Hold down **Alt** and double-click **My Computer** to display the System Properties dialog box, as shown in Figure 10.1. The General Tab displays the operating system type and version number, the type of processor, and the amount of RAM. Click the **Device** tab and click the plus sign next to a device type to view the make and model number; for instance, click the plus sign next to Display Adapters to determine the type of video card that's installed.

Figure 10.1

The System Properties dialog box can tell you a lot about your computer.

The operating system and version number

The type of processor

The amount of RAM (memory)

Do You Have Enough Disk Space?

Most new computers sport a four-plus gigabyte hard drive that has enough free space to last you well into the 21st century. However, you should make sure that your new program will fit on the disk before you start the installation. If you try to stuff a program on a hard disk that's nearly full, you'll have some serious warning messages to deal with.

Checking the available disk space is easy. Right-click the icon for your hard disk drive in My Computer or Windows Explorer and click **Properties**. The Properties dialog box displays the total disk space, the amount in use, and the amount that's free, as shown in Figure 10.2.

Figure 10.2

Windows displays the available space remaining on the disk.

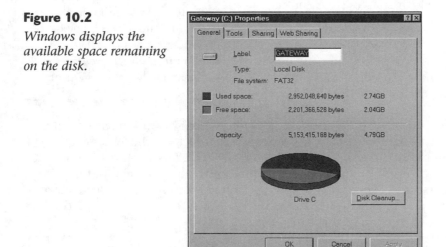

If your hard disk does not have sufficient free space for installing the program, you can free up some disk space by taking the following steps:

➤ Display the disk's Properties dialog box. On the General tab, click the **Disk Cleanup** button (see the previous figure) and follow the onscreen instructions to clear unnecessary files from the disk. If you have an older version of Windows (Windows 3.1 or Windows 95 without the Internet Explorer upgrade), the Disk Cleanup button is unavailable.

➤ Uninstall any programs you no longer use, as explained later in this chapter.

➤ Make sure the Recycle Bin does not contain any files you might need by double-clicking the Recycle Bin icon. To empty the Recycle Bin, open the **File** menu and click **Empty Recycle Bin**.

➤ Run Windows Setup again, as explained in Chapter 4, "Warming Up with Some Computer Games," and remove any Windows components you no longer use.

Installing Your New Program

Nearly every program on the market comes with an installation component (called setup or install) that does everything for you. If the program is on CD-ROM, you can usually pop the disc into your CD-ROM drive, click a few options to tell the program that it can install itself according to the default settings, and then kick back and watch the installation routine do its thing.

If the program comes on floppy disks or the setup component on the CD doesn't start automatically when you insert the disc, take the following steps to kick-start the setup routine:

1. If you haven't inserted the program CD or the first floppy disk into the drive, insert the CD or disk now.

2. Double-click **My Computer** on the Windows desktop.

3. Double-click the icon for your CD-ROM or floppy drive. This displays a list of files and folders on the disk or CD.

4. Double-click the file named **Setup**, **Install**, or its equivalent (refer to the program's installation instructions, if necessary). This starts the installation utility.

5. Follow the onscreen instructions to complete the installation.

No Install or Setup File?

99.9% of the programs you encounter have an Install or Setup file, so you shouldn't have any problem. However, if the program does not have its own setup utility, take the following steps to copy the program files to a folder on your computer's hard disk:

1. In My Computer, double-click the icon for drive C.

2. Right-click a blank area in the window, point to **New**, and click **Folder**.

3. Type a unique name for the folder and then double-click the folder icon to open it.

Tech Terms

Deleting Temporary Files

Many programs create temporary files and then forget to delete them. Click **Start**, **Find**, **Files or Folders**. In the **Named** text box, type ***.tmp**. In the **Look In** text box, type **c:**. Make sure **Include Subfolders** is selected and then click **Find Now**. Open the **Edit** menu, choose **Select All**, and then press the **Delete** key.

Panic Attack

I Can't Find the Setup File!

If you cannot find the Setup or Install file, Windows can help you locate the file that initiates the installation routine. Open the **Start** menu, point to **Settings**, and click **Control Panel**. Double-click the **Add/Remove Programs** icon. Click the **Install** button and follow the onscreen instructions.

Copy Files to a Disk in Drive A

To quickly copy a file from your hard disk to a floppy disk in drive A, right-click the file, point to **Send To**, and click **Floppy A**.

4. Open another My Computer window and change to the drive that contains the program disk or CD.

5. Press **Ctrl+A** to select all of the files on the disk or CD, and then press **Ctrl+C** to copy them.

6. Change to the folder you just created and press **Ctrl+V** to paste the files into the folder.

The file for running the program is typically marked with an icon that looks like the program's logo. Using the right mouse button, drag and drop this icon onto the Windows desktop, and then click **Create Shortcut(s) Here**. You can now use this icon to run the program.

Selectively Installing Components

Many newer programs can consume several hundred megabytes of disk space, making it unwise to install the entire program on your hard disk. These large programs typically offer the option to run the program from the CD or install only the most commonly used components.

If the setup routine gives you the option of running the program from the CD or hard disk and your hard disk has plenty of free space, choose to run the program from the hard disk. You'll find that the program runs much faster, and you won't have to insert the CD every time you want to use the program. Choose to run the program from the CD only if your hard disk is running out of space.

Many setup routines provide an option for running the standard (typical), minimal, or custom installation, as shown in Figure 10.3. Again, unless your hard disk is running out of storage space, choose the standard installation. This installs the most common components. If you'd like to see what's available and order *à la carte*, perform a custom installation.

Figure 10.3

When in doubt, choose the standard or typical installation.

Setup Type

Click the type of Setup you prefer, then click Next.

○ Typical   Program will be installed with the most common options. Recommended for most users.

○ Compact   Program will be installed with minimum required options.

○ Custom   You may choose the options you want to install. Recommended for advanced users.

Destination Directory

C:\...\Chronicle Encyclopedia of History   Browse...

< Back   Next >   Cancel

Does Anyone Use Floppy Disks Anymore?

Floppy disks are fast becoming extinct, but you might still receive small programs on floppy disks. Before installing a program from floppy disks, it's a good idea to write-protect the disks if they are not already write-protected. Write protection locks the disk, preventing the disk drive from making any changes to it. If you hold the disk with the label facing up and away from you, the write-protect tab is in the upper-left corner of the disk. Slide the tab up so you can see through the hole in the disk.

Removing a Program That You Never Use

Your hard disk isn't an ever-expanding universe on which you can install an unlimited number of programs. As you install programs, create documents, send and receive email messages, and view Web pages, your disk can quickly become overpopulated.

One of the best ways to reclaim a hefty chunk of disk space is to remove (uninstall) programs you don't use. Unfortunately, you cannot just nuke the program's main folder to purge it from your system. When you install a Windows program, it commonly installs files not only to the program's folder, but also to the \WINDOWS, WINDOWS\SYSTEM, and other folders. It also edits a complicated system file, called the Windows Registry—if you remove files without removing the lines in the Registry that refer to those files, you may encounter some serious problems. In short, you can't remove a program from your computer simply by deleting the program's files.

To remove the program safely and completely, you should use the Windows Add/Remove Programs utility:

1. Click the **Start** button, point to **Settings**, and click **Control Panel**.
2. Click the **Add/Remove Programs** icon. The Add/Remove Programs Properties dialog box appears (see Figure 10.4).

Computer Cheats

Now It Won't Run!

Some programs allow only a certain number of installations or require you to enter a password or registration number during installation. The installation utility then records this information on the floppy disk. In such cases, you may need to remove write-protection in order to proceed.

Inside Tip

The Program's Not Listed

If the name of the program you want to remove does not appear in the Add/Remove Programs list, use the program's own setup utility to remove the program. Search the program's submenu on the Start, Programs menu or in the program's folder for a Setup or Install option.

3. Click the **Install/Uninstall** tab if it is not already selected. At the bottom of the window is a list of installed programs.

4. Click the name of the program you want to remove, as shown in Figure 10.4.

5. Click the **Add/Remove** button.

6. One or more dialog boxes lead you through the uninstall process, asking for your confirmation. Follow the onscreen instructions to complete the process.

7. If the program you removed has a shortcut icon on the desktop, you might have to delete this manually. Right-click the icon, and click **Delete**.

Figure 10.4

Let Windows remove the program for you.

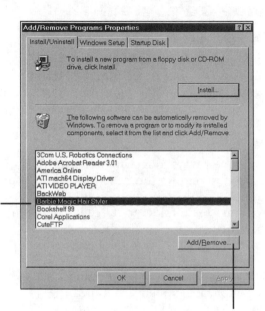

Click the program you want to remove.

Click the **Add/Remove** button.

The Least You Need to Know

Without software, computer hardware is nothing more than an oversized, over-priced paperweight. For your computer to do anything useful (or fun), it needs the right software installed. To make sure your computer has the software it needs, you should know the following:

➤ Software provides the instructions your computer needs to perform a task.

➤ Not all programs run on all computers. Before buying a program, make sure your computer meets the requirements that are printed on the program's box.

➤ Alt+double-click **My Computer** to view important information about your computer.

➤ In most cases, you can simply pop a CD-ROM program into your computer's CD-ROM drive to start the installation routine.

➤ To install a program, use My Computer to change to the CD-ROM or floppy drive in which the program diskette or CD is loaded and double-click the Setup or Install icon.

➤ To remove a program you no longer use, open the Windows Control Panel and double-click the Add/Remove Programs icon.

Part 3

Creating Letters and Greeting Cards

Playing Solitaire and fiddling with the Windows desktop can keep you entertained for hours, but you didn't lay down a thousand bucks for a computer only to use it as a 99-cent deck of playing cards. You want to make something, print something, poke around on the Internet— you want to use the computer to get more out of life!

In this part, you begin to become productive with your computer as you learn how to type and format a letter or greeting card, add images, and print your letter or custom publication. Along the way, you'll even learn how to perform some basic tasks, such as saving, naming, and opening your documents.

Chapter 11

I Just Want to Type a Letter!

In This Chapter

➤ Typing on an electronic page

➤ Inserting the date and time from your computer

➤ Making your text big and pretty

➤ Shoving your paragraphs around on a page

➤ Saving the document you created

When my wife and I purchased a new computer for our home, I was dazzled by the hardware: the state-of-the-art processor, the all-in-one fax-copier-scanner-printer, the big-screen monitor, the surround sound audio system, and the super-speed ISDN modem! With this bad boy, we'd be cruising, rather than surfing, the Internet; building our own Web sites; scanning in family photos; editing videos!

As I ran down a list of all the cool things we could do with our new computer, my wife just stared at the screen. When I finished, she looked at me and said, "I just want to type a letter."

With the popularity of the Internet and other computer technologies, it's easy to forget that many people still use a computer primarily to type and print documents. In this chapter, you learn how to type, format (style), and save a document using the most popular word processor on the planet—Microsoft Word.

Making the Transition to the Electronic Page

When you run Word (or whatever word processor is installed on your computer), it displays a blank "sheet of paper." The program also displays a vertical line called the *cursor* or *insertion point* to show you where the characters will appear when you start typing. Just below the insertion point is a horizontal line that marks the end of the document, as shown in Figure 11.1. As you type, this line moves down automatically.

But I Don't Have Microsoft Word!

Don't worry if you're using a different word processor. The basic features and commands covered in this chapter differ only slightly among word processing programs.

The best way to learn how to type in a word processor is to start typing. As you type, keep the following information in mind:

➤ If the text is too small to read, open the **Zoom** list, as shown in Figure 11.1 and pick 100%. If the text is still too small, make it bigger as explained in "Making the Text Bigger or Smaller," later in this chapter.

➤ Press the **Enter** key only to end a paragraph and start a new paragraph. Within a paragraph, the program automatically *wraps* the text from one line to the next as you type.

➤ Don't press the Enter key to insert a blank line between paragraphs. Later in this chapter, I will show you a better way to add space between paragraphs.

➤ Use the mouse or the arrow keys to move the insertion point around in the document. If you're working on a long document, use the scrollbar to move more quickly.

➤ To delete a character, move the insertion point to the left of the character and press the **Delete** key, or move the insertion point to the right of the character and press the **Backspace** key.

➤ Delete to the right; Backspace to the left. To delete a character that the insertion point is on (or under) or a character to the right of the insertion point, press the **Del** (Delete) key. To delete characters to the left of the insertion point, press the **Backspace** key.

Choose 100% to view the text as it will appear in print.

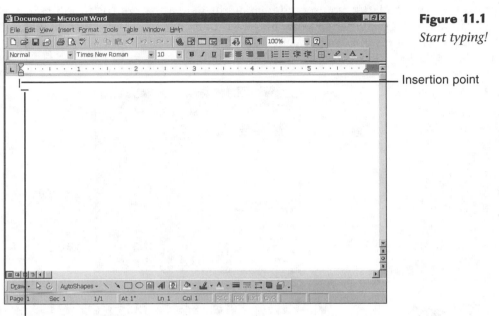

Figure 11.1
Start typing!

Insertion point

End of document

What's with the Squiggly Red and Green Lines?

As you type, you might get a strange feeling that your sixth-grade English teacher is inside your computer, underlining your spelling mistakes. Whenever you type a string of characters that does not match a word in Word's spelling dictionary, Word draws a squiggly red line under the word to flag it for you so that you can immediately correct it. If the word is misspelled, right-click the word and choose the correct spelling from the context menu. (A squiggly green line marks a questionable grammatical construction.)

If the squiggly lines annoy you, you can turn off automatic spell checking. Open the **Tools** menu and click **Options**. Click the **Spelling & Grammar** tab, and turn off both **Check Spelling As You Type** and **Check Grammar As You Type**. Click **OK**.

Wrong Date?

If the date or time is not current, your computer has the wrong information. Double-click the time display on the right end of the Windows taskbar and use the resulting dialog box to reset the date or time.

Inserting Today's Date

When you're typing a letter, you should include the date as part of the heading, just below your address. Of course, you could type the date, but that's too much like work. Have Word insert the date for you. Open the **Insert** menu and click **Date and Time**. Click the desired format and click **OK**, as shown in Figure 11.2.

Figure 11.2

You can have your word processor insert the date or time for you.

Click the desired format.

Click **OK**.

Making the Text Bigger or Smaller

When you first start to type, you might notice that there's nothing fancy about the text. Word processors choose the dullest, dreariest-looking typestyle available. To give your text a facelift, try choosing a different typestyle (or *font*) and varying the size and attributes of the text.

To change the appearance of existing text, drag over the text to highlight it. Highlighting displays white text on a black background to indicate that the text is selected. Then, choose the desired formatting options from the Formatting toolbar, as shown in Figure 11.3. (By the way, you can change the properties of the text before you start typing.)

Font

Technically, a *font* is a collection of characters that share the same typestyle and size. (Type size is measured in *points*; a point is approximately 1/72 of an inch.) Most programs use the terms "font" and "typestyle" interchangeably.

Choose a different text color.

Make text bold, italic, or underlined.

Highlighted text   Select the text size.

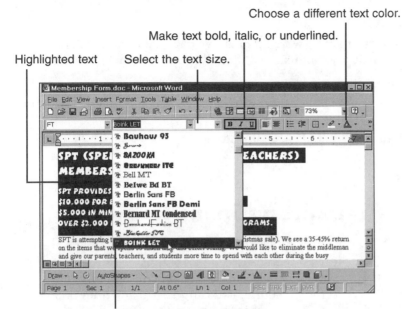

Figure 11.3
Use the Formatting tool-bar to quickly change the text's appearance.

Pick a different typestyle.

Shoving Text Left, Right, or Center

As you type a document, you might want to center a heading or push a date or address to the right side of the page to set it apart from surrounding text. To quickly change the text alignment, click anywhere inside the paragraph and then click one of the following buttons in the Formatting toolbar:

 Align Left pushes all lines of the paragraph against the left margin.

Center positions the text at an equal distance between the left and right margins.

Align Right pushes all lines of the paragraph against the right margin. This is a useful option for placing a date in the upper-right corner of a page.

Justify inserts spaces between the words as needed to make every line of the paragraph the same length, as in newspaper columns.

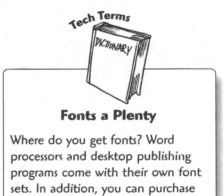

Fonts a Plenty

Where do you get fonts? Word processors and desktop publishing programs come with their own font sets. In addition, you can purchase font collections on CD or download (copy) fonts from the Internet.

 The formatting toolbar also contains buttons for creating numbered and bulleted lists. Simply highlight the paragraphs you want to transform into a list and then click the desired button: **Numbering** or **Bullets**.

Changing the Line Spacing

Here's a section just for kids. If you're working on a five-page paper for school, and you have only two and a half pages of material, stretch it out by double-spacing:

1. Press **Ctrl+A** to select all of the text.
2. Open the **Format** menu and click **Paragraph**. The Paragraph dialog box pops up on your screen.
3. Open the **Line Spacing** list and click **Double**.
4. Click **OK**.

Computer Cheats

More Subtle Ways to Stretch Your Essay

If your teacher wises up and issues formatting restrictions on your next assignment, try bumping up the text size by one point (barely noticeable), using the File, Page Setup command to trim the margins, and increasing the line spacing by only a few points rather than double-spacing. An even more subtle technique is to use larger fonts—some fonts, such as Arial and Times New Roman, take up more space at the same point size than other fonts.

Inserting Space Between Paragraphs

Leaving space between paragraphs helps the reader easily see where one paragraph ends and another begins. Of course, you can insert blank lines between paragraphs simply by pressing the **Enter** key twice at the end of a paragraph, but that's a sloppy technique that reduces your control over paragraph spacing.

By specifying the exact amount of space you want inserted between paragraphs, you ensure that the amount of space between paragraphs is consistent throughout your document.

To change the space between paragraphs, drag over the paragraphs to highlight at least a portion of each paragraph. (You need not highlight the entire first and last paragraphs.) Open the **Format** menu and click **Paragraph**. Under **Spacing**, click the arrows to the right of **Before** or **After** to specify the amount of space (measured in points) you want to insert before or after each paragraph. Click **OK**.

Save It or Lose It

Unless you're the type of person who loves the thrill of risking everything for no potential gain, you should save your document soon after you type a paragraph or two. Why? Because right now, your computer is storing everything you type in RAM (Random Access Memory). A little dip in your local electric company's power grid can send your document off to Never Never Land. To prevent losing your work, save it to a permanent storage area—your computer's hard disk.

The first time you save a document, your program asks for two things: a name for the document and the name of the drive and folder where you want the document stored. Here's the standard operating procedure for saving documents in most Windows programs:

1. Click the **Save** button or open the **File** menu and click **Save**. The Save As dialog box appears, asking you to name the file.

2. Click in the **File Name** text box and type a name for the file, as shown in Figure 11.4. The name can be up to 255 characters long and you can use spaces, but you cannot use any of the following taboo characters: \ / : * ? " < > or |.

3. Open the Save In list and click the letter of the disk on which you want to save the document (typically drive C).

4. In the file/folder area, double-click the folder in which you want the document saved. (To save the document in a folder that's inside another folder, repeat this step.)

5. Click the **OK** or **Save** button. The file is saved to the disk.

Computer Cheats

I Clicked the Wrong Folder!

If you pass up the folder you wanted to select, you can back up. Click the **Up One Level** button.

Select the folder here.

Select the disk drive here.

Type a filename here.

Figure 11.4

Use the Save As dialog box to save your document to your computer's hard disk.

From now on, saving this document is easy; you don't have to name it or tell the program where to store it ever again. The program saves your changes in the document you already created and named. You should save your document every 5 to 10 minutes to avoid losing any work. In most programs, you can quickly save a document by pressing **Ctrl+S** or by clicking on the **Save** button in the program's toolbar.

Printing Addresses on Envelopes

Are you one of those people who carefully types and formats a letter and then addresses the envelope by hand? You're not the only one. Many people become frustrated trying to figure out how to print an address on an envelope. Fortunately, Word can help.

To print one envelope, open the **Tools** menu, click **Envelopes and Labels**, and make sure the Envelopes tab is up front (see Figure 11.5). Type the recipient's name and address in the **Delivery Address** text box. Tab to the **Return Address** text box and type your address. You can format selected text in the Delivery or Return Address text boxes by highlighting the text and pressing the key combination for the desired formatting—for example, **Ctrl+B** for bold. You can also right-click the text to choose additional formatting options.

Printing for a Mailing List

Chapter 15, "Form Letters, Mailing Labels, and Envelopes," shows you how to integrate a mailing list with documents, enabling you to print multiple envelopes at one time.

Figure 11.5

Make your envelope look as professional as your letter.

Enter the recipient's address.

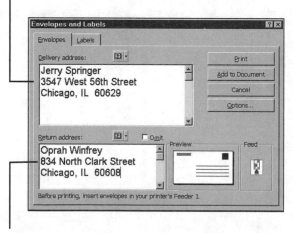

Type your address.

Before you print, click the **Options** button. This displays the Envelope Options dialog box, which enables you to specify the envelope size and the fonts for the delivery and return addresses. The Printing Options tab enables you to specify how the envelopes feed into your printer. Enter your preferences and click the **OK** button.

If you need to manually load the envelope into your printer, load away. All printers are different; check your printer's documentation to determine the proper loading technique. When the envelope is in position, click the **Print** button to print it.

Dry Run

Before printing on a relatively expensive envelope, print on a normal sheet of paper to check the position of the print. You can then make adjustments without wasting costly supplies.

The Least You Need to Know

If you know your way around a typewriter, you don't need to know much to create your first document. Just start typing. After you have something on the screen, you can get down to work. Just make sure you know the following information:

➤ Use the Zoom list to zoom in if the text is too small.

➤ Use the arrow keys or the mouse to move the insertion point.

➤ Use the Insert, Date and Time command to insert the current date from your computer.

➤ Drag the mouse pointer over text to highlight it.

➤ Use the buttons in the Formatting toolbar to quickly style and align your text.

➤ To avoid losing your document, press **Ctrl+S** to save it to your computer's hard disk.

➤ Save early and save often.

Chapter 12

Editing and Printing Your Letter

In This Chapter

➤ 10 quick ways to highlight text

➤ Cutting, copying, moving, and dragging text

➤ Saving your own neck with the Undo button

➤ Tweaking the page margins

➤ Printing your masterpiece

➤ Designing your own letterhead

Is your letter perfect? Are you sure? Take a 10-minute break, come back, and read it again with fresh eyes. Chances are that your letter has at least a couple of minor flaws and possibly even some major organizational problems. To perform the required fixes and purge common errors from your letter, you need to master the tools of the trade. This chapter shows you how to use your word processor's editing tools to copy, move, and delete text, and to check for and correct spelling errors and typos.

And after your letter is perfect, this chapter shows you how to transform the document displayed onscreen into a printed product. If you stick with me to the end of the chapter, I'll even show you how to combine text and graphics to create your own custom letterhead.

Selecting Text

Before you can do anything with the text you just typed, you must select it. You can always just drag over text to select it (as explained in the previous chapter), but Word offers several quicker ways to select text. Table 12.1 describes these techniques:

Table 12.1   Quick Text Selection Techniques

To Select This	Do This
Single word	Double-click the word.
Sentence	**Ctrl+click** anywhere in the sentence.
Paragraph	Triple-click anywhere in the paragraph. Alternatively, position the pointer to the left of the paragraph until it changes to a right-pointing arrow, and then double-click.
Several paragraphs	Position the pointer to the left of the paragraphs until it changes to a right-pointing arrow. Then double-click and drag up or down.
One line of text	Position the pointer to the left of the line until it changes to a right-pointing arrow, and then click. (Drag to select additional lines.)
Large block of text	Click at the beginning of the text, scroll down to the end of the text, and **Shift+click**.
Entire document	Position the pointer to the left of any text until it changes to a right-pointing arrow. And then triple-click, or press **Ctrl+A**.
Extend selection	Hold down the **Shift** key while using the arrow keys, Page Up, Page Down, Home, or End.

Cutting and Pasting Without Scissors

Every word processor features the electronic equivalent of scissors and glue. With the cut, copy, and paste commands, you can cut or copy selected text and then insert it in a different location in your document. You can even copy or cut text from one document and paste it into another document!

To cut or copy text, select it, and then click either the **Cut** or the **Copy** button in the toolbar. Move the insertion point to where you want the text inserted and then click the **Paste** button.

Whenever you cut or copy data in any Windows program, Windows places the data in a temporary storage area called the *Clipboard*. In the old days, the Clipboard could store only one chunk of data. If you cut one selection and then cut another selection, the second selection would bump the first selection off the Clipboard. Word 2000 upgrades the Clipboard, enabling it to store multiple selections. When you cut or copy two or more selections, the Clipboard toolbar appears, displaying an icon for each copied or cut selection. To paste the selection, click its icon. To paste all of the cut or copied selections, click the **Paste All** button. If the Clipboard toolbar does not appear, right-click any toolbar and click **Clipboard**.

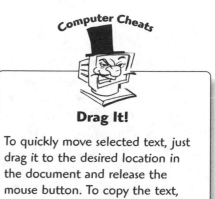

Computer Cheats

Drag It!

To quickly move selected text, just drag it to the desired location in the document and release the mouse button. To copy the text, hold down the **Ctrl** key while you drag.

Oops! Undoing Changes

What if you highlight your entire document intending to change the font size and then press the Delete key by mistake? Is your entire document gone for good?

Nope.

As you cut, paste, delete, and perform similar acts of destruction, your Word processor keeps track of each command and enables you to recover from the occasional blunder. To undo the most recent action, open the **Edit** menu and choose **Undo**, or click the **Undo** button in the Standard toolbar. You can continue to click the **Undo** button to undo additional actions.

Whoa!

No Undoing After Closing

After you save your document and close it, you cannot reopen it and undo actions you performed during a previous work session.

Checking Your Spelling and Grammar

In the previous chapter, you learned that Word automatically checks for typos and spelling errors as you type. If you turned off that option, you can still initiate a spelling check by opening the **Tools** menu and selecting **Spelling and Grammar** or by clicking the **Spelling and Grammar** button in the Standard toolbar.

Word starts checking your document and stops on the first questionable word. The Spelling and Grammar dialog box displays the word in red and usually displays a list of suggested corrections, as shown in Figure 12.1. (If the word appears in green, the grammar checker is questioning the word's usage, not its spelling.) You have several options:

➤ Double-click the word in the Not in Dictionary text box, type the correction, and click **Change**.

➤ Click **Ignore** if the word is spelled correctly and you want to skip it just this once. Word stops on the next occurrence of the word.

➤ Click **Ignore All** if the word is spelled correctly but is not in the dictionary and you want Word to skip any other occurrences of this word in this document.

➤ Click **Add** to add the word to the dictionary so that the spelling checker never questions it again in any of your Office documents (the dictionary is shared by all Office applications).

➤ If the word is spelled incorrectly and the Suggestions list displays the correct spelling, click the correct spelling and click **Change** to replace only this occurrence of the word.

➤ To replace this misspelled word and all other occurrences of the word in this document, click the correct spelling in the Suggestions list and click **Change All**.

Figure 12.1

If Word finds a misspelling and displays the correct spelling, your options are easy.

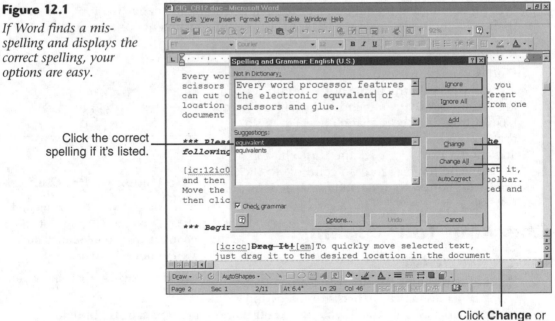

Click the correct spelling if it's listed.

Click **Change** or **Change All**.

When Word completes the spelling check, it displays a dialog box telling you so. Click **OK**.

Setting Your Margins and Page Layout

After typing a document, you might be tempted to just click the **Print** button in the Standard toolbar to crank out a paper copy of the document. Avoid the temptation. You usually just end up wasting paper and being sorely disappointed with the results. Before you print, you should first check the Page Setup options.

To display the Page Setup options, open the **File** menu and select **Page Setup**. The Page Setup dialog box appears, presenting four tabs for changing various page and print settings. In the following sections, you learn how to use this dialog box to set margins and control the way Word prints text on the pages.

Check a Word

To check the spelling of a single word or paragraph, double-click the word or triple-click the paragraph to select it before you start the spelling checker. When Word is done checking the selection, it displays a dialog box asking if you want to check the rest of the document.

Setting the Page Margins

The very first time the Page Setup dialog box appears, the Margins tab is up front, as shown in Figure 12.2. If it's hiding, click it to bring it to the front. This tab enables you to change the top, bottom, left, and right margins. Click the up or down arrow to the right of each margin setting to change the setting in increments of .1 inch, or click in a margin setting text box and type a more precise measurement.

The Margins tab offers several additional options for special printing needs:

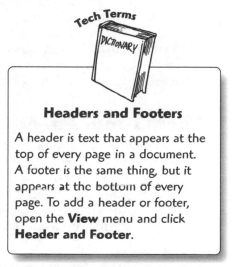

Headers and Footers

A header is text that appears at the top of every page in a document. A footer is the same thing, but it appears at the bottom of every page. To add a header or footer, open the **View** menu and click **Header and Footer**.

➤ *Gutter* enables you to add margin space to the inside margin of the pages, in case you plan to insert the pages into a book or binder.

➤ *From Edge* specifies the distance from the top of the page to the top of the header and from the bottom of the page to the bottom of the footer.

➤ *Mirror Margins* is useful if you plan to print on both sides of a page. When this option is on, Word makes the inside margins of facing pages equal.

➤ *2 Pages per Sheet* shrinks the pages of your document so Word can print two pages on a single sheet of paper.

➤ *Apply To* enables you to apply the margin settings to the entire document, from this point forward in the document, or only to selected text. This is useful for long documents that might require different page layouts for some sections.

Figure 12.2

Set the page margins for the entire document.

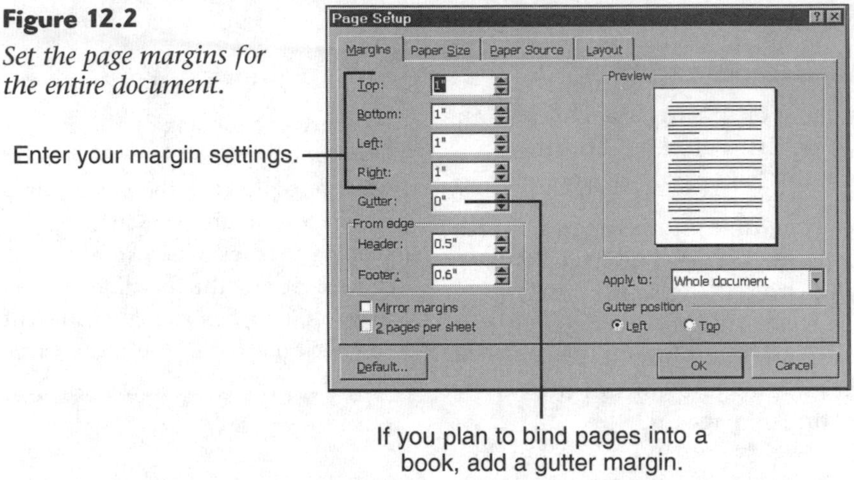

Enter your margin settings.

If you plan to bind pages into a book, add a gutter margin.

Picking a Paper Size and Print Direction

Usually, you print a document right side up on 8.5 × 11-inch paper. In some cases, however, you might need to print on legal-size paper or print a wide document, such as an announcement or sign, sideways on the page. If that's the case, check out the Paper Size tab. On this tab, you can pick from a list of standard paper sizes or specify a custom size. You can also select a print orientation: **Portrait** (to print normally, as in this book) or **Landscape** (to print sideways on the page). Landscape is especially useful if you choose the 2 Pages per Sheet option.

Where's Your Paper Coming From?

If you always print on standard 8.5 × 11-inch paper, you don't really need to worry about where the paper is coming from. Your printer is set up to use the default paper tray, which is typically loaded with 8.5 × 11-inch paper, and all your programs know that. If, however, you need to print envelopes, banners, or any other paper that's not 8.5 × 11-inch, check the Paper Source tab before you start printing just to make sure that Word is set up to use the right tray.

Laying Out Your Pages

The last tab in the Page Setup dialog box is the Layout tab. You can safely ignore most of the options on the Layout tab. Just be sure you don't miss the following three options:

Vertical Alignment   The Vertical Alignment list is very useful for making one-page documents (such as a short letter) look good on the page. Open the list and select **Center** to center the document on the page. This option is especially useful for printing cover pages and letters. To make the document fill the page, select **Justified**.

Line Numbers   The Line Numbers button is useful for legal and literary pieces. These types of documents often contain line numbers so that people can refer to the line numbers when discussing the documents, instead of quoting entire lines and sounding really boring. To insert line numbers, click the button and enter your preferences.

Borders   The Borders button opens the Borders and Shading dialog box, which allows you to add a border around your entire page or at the top, bottom, left, or right margin.

Saving Paper: Previewing Before Printing

Before you print the document, click the **Print Preview** button in the Standard toolbar. This gives you a bird's-eye view of the page, enables you to quickly flip pages, and provides rulers you can use to drag the margin settings around.

Sending Your Letter Off to the Printer

When you have your printer working successfully with any of your Windows applications, printing is pretty simple. Make sure your printer has plenty of paper and ink or toner, turn on the printer, open your document, and click the **Print** button.

To take more control of the printing—to print extra copies, print sideways on the page (landscape mode), collate copies, select a print quality, or enter other settings—you must display the Print dialog box. To do this, open the **File** menu and select **Print** instead of clicking the Print button. You can then use the Print dialog box, shown in Figure 12.3, to enter your preferences.

Computer Cheats

Shrink to Fit

If you have a short document with just a few lines of text stranded on the last page, click the **Shrink to Fit** button in the Print Preview toolbar. Word automatically decreases the font size of all the text to pull the excess text to the bottom of the previous page.

Figure 12.3

Enter your printing preferences.

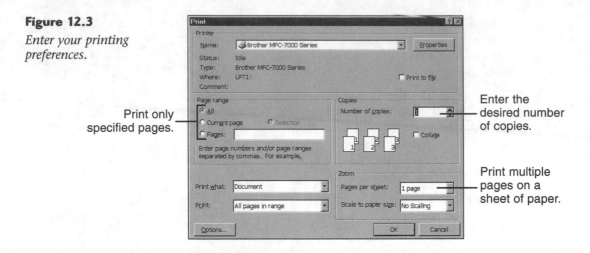

Print only specified pages.

Enter the desired number of copies.

Print multiple pages on a sheet of paper.

Hey, It's Not Printing!

If Word refuses to start printing your document, you'll have to do a little troubleshooting. The following questions can help you track down the cause:

➤ Is your printer plugged in and turned on?

➤ Does your printer have paper? Is the paper tray inserted properly?

➤ Is the printer's On Line light on (not blinking)? If the On Line light is off or blinking, press the **On Line** button to turn on the light.

➤ Display the Print dialog box again and make sure Print to File is not selected. This option sends the document to a file on your disk instead of to the printer.

➤ Is your printer marked as the default printer? In My Computer, double-click the **Printers** icon. Right-click the icon for your printer and make sure that Set as Default is checked. If there is no check mark, select **Set As Default**.

➤ Is the printer paused? Double-click the printer icon on the right end of the taskbar, open the **Printer** menu, and make sure that Pause Printing is not checked. If there is a check mark, click **Pause Printing**.

➤ Is the correct printer port selected? In My Computer, double-click the **Printers** icon and then right-click the icon for your printer and choose **Properties**. Click the **Details** tab and make sure the correct printer port is selected—LPT1 in most cases.

Project Time! Making Your Own Letterhead

A plain-vanilla, text-only letter is fine if you're writing to your accountant, but if you're trying to impress a prospective employer or add a personal touch to a friendly letter, try creating your own letterhead. All you need to do is add a clip art graphic, your address, and a code for inserting the date. The following instructions lead you step by step through the process:

1. Click the **New Blank Document** button.

2. Open the **Insert** menu, point to **Picture**, and click **Clip Art**.

3. Use the Insert ClipArt dialog box to find the picture you want to use for your letterhead.

4. Click the desired clip art image and click the **Insert Clip** button. (Close or minimize the Insert ClipArt dialog box when you're done.)

5. Right-click the image that you inserted in Step 4 and click **Format Picture**.

6. Click the **Layout** tab, click **In Front of Text**, and click **OK**. This lets you move the image without affecting the text you will type later.

7. Resize and move the image, as desired, to place it in the upper-left corner of the page.

8. Drag the Left Indent marker to the right to move the insertion point out from under the image, as shown in Figure 12.4.

9. Type your name and address (or your business name and address) on separate lines, as you would type the inside address in any letter.

10. Open the **Insert** menu and click **Date and Time**.

11. Click the desired format for the date, make sure **Update Automatically** is checked, and click **OK**. Word inserts the date as a code, so whenever you open this letterhead, Word will insert the current date.

12. (Optional) Right-click any toolbar and click **Drawing** to turn on the drawing toolbar.

13. Click the **Line** button in the drawing toolbar.

14. Hold down the **Shift** key and drag a line from left to right, just below your address, as shown in Figure 12.4. When you release the mouse button, a line appears.

15. Click the **Line Style** button and click the desired line thickness.

16. Click the **Line Color** button and click the desired line color.

Use a Page Border

You can use a page border to create some fancy stationery. Open the **Format** menu and click **Borders and Shading**. Choose the desired line style or open the Art list and choose a graphic border. In the Preview area, click the top and right border lines to leave only the left and bottom border lines in place.

When you're finished, press **Ctrl+S**. Open the **Save As Type** list and click **Document Template (*.dot)**. Name the document and save it as you normally would. By saving your letterhead as a template, you can use the File, New command to open it and use it to create a new letter without affecting the original template.

Figure 12.4

Create your own letterhead.

Drag the left indent marker to indent the inside address to the right of the picture.

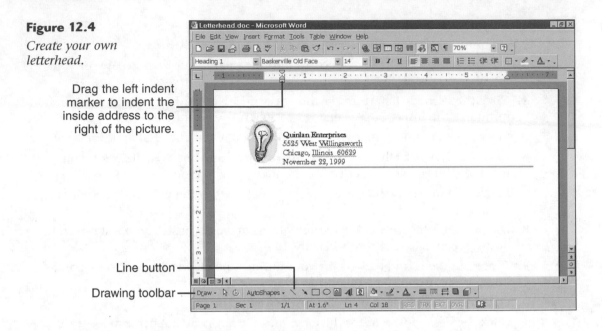

Line button

Drawing toolbar

The Least You Need to Know

This chapter is chock-full of important information on how to check your letter (or any document) for errors, edit your letter, print it, and even create your own fancy letterhead. You don't need to remember everything, but make sure the following points stick to your brain cells:

➤ To select a single word, double-click it; a sentence, **Ctrl+click** it; a paragraph, triple-click it.

➤ To move selected text, drag it to the desired location and release the mouse button. To copy text, hold down the **Ctrl** key while dragging.

➤ Click the **Undo** button to reverse the last action you performed or command you entered.

➤ To initiate a spelling check, click the **Spelling and Grammar** button.

➤ Before you print a document, open the **File** menu, click **Page Setup**, and check the page layout options.

➤ To quickly print a document, no questions asked, click the **Print** button. For more control over printing, choose **File**, **Print**.

➤ If your document doesn't start printing, double-click the printer icon on the right end of the taskbar to determine what's wrong.

Chapter 13

Designing Personalized Greeting Cards, Banners, and Other Publications

In This Chapter

➤ Getting started with a desktop publishing program

➤ Picking a greeting card off the rack

➤ Customizing greeting cards and other publications

➤ Combining pictures and text (without losing anything)

➤ Printing a banner for your next party

Word processors make great blue-collar programs. They're excellent for typing and printing memos, letters, and reports, but they fall short when it comes to creating fancy, designer publications that dazzle the eye. Unless you're a master of page layout, you'll find it nearly impossible to create a greeting card, banner, or tri-fold brochure using a word processor.

To create these specialized publications, you need a program that provides precise control over pictures and text. You need a desktop publishing program. In this chapter, you learn how to use a desktop publishing program to design and build your own greeting cards, banners, business cards, and other custom publications.

What You Need to Get Started

Before you get too excited over the possibilities, first make sure you have a desktop publishing program installed on your computer. Many new computers include Microsoft Publisher or Broderbund's Print Shop Deluxe. If you have Microsoft Publisher, you've hit pay dirt, because this chapter uses Publisher to illustrate the cool publications you can create. If you don't have Publisher, don't worry—most desktop publishing programs offer similar tools and commands for creating publications and for inserting and manipulating text and graphics.

Check Your Printer Software

If your computer didn't come with a desktop publishing program, check the CD or diskettes that came with your printer. Many printer manufacturers include a copy of a basic desktop publishing program to show off the capabilities of the printer.

Starting with a Prefab Greeting Card

Popular desktop publishing programs pride themselves on never leaving you with a blank screen. On startup, the program typically displays a window or dialog box that lists the available publication types: greeting card, brochure, flyer, business card, banner, and so on. You simply choose the desired type of publication and click the **OK** or **Next** button to initiate a publication wizard or open a ready-made publication.

If Microsoft Publisher is installed on your system, take the following steps to initiate the publishing wizard and create your own custom greeting card. If you don't have Publisher, follow along to see how it's done:

1. Click the **Start** button, point to **Programs**, and click **Microsoft Publisher**. The Microsoft Publisher Catalog appears, displaying a list of publication types.

2. Click **Greeting Cards** to view a list of greeting card types.

3. Click the desired greeting card type. The preview area on the right displays the available ready-made cards, as shown in Figure 13.1.

4. Click the card that best suits your tastes.

5. Click the **Start Wizard** button.

6. Follow the wizard's instructions to enter your preferences.

7. When you've entered your final preference, click the **Finish** button. The wizard announces that you've done everything you needed to do and offers to create the publication.

8. Click **Create It**, and then sit back and watch as the Wizard does its paste-up work.

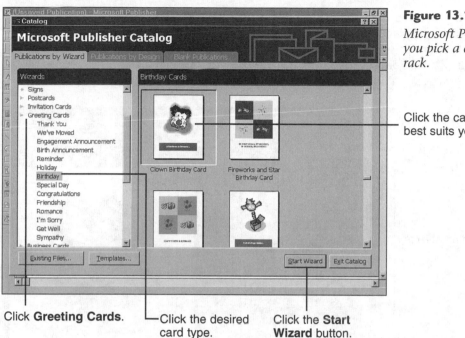

Figure 13.1
Microsoft Publisher lets you pick a card off the rack.

Click the card that best suits your tastes.

Click **Greeting Cards**. Click the desired card type. Click the **Start Wizard** button.

When Publisher is done slapping together your greeting card, Publisher displays it in the work area on the right. To the left of the work area is the Wizard pane, where you can change the overall design, layout, color scheme, and other settings that control your publication. To make a change, click the desired category in the Wizard list at the top, and then click the desired setting or enter the requested information at the bottom. You can hide the Wizard pane at any time by clicking the **Hide Wizard** button below the pane.

Microsoft Publisher Survival Guide

Your first glance at the publication that the wizard created might just turn you to stone. The page is dinky, the graphics look sloppy, and the text looks as if the wizard were trying to fit it on the head of a pin. Before you can do anything, you need to know how to zoom in and out and flip from one page to the next.

Panic Attack

This Isn't What I Wanted!

Most of the options that the desktop publishing program displays are rather limited. Just pick the least objectionable options for now. You'll learn how to customize your greeting card in the following sections.

First, zoom in. Open the **Zoom** drop-down list in the standard toolbar and choose the desired zoom percentage—75% is usually sufficient. Just below the work area are the page flippers, as shown in Figure 13.2. Click the icon for the desired page to quickly display it. You already know how to use the scrollbars; you'll get plenty of scrollbar practice in Publisher.

Figure 13.2

Before you can start working, make sure you can see everything.

Tools for inserting objects

You can hide the Wizard for more room to work.

Use the Page Navigation buttons to flip pages.

Choose the desired zoom percentage.

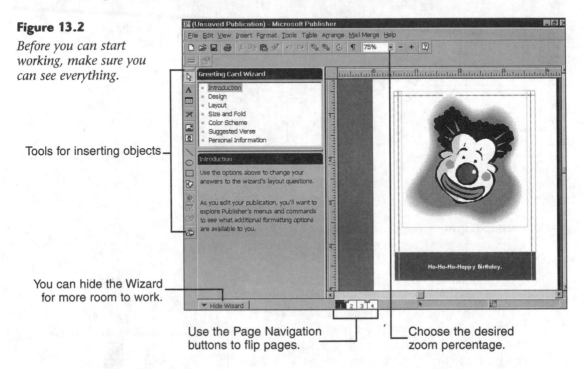

After you have everything in plain sight, you're ready to fiddle with the publication. However, there are a few additional things that might not seem obvious at first:

➤ Every 15 minutes, a dialog box pops up on your screen, reminding you to save your work. Reply the first time and save your file, but if this dialog box becomes too annoying, turn it off. Choose **Tools**, **Options**, click the **User Assistance** tab, and click **Remind to Save Publication** to remove the check mark.

➤ The **Undo** button doesn't have a drop-down list as in Word, but it can undo more than one action by clicking on the button several times.

➤ You will encounter two types of text boxes, normal and WordArt, which might look the same. To edit text in a normal text box, click in the text box to position the insertion point and type your changes (just pretend that you're working in Word). For WordArt "text boxes," double-click the box to display a dialog box for editing the text. Edit your text and click **OK**.

➤ The dotted lines are page layout guides. They don't print. They just help you align stuff more precisely.

➤ Some publications have a text frame off to the side that displays information about the publication. This won't print. In fact, nothing placed on the gray area outside the page will print. You can drag objects onto this work area as you lay out your pages.

➤ A greeting card may have a graphic on the first page that looks as though it doesn't fit on the page. Don't worry about it. Publisher does this wrap-around thing with the graphic so it prints on both the front and back of the card. It's actually pretty cool.

Playing with Pictures

Whenever you start with a ready-made greeting card, the desktop publishing program chooses the picture to place on the front and any other graphics for the inside and back of the card. What happens if you don't like the picture? Are you stuck with it? Should you run the wizard and try a different design? No! Simply replace the picture with a different clip art image.

In most desktop publishing programs, including Microsoft Publisher, you simply double-click the existing image and select a new image from the program's clip art library. If that doesn't work, click the image and press the **Delete** key to get rid of it. Choose the **Insert**, **Picture**, **Clip Art** command; click the desired image; and click the **Insert Clip** button.

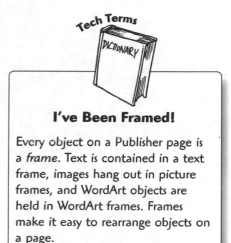

Tech Terms

I've Been Framed!

Every object on a Publisher page is a *frame*. Text is contained in a text frame, images hang out in picture frames, and WordArt objects are held in WordArt frames. Frames make it easy to rearrange objects on a page.

If the picture ends up in the wrong location or is too big or too small, move or resize it as needed. First, click the image to select it and display its handles (small black squares that allow you to resize the image). Drag the image to move it or drag a corner handle to resize it. Microsoft Publisher also features a cropping tool that enables you to "trim" the edges of the image. Click the **Crop** button as shown in Figure 13.3 and then drag a handle toward the center of the image to trim an edge off the image. (If you crop too much, drag the handle away from the image to uncrop it.)

Figure 13.3

Trim an image to remove unwanted parts.

Crop button ⌐

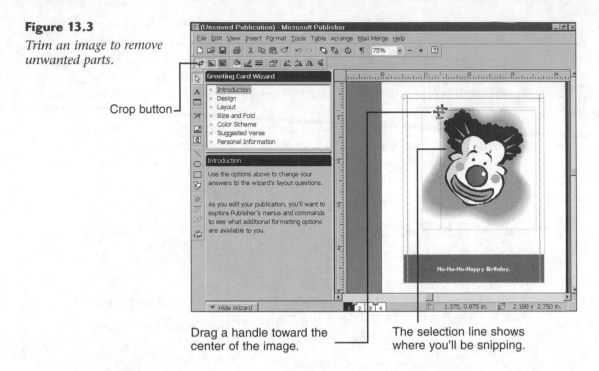

Drag a handle toward the center of the image.

The selection line shows where you'll be snipping.

Text-in-a-Box

Unlike word processors, which enable you to type right on a page, desktop publishing programs won't let you place anything on a page unless it's in a *frame* or *box*. To place text in your publication, you must first draw a text box and then type something in that box. As you fine-tune your publication, you can drag and stretch the box as needed to position it on the page and accommodate your text.

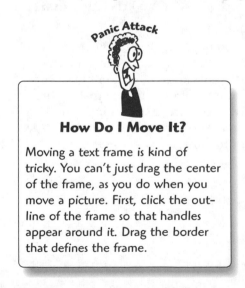

How Do I Move It?

Moving a text frame is kind of tricky. You can't just drag the center of the frame, as you do when you move a picture. First, click the outline of the frame so that handles appear around it. Drag the border that defines the frame.

A To create a text frame, click the **Text Frame Tool**. The mouse pointer turns into a crosshair pointer. Position the pointer where you want the upper left corner of the frame to appear and then drag down and to the right to create a frame of the desired height and width. When you release the mouse button, Word inserts the text frame. Type your text in the frame and use the Formatting toolbar to style the text.

If you fill the frame, Publisher displays a dialog box asking if you want to flow the excess text into a new text frame. To have Publisher create a new text frame for you and link the two frames, click **Yes**. If you want all of your text in one frame, click **No**, and then resize the frame or choose a smaller type size. To link two frames yourself, click one frame, click the **Connect Text Frames** button, and click inside the second frame.

Layering Pictures and Text Boxes

Working with two or more frames on a page is like making your own collage. The trouble with frames is that when you place one frame on top of another, the top frame blocks the bottom one and prevents you from selecting it. You have to flip through the stack to find the frame that you want.

Inside Tip

Linking Frames in a Newsletter

Linked frames are great for newsletters. You can start a story on the front page and then print the rest of the story in a frame on the next page or anywhere in the newsletter.

Publisher and most other desktop publishing programs offer tools to help you rearrange the frames in a stack. You can send an object that's up front back one layer or all the way to the bottom of the stack, or you can bring an object from the back to the front. First, click the object you want to move (if possible). Some objects are buried so deeply that you can't get to them. In such a case, you have to move objects from the front to the back to get them out of the way until you find the one you want.

After selecting the object that you want to move, open the **Arrange** menu and select the desired movement: **Bring to Front**, **Send to Back**, **Bring Forward**, **Send Backward**, **Bring in Front of Text**, or **Send Behind Text**.

Inside Tip

Grouping Frames

If you have a half dozen frames on a page and want to nudge them all to the right, you don't have to move each frame individually. Click the **Pointer Tool** and **Shift+click** each object you want to move. Drag one of the frames, and all the rest will follow like little sheep. To group the objects and make them act as a single object, right-click one of the objects and click **Group**. (To ungroup the objects, right-click the grouped object and click **Ungroup**.)

Do-It-Yourself Banners

You're throwing a birthday party for your friend, and you've already created a custom birthday card and churned out the party invitations. With the big date fast approaching, you realize that a banner would jazz up the party décor, but you have no idea where to start. Never fear, your handy-dandy desktop publishing program has just the thing you need.

If you're using Microsoft Publisher, choose **File**, **New**, and click **Banners** in the Wizards list. The steps you use to pick a banner and initiate the publishing wizard are nearly identical to those given earlier in this chapter for creating a greeting card. The only difference is that in Step 2, you choose **Banners** instead of Greeting Cards. After starting the Wizard, simply follow the onscreen instructions and enter your preferences.

Although creating a banner is easy, printing a banner may be fairly complicated, depending on your printer. Many printers require you to flip levers or follow a special procedure for loading banner paper into the printer. In addition, you may need to change the print settings in Windows to indicate that you're printing a banner. Even if you're printing the banner on standard 8.5-by-11-inch sheets of paper (to tape together after printing), you might need to specify that you're printing a banner. Failing to do so might cause the printer to chop off the print area where you tape together the sheets that make up the banner.

In most cases, you choose the **File**, **Print** command and then click the **Properties** button to access the setting for printing a banner. Click the **Paper** tab, and then choose **Banner**, as shown in Figure 13.4. Enter any other settings as desired and click **OK**. Load your banner paper as specified in your printer documentation, and then click **OK** to start printing.

Figure 13.4

Some printers require that you enter a special print setting to print banners.

Click the **Paper** tab.

Click **Banner**.

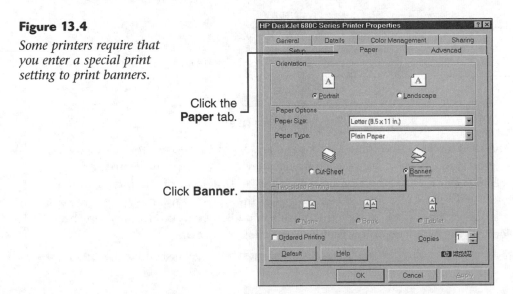

Other Cool Desktop Publishing Stuff

Just a few short years ago, home-based desktop publishing programs focused primarily on greeting cards and banners. However, with more and more people starting their own small businesses, these programs have expanded their offerings to include flyers, business cards, newsletters, catalogs, brochures, and even Web pages! Figure 13.5 displays a portion of a 3-fold brochure created with Publisher.

Figure 13.5

A brochure is a great tool for advertising products.

As long as you have the skills required for moving and resizing graphics and text frames, you can create and customize any personal or business publication you need.

Inside Tip

Printing on Card Stock

If you plan on printing your publication on thicker paper or card stock (for business cards), make sure you adjust the thickness setting on your paper feeder. Otherwise, the paper might become jammed or fail to feed through the printer.

The Least You Need to Know

Although desktop publishing programs are fairly complicated, most come with a robust collection of ready-made publications, which you can customize for your personal or business use. When you're ready to start creating your own publications, keep the following information at your fingertips:

➤ To create a new publication, enter the **File**, **New** command and follow the onscreen instructions.

➤ To add text to a publication, you must first draw a text box or text frame.

➤ To insert a clip art image, open the **Insert** menu, point to **Picture**, and click **Clip Art**.

➤ To resize a graphic or text frame, first click the frame or graphic and then drag one of its handles.

➤ To move a text frame, click the outline of the frame and then drag the frame's border.

➤ To send a frame back one layer in a stack, click the frame, open the **Arrange** menu, and click **Send Backward**.

Creating an Address Book and Other Listy Stuff

Unless you're a hermit, you probably have an address book packed with the names, addresses, and phone numbers of your friends and relatives. You might have a day planner that contains a list of business contacts or a wallet or purse packed with business cards. If you're a parent, team lists, practice schedules, and important school dates dangle from your refrigerator or cabinet doors. You might even have Post-It notes stuck to the walls and countertops to remind you of important dates.

How would you like to consolidate this loose collection of notes and papers and keep it in one location—on your computer? In this chapter, you learn how to use various programs to organize and manage names, addresses, phone numbers, dates, and other important information.

Tables, Spreadsheets, Databases, and Address Books

Now don't get all excited and start typing a list of names and addresses in your word processor. Doing so will create a mess you'll only have to clean up later. First, pick the right tool for the right job:

➤ To create a simple address book, membership directory, or other list without leaving your word processor, use a table as explained in the following section.

➤ To create a full-featured address book for personal or business use, enter your data in a personal information manager, such as Microsoft Outlook (see "Using an Electronic Day Planner" later in this chapter). You can use an address book to store names, mailing addresses, email addresses, phone and fax numbers, and pertinent information about each contact.

➤ If you want more control over the layout of your records or have numerical data, such as membership fees you need to track, enter your data in a spreadsheet, as explained in "Automating Calculations with Spreadsheets" later in this chapter.

➤ For more flexibility and control over your data, use a database, as explained in "Managing Records in a Database." A database is great for generating reports. A *relational database*, such as Access, can even extract and combine data from two or more databases.

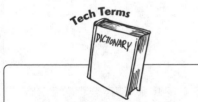

Tech Terms

Relational Database

A *relational database* is a data management program that can extract data from two or more databases (a collection of records) and combine the data in a single report. In a relational database, for instance, you can create an invoice that combines part numbers and prices from one database and customer names and addresses from another database.

Making a Simple Address Book with a Word Table

Are you looking for a no-frills address book that doesn't require you to learn another program? Consider creating your address book using Word's table feature. You simply create a table consisting of several columns and rows and then type in the names and addresses, as shown in Figure 14.1. You can even use the table along with Word's mail merge feature to automate mass mailings, as explained in Chapter 15, "Form Letters, Mailing Labels, and Envelopes." For details on creating a table in Word, see "Setting Up Your Own Table" later in this chapter.

Figure 14.1

Word's table feature enables you to create a basic address book.

Title	Lname	Fname	Street	City	State	ZIP	Phone
Mr.	Fink	Bart	212 N. Acre St.	San Francisco	CA	94108	(415)555-5555
Ms.	Lane	Lois	1111 W. Fagon Ave.	San Francisco	CA	94110	(415)555-1212
Mr.	Strap	Greg	1308 S. Naples St.	Chicago	IL	60629	(312)555-5555

Using an Electronic Day Planner

Many computers come with an electronic version of a day planner, commonly called a *personal information manager* (*PIM* for short). One of the most popular PIMs is Microsoft Outlook, shown in Figure 14.2. With Outlook, you can send and receive email messages, keep track of appointments and special dates (such as anniversaries and birthdays), create a to-do list, and even manage your documents.

Of course, I can't cover all of that nifty stuff in this section, but I can tell you how to create your own address book in Outlook. First, click the **Contacts** icon. Click the **New Contact** button (on the left end of the button bar). The New Contact dialog box appears. Enter the person's name, address, phone number, email address, and other contact information. Click the **Save and New** button to save the address card and display a new blank card, or click **Save and Close** to close the window.

Inside Tip

Multifunction Tables

Tables are great for aligning text in columns. For example, you can create a two-column table for laying out your résumé. Use the left column to list dates and the right column for job descriptions and information about training and education.

127

Figure 14.2

Outlook can help you manage your life.

Send and receive email.

Log appointments.

Create an address book.

Create and check your to-do list.

Write notes to yourself.

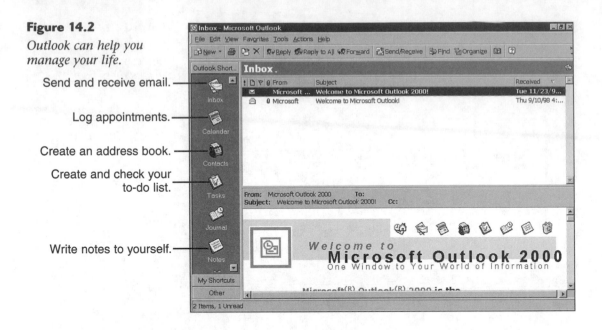

Automating Calculations with Spreadsheets

Generally speaking, PIMs and databases are better tools for entering, locating, and extracting information. However, if your data consists primarily of numerical entries and you need to analyze that data or perform calculations using those entries, use a spreadsheet.

A spreadsheet program, such as Microsoft Excel, displays a grid consisting of multiple rows and columns that intersect to form little boxes called *cells*. Each cell has an *address* consisting of its column letter and row number; for example, the cell in the upper left corner is A1. You type your entries just as you would type them in a table. Press the **Tab** or **Down Arrow** key to move from one cell to the next, and then type your entries in each cell.

Cheap Address Book

You can use an Excel spreadsheet to keep track of names and addresses, just as you can use a Word table. Make sure you type column headings in the top column ("LastName," "FirstName," and so on) to label your entries.

What makes spreadsheets special is that you can enter a formula in a cell that performs a calculation and displays the results. For example, the formula =(A1+B1+C1)/3 totals the values in the cells A1, B1, and C1 and divides the total by three to determine the average. Later in this chapter, you learn how to enter basic formulas in a Word table.

Managing Records in a Database

The Cadillac of data management tools is the database program. A database program enables you to design your own forms for collecting data, making data entry as easy as filling-in-the-blanks. As shown in Figure 14.3, the form represents a single *record* in the database, consisting of several *field* entries.

Figure 14.3

With a database program, you complete forms to enter records into the database.

The completed form represents a database record.

Each record consists of several field entries.

After you have entered the data for several records, you can use the database tools to find, sort, or filter records. *Filtering* consists of restricting the number of records the database displays; for example, you can tell the database to display only those records for February, 1999. In addition, you can create reports that pull data from one or more databases and then organize and summarize the data.

Setting Up Your Own Table

Early in this chapter, I promised to show you how to create a simple address book using a Word table, so let's get started. First, click the **Insert Table** button. This opens a list showing a graphic representation of the columns and rows that make up a table. Drag down and to the right to highlight the desired number of

Help Is on the Way!

Most database programs have sample databases, wizards, and other tools to help you create forms and reports. Use these tools to create basic forms and reports and then customize the forms and reports to suit your needs. Don't try to go it alone when you're first learning about databases. This is pretty complicated stuff.

rows and columns. If you need more columns or rows than first shown, drag beyond the bottom or right side of the grid to expand it (see Figure 14.4). When you release the mouse button, Word inserts the table.

Figure 14.4

Use the Insert Table button to set the number of rows and columns.

Click the
Insert Table —
button.

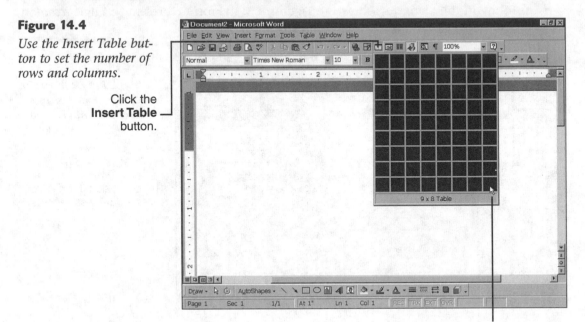

Drag over the desired
number of columns and rows.

No Spaces in the Column Headings

When typing column headings, don't type any spaces. For example, use "LName" or "LastName" instead of "Last Name." Using spaces will confuse the mail merge feature in Chapter 15.

Typing in the Little Boxes

After the table is in place, start typing your entries. In the top row, type headings for each column; for instance, type LastName, FirstName, and Address. The headings enable Word to find and extract data from the table to create mailing labels and personally addressed letters, as explained in the next chapter.

If an entry is too wide for the column, Word automatically resizes the columns or wraps text inside a cell to accommodate the entry. If you would prefer resizing the columns and rows yourself, skip ahead to the next section.

Press the **Tab** key to move from one cell (box) to the next or click in the cell. When you reach the end of the row, press the **Tab** key to move to the next row. If you're in the last cell of the last row, pressing the Tab key creates a new row so you can continue typing entries.

Rearranging and Resizing Columns and Rows

A table never turns out perfect the first time. Maybe you want more space between the top row and the rest of the table or you just don't like the way that Word is wrapping entries in the cells. In the following sections, you learn all the tricks for restructuring your table.

Adjusting the Row Height and Column Width

The easiest way to adjust the row height and column width is to drag the lines that divide the columns and rows. When you move the mouse pointer over a line, the pointer changes into a double-headed arrow; that's when you can start dragging. If you hold down the **Alt** key and drag, the horizontal or vertical ruler shows the exact row height or column width measurement. (You can also drag the column or row markers inside the rulers to change the row height and column width.)

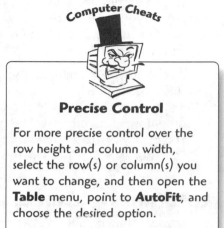

Computer Cheats

Precise Control

For more precise control over the row height and column width, select the row(s) or column(s) you want to change, and then open the **Table** menu, point to **AutoFit**, and choose the desired option.

Inserting and Deleting Columns and Rows

When you start typing entries in a table, you might find that you have either too many rows or columns or too few. Either problem is easy to correct:

➤ To insert one or more rows, click in the row where you want the new row added (or drag over the desired number of rows) and choose **Table**, **Insert**, **Rows Above**, or **Rows Below**.

➤ To insert one or more columns, first select an existing column (to insert two columns, select two columns). Then choose **Table**, **Insert**, **Columns to the Left**, or **Columns to the Right**.

➤ To delete rows or columns, drag over the rows or columns you want to delete and choose **Table**, **Delete**, **Rows**, or **Columns**. (If you press the Delete key instead, Word removes only the contents of the rows or columns.)

Inside Tip

Splitting and Merging Cells

You can merge two or more cells to create a cell that spans multiple columns or rows. Drag over the cells that you want to transform into a single cell, open the **Table** menu, and select **Merge Cells**. To split a cell, select the cell and choose **Table**, **Split Cells**.

Sorting Your List

Tables commonly contain entries that you need to sort alphabetically or numerically. If you create a table of phone numbers for people and places you frequently call, for example, you might want to sort the list alphabetically to make it easy to find people.

To sort entries in a table, first select the entire table (or the portion that contains the entries you want to sort). If you have a row at the top that contains descriptions of the contents in each column, make sure it is not selected; otherwise, it is sorted along with the other rows.

Open the **Table** menu and select **Sort**. Open the **Sort By** list and select the column that contains the entries to sort by. (For example, if you want to sort by last name and the last names are in the second column, select Column 2.) Open the **Type** drop-down list and select the type of items you want to sort (**Number**, **Text**, or **Date**). Select the desired sort order: **Ascending** (1,2,3 or A,B,C) or **Descending** (Z,Y,X or 10,9,8). Click **OK** to sort the entries.

Automating Calculations with Formulas

If your table includes numerical entries, such as membership dues or contributions, you might want to include a basic formula that totals a column of numbers.

Although a Word table is not designed to perform the complicated mathematical operations that an Excel spreadsheet can handle, tables can perform some basic calculations. For example, to total a column of numbers, take the following steps:

1. Click in the cell directly below the column of numbers you want to total.
2. Open the **Table** menu and click **Formula**. By default, the Formula dialog box is set up to total the values directly above the current cell.
3. Click **OK** to total the numbers.

Decorating Your Table with Lines and Shading

Your table might appear bland at first sight, but you can spice it up with some borders and shading. By far, the easiest way to embellish your table is to use the AutoFormat feature. Click anywhere inside the table, open the **Table** menu, and select **Table AutoFormat**. Select the desired design for your table and click **OK**.

If you don't like the prefab table designs that Word has to offer, you can design the table yourself using the Borders and Shading dialog box. To change the borders or add shading to the entire table, make sure the insertion point is somewhere inside the table; you don't have to select the entire table. To add borders or shading to specific cells, select the cells. Then open the **Format** menu and select **Borders and Shading** to display the Borders and Shading dialog box.

To add borders around cells or around the entire table, click the **Borders** tab. Select any of the border arrangements on the left, or create a custom border by inserting lines of a specific thickness, design, and color. Open the **Apply To** drop-down list, and choose **Table** (to apply the lines to the entire table) or **Cell** (to apply lines only to selected cells). You can turn individual border lines on or off by clicking them in the Preview area, as shown in Figure 14.5.

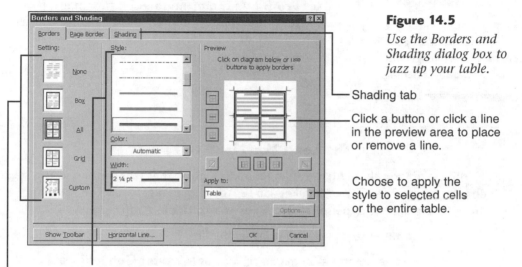

Figure 14.5

Use the Borders and Shading dialog box to jazz up your table.

Shading tab

Click a button or click a line in the preview area to place or remove a line.

Choose to apply the style to selected cells or the entire table.

Select a pre-designed border arrangement.

Select a line style, thickness, and color.

To shade cells with color or gray shading, click the **Shading** tab. In the Fill grid, click the color that you want to use to shade the table or selected cells. Under Patterns, click a color and percentage to add a pattern of a different color to the shading. For example, you might choose green as the fill and use a 50% yellow pattern to brighten the green. When you finish entering all of your border and shading preferences, click **OK** to apply the changes to your table.

What About Pictures?

Can you add pictures to a table? Of course! In fact, a table is the perfect tool for aligning graphics and text. For example, you can use a

Computer Cheats

Use the Toolbar

For quick formatting, use the Tables and Borders toolbar. Right-click any toolbar and click **Tables and Borders**. In addition to buttons for formatting tables, this toolbar contains the **Eraser** button, which enables you to quickly erase the lines that define cell boundaries.

Résumé Design

Use a two-column table to lay out your résumé. In the upper-left cell, insert a clip art image that's appropriate for the job opening.

table to create your own catalog. Simply insert graphics in the left column and type product descriptions and prices in the right column.

Before you insert a picture, make sure the insertion point is in the cell into which you want to insert the picture. Use the **Insert**, **Picture**, **Clip Art**, or **From File** command to insert the image. If you resize the image, you may need to resize the cell.

The Least You Need to Know

At this point, you should have a simple address book that you can use in the next chapter to create your own mailing labels. You should also know the following in order to organize your personal and business records more efficiently:

➤ Use a table to create and print simple lists.

➤ A personal information manager, such as Microsoft Outlook, features superior tools for creating and using an address book.

➤ Use a spreadsheet for any data on which you need to perform calculations.

➤ A database is most useful for heavy-duty data management and for producing forms and reports.

➤ To create a table in Word, click the **Insert Table** button and drag over the desired number of rows and columns.

➤ If you use a table for creating your address book, type column headings in the first row.

➤ To adjust the width of a column, drag the line on the right side of the column.

➤ To sort the records (rows) in a table, select all of the records and then enter the **Table**, **Sort** command.

Chapter 15

Form Letters, Mailing Labels, and Envelopes

In This Chapter

➤ Making your very own form letter

➤ Automating mass mailings

➤ Printing mailing labels for your Christmas cards

➤ Printing a stack of envelopes

Whether you run your own small business or just have lots of friends and relatives, mailing announcements, invitations, and greeting cards can become a major ordeal. Fortunately, Microsoft Word and most other popular word processors include a mail merge feature that can automate the task for you.

In this chapter, you learn how to create your own form letter and use Word's Mail Merge Helper to merge the form letter with a list of names and addresses to generate a stack of personally addressed letters. You also learn how to use the Mail Merge Helper to print a stack of matching envelopes. By the end of this chapter, all you'll have to do is stuff the envelopes and peel and stick the stamps.

The Incredible Power of the Mail Merge Feature

The mail merge feature is a powerful tool that merges a standard document, such las a form letter or mailing label, with a data source, such as an address list, to generate a series of unique documents. For example, the mail merge feature can

Data Source

A data source can be any document that contains a collection of records consisting of data entries. A data source may be a table, spreadsheet, database, or address book.

merge a form letter with an address list to generate a stack of letters personally addressed to each person on the list.

Here's how it works: First, you create a form letter with *field codes* that specify the location of the data entries in the data source. For instance, the field code <<LastName>> tells mail merge to grab data entries from the LastName column in the data source. When you execute the mail merge operation, mail merge generates a single document for each record (row) in the data source. You can use mail merge to generate your form letters and print matching envelopes or mailing labels, as shown in Figure 15.1.

Figure 15.1

Mail merge generates a unique document for each record in a table.

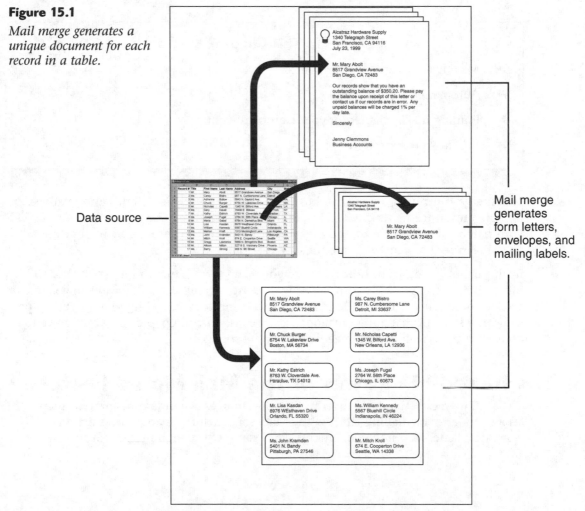

Data source

Mail merge generates form letters, envelopes, and mailing labels.

The Making of a Form Letter

How you compose your form letter is your business. You can type it from scratch, use a template, or seek help from the Letter Wizard. Omit any information that Word obtains from the data source during the merge, such as the person's name and address. After you complete the letter, you will insert field codes into the letter (one for the person's name, one for the address, and so on). These codes tell mail merge which entries to extract from the data source and where to insert those entries.

Inserting the Secret Codes

Assuming you created an address book in the previous chapter, you should have everything you need to perform a mail merge: a form letter and a data source. You can now run the Mail Merge Helper and use it to insert field codes in your form letter:

1. With your form letter displayed onscreen, crank down the **Tools** menu and select **Mail Merge**. The Mail Merge Helper dialog box appears, which will lead you step-by-step through the merge operation.

2. Click **Create** (under Main Document), select **Form Letters**, and click **Active Window**. This tells Word to use your letter as the main document in the merge.

3. Under Data Source, click **Get Data** and **Open Data Source**.

4. Select the document that contains the desired records and click **Open**. (This may be a Word document containing a table, a spreadsheet, or a database file.)

5. The Microsoft Word dialog box appears, telling you that your form letter has no merge fields (as if you didn't know). Click **Edit Main Document**. Word returns you to your form letter and displays the Mail Merge toolbar.

6. Position the insertion point where you want to insert a piece of data from the database. For example, you might move the insertion point a couple lines down from the date to insert the person's name and address.

7. Open the **Insert Merge Field** drop-down list and click the desired field, as shown in Figure 15.2. This inserts a code (such as <<FirstName>>) that will pull specified data (a person's first name, in this case) from the data source and insert it into your letter.

Computer Cheats

Use the Letter Wizard

The easiest way to write and format a letter is to use the Letter Wizard. Choose **File, New**, click the **Letters & Faxes** tab, and double-click **Letter Wizard**. The Letter Wizard dialog box displays a fill-in-the-blanks form that you can use to specify your preferences and enter information, such as the inside address, the salutation, and the closing.

Click **Insert Merge Field.**

Figure 15.2

Insert field codes by selecting them from the Insert Merge Field list.

Click the desired field.

Word plugs in the field codes at the insertion point.

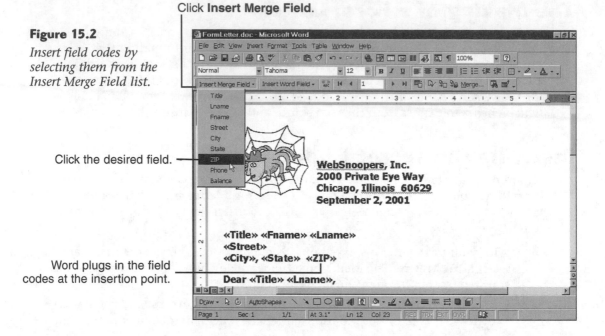

8. Repeat step 7 to insert additional merge field codes. Add punctuation and spaces between the codes as necessary. For example, if you are assembling codes to create an inside address, you need to add spaces and commas in the following way:

```
<<Title>> <<FirstName>> <<LastName>>[sr]
<<Address>>[sr]
<<City>>, <<State>>   <<ZIP>>
```

9. If your database contains information that you want to insert in the salutation or body of the letter, insert a field merge code wherever you want that information to appear. You might, for example, use the following salutation:

```
Dear <<Title>> <<LastName>>,
```

Initiating the Merge Operation

Now for the fun part. After you have inserted the desired field codes, you're ready to initiate the merge operation and generate your personalized letters:

1. Click the **Merge** button (in the Merge toolbar). The Merge dialog box appears, as shown in Figure 15.3, offering the following options for controlling how Word merges the form letter and data source:

   Merge To: Enables you to merge to the printer, to a new document, or to your email program. It's a good idea to merge to a new document so that you can check for errors before printing. You can also flip through the merged document and personalize the form letters that Word generates.

Records to Be Merged: Enables you to select a range of records (so you can create letters for only selected records in the data source).

When Merging Records: Tells Word whether to insert blank lines when a particular field in a record is blank.

Query Options: Displays a dialog box that enables you to sort the merged letters or create letters for a specific collection of records.

Don't Type the Field Codes

Typing field codes into your form letter doesn't work. No matter how easy it is, Word just doesn't recognize these codes. You must select the code from the Insert Field Code list.

2. Enter your merge preferences, and then click the **Merge** button. If you choose to merge to the printer, Word starts printing the letters. If you choose to merge to a new file, Word opens a new document window and places the merged letters in this window. You can then print them.

Enter your mail merge preferences.

Click **Merge**.

Figure 15.3

Use the Merge dialog box to initiate the mail merge operation.

Printing Addresses on Mailing Labels

Now that you have a stack of letters, you need to address them. You can do this by using a mailing label as your main document and merging it with the data source. Here's what you do:

1. Open the **Tools** menu and select **Mail Merge**. The Mail Merge Helper dialog box appears.

2. Click **Create** (under Main Document) and select **Mailing Labels**. The Microsoft Word dialog box pops up and asks whether you want to change the document type or create a new main document.

3. Click **New Main Document**.

4. Under Data Source, click **Get Data** and click **Open Data Source**.

5. Select the same data source document you used for your form letter and click **Open**. The Microsoft Word dialog box appears, telling you it needs to set up the main document.

6. Click **Set Up Main Document**. The Label Options dialog box appears, asking you to specify the type and size of the mailing labels on which you intend to print.

7. Choose the correct label type and size (as found on the box the labels came in), enter any additional printing preferences for your mailing labels, and click **OK**. The Mail Merge Helper displays the Create Labels dialog box, which prompts you to insert the merge field codes for creating the label.

8. Click the **Insert Merge Field** button and select the desired field code.

9. Repeat step 8 to insert additional field codes. Type any required punctuation and spaces between codes. (To change the font used for the label, drag over the codes, right-click the selection, and click **Font**.)

10. Click **OK**.

After you have entered the field codes, you're ready to execute the merge operation and print your mailing labels. Follow the same steps you performed earlier in this chapter in "Initiating the Merge Operation."

Mailing Newsletters or Brochures

If you're mailing out three-fold newsletters or brochures, you don't need an envelope. Simply create a new main document and position the field codes where you want the addresses printed (typically the center of the page). You can then print the addresses directly on the back of the brochure or newsletter.

Printing a Stack of Envelopes for Mass Mailing

At the beginning of this chapter, I promised that after you learned how to use mail merge, all you would need to do is stuff envelopes and peel and stick mailing labels. I lied. You can reduce your workload even more by printing the addresses directly on your envelopes.

To use the mail merge feature to print envelopes, perform the same steps you followed to create mailing labels. However, in step 2 instead of choosing to create mailing labels, click the **Create** button and click **Envelopes**. After you enter the field codes and give your okay, Mail Merge Helper returns you to the main document, where your field codes are laid out on an "envelope." Type your name and return address in the upper-left corner to have it printed on the envelope. Click the **Merge** button (in the Merge toolbar) and execute the merge.

Print on Cheap Paper First

Print your mailing labels on some inexpensive printer paper and hold the printed addresses over a sheet of labels to check for alignment. You can move the addresses down by adding blank lines before the field codes or move the addresses to the right by adding spaces to the left of each line.

The Least You Need to Know

With a little assistance from the Mail Merge Helper, you can churn out hundreds of personally addressed form letters and matching envelopes without typing a single character. Just keep the following information in mind:

➤ To use the mail merge feature, you need a main document and a data source.

➤ Field codes tell mail merge where to obtain each data entry.

➤ To run Mail Merge Helper, open the **Tools** menu and click **Mail Merge**.

➤ Use the Mail Merge Helper's **Create** list to specify the type of document you want to create: a form letter, mailing labels, or envelopes.

➤ Use the Mail Merge Helper's **Get Data** list to specify the location of the data source.

➤ To insert a field code in the main document, open the **Insert Merge Field** list and click the desired field.

➤ To initiate the merge, click the **Merge** button in the Merge toolbar.

Part 4
Getting Wired on the Internet

Faster than Federal Express. More powerful than the Home Shopping Network. Able to leap wide continents in a single click. Look, up on your desktop. It's a phone! It's a fax machine! No, it's the Internet!

With your computer, a modem, and a standard phone line, you have access to the single most powerful communications and information network in the world—the Internet. The chapters in this part show you how to get wired to the Internet and use its features to exchange electronic mail, chat with friends and strangers, shop for deals, manage your investments, plan your next vacation, research interesting topics, and even publish your own creations!

Connecting to the Outside World with a Modem

How would you like to access the latest news, weather, and sports without stepping away from your computer? Track investments without having to call a broker or wait for tomorrow's newspaper? Connect to an online encyclopedia, complete with sounds and pictures? Order items from a computerized catalog? Send a postage-free letter and have it arrive at its destination in a matter of seconds? Mingle with others in online chat rooms? Transfer files from your computer to a colleague's computer anywhere in the world?

With your computer, a modem, and a subscription to an online service or Internet service provider, you can do all this and more. This chapter introduces you to the wonderful world of modems and shows you how to connect your computer to the outside world.

What Can I Do with My Modem?

A modem is the single most liberating tool for your computer. With a modem and a computer, you can connect to other computers located down the block, across town, or anywhere in the world—assuming the remote computer lets you in. Here's a sample of some of the cool stuff you can do with your modem:

➤ Get the latest news, up-to-the-minute stock prices, sports scores, weather reports, and travel information.

➤ Shop anywhere in the world, track down hard-to-find products, and even place an order on the Web.

➤ Research any topic imaginable without leaving your home or office.

➤ Take classes on everything from using your computer to speaking Spanish.

➤ Exchange email messages with anyone in the world who has an email account.

➤ Chat with friends, relatives, and complete strangers by typing and transmitting messages back and forth.

➤ Save on long-distance service by placing long distance calls over the Internet.

➤ Play games in two-player mode. If you have a game that enables you to play games in two-player mode by using a modem, the program probably contains all the tools you need to play the game over the phone lines. Refer to the user manual that came with the game.

➤ Transfer files between your computer at work and your computer at home.

➤ Publish your own documents electronically on the Web. You can publish a personal page, family page, or business page, including photos, original drawings, and even audio and video clips.

How This Modem Thing Works

A modem (short for MODulator DEModulator) is essentially a phone for computers. A phone converts incoming signals from a phone line into audio output that you can hear. In a similar manner, a modem converts the analog signals that travel over phone lines into digital signals that the computer can process. To send a signal, a modem converts the digital signal from your computer into an analog signal that can be transmitted over phone lines.

Modems transfer data at different speeds, commonly measured in *bits per second (bps)*. The higher the number, the faster the modem can transfer data. Common rates include 28,800bps, 33,600bps, and 56,800bps. Because these modem speed numbers are becoming so long, manufacturers have started to abbreviate them. You'll commonly see speeds listed as 33.6Kbps. When they start dropping the bps and list something like 56K, you know it's really fast. Although you pay more for a higher transfer rate, you save time and decrease your phone bill by purchasing a faster modem.

Modem Types: Standard, ISDN, DSL, and Cable

If your computer is not equipped with a modem, you need to do a little shopping. However, before you visit your local computer store, you should do a little homework and check out your modem options. The following sections explain the major differences between modems and introduce special features you may want to consider.

Chugging Along with Standard Modems

Because standard modems are the least expensive of the lot and because they can send and receive signals over standard phone lines, they remain the most popular type of modems. However, not all modems are created equal. As you shop for a modem, you should consider the following features:

➤ **Speed**   Don't settle for anything slower than 56Kbps.

➤ **Internal Versus External**   Most computers come with an internal modem that's built into the computer. All you see of the modem are jacks for connecting the modem to a phone line and (optionally) plugging in a phone. An external modem sits outside the computer and connects to the computer's serial (COM or communications) port using a cable.

➤ **ITU or V.90 Support**   ITU is the international standard for 56K modems. If given the option of buying an x2, 56KFlex, or ITU, get the ITU. Because x2 and 56KFlex are competing 56K standards, a 56KFlex modem can't connect to a 56K x2 modem at full speed.

➤ **Fax support**   Like fully equipped fax machines, a fax/modem allows you to exchange faxes with a conventional fax machine or another computer that has a fax/modem.

➤ **Voice support**   If you plan on having your computer answer the phone and take messages, make sure the modem offers voice support. Without voice support, your modem can answer the phone, but it can only emit annoying screeching noises—which is useful for making telemarketers back off.

➤ **Video conferencing support**   Some modems are also designed to handle video calls, sort of like on *The Jetsons*. Of course, you'll need a video camera to take advantage of this feature.

56K Limits

56K pushes the limits of phone line communications. The phone company limits connection speeds to 53K, although there is some talk of raising the speed limit. You will rarely see data transfers at 56Kps. Expect a maximum speed of about 40Kbps–45Kbps, and that's only when your modem is receiving data. A 56K modem still sends data at 28.8Kbps–33.6Kbps due to other limitations, such as line noise.

Standard modems offer three benefits: The modem itself is inexpensive and easy to install, the modem plugs into a standard phone jack, and online services offer modem connections at bargain rates. However, for speedy Internet connections, consider the options described in the following sections.

Speeding Up Your Connections with ISDN

Unlike standard modems that must perform analog-to-digital conversions, ISDN deals only with digital signals, supporting much higher data transfer rates: 128Kbps, which is more than twice as fast as 56K modems. ISDN modems use two separate 64Kbps channels, called *B channels*, that, when used simultaneously, achieve the 128Kbps transfer rates. This two-channel approach also enables you to talk on the phone while surfing the Web; one channel carries your voice, while the other carries computer signals at 64Kbps (half speed). When you hang up, the modem can use both channels for computer communications. A third, slower channel (channel D) is used by the phone company to identify callers and do basic line checking, so you don't really need to think about it.

Whoa!

Calculate the Total Cost

Although ISDN may sound like the ideal solution for home and small-business use, ISDN setup and service can be expensive. Call your phone company and add up the costs before you decide.

Shop for the ISDN service before you shop for an IDSN modem or adapter and ask your phone company for recommendations. The performance of your ISDN connection relies on how well your ISDN adapter works with your phone company's connection.

The New Kid on the Block: DSL Modems

Short for *digital subscriber line*, DSL promises to put a big dent in the ISDN market and challenge cable companies. Using standard phone lines, DSL can achieve data transfer rates of up to 1.5Mbps, or even 9Mbps if you're within two miles of an ADSL connection center—with Mbps being 1,000 times faster than Kbps. DSL achieves these rates over standard, analog phone lines by using frequencies not used by voice signals. The only drawback is that DSL is a relatively new product (although the technology has been around awhile) and may not be available in your area or supported by your online service.

Because there is no single DSL standard, don't purchase a modem without first checking with your phone company. Most DSL providers market their service as a package deal and include a DSL modem that works with the service.

The Pros and Cons of Cable Modems

Like cable television connections, a cable Internet connection supports high-speed data transfers to your PC, allowing you to cruise the Internet at the same speed you can flip channels. In addition to speed, cable modems are relatively inexpensive (starting at about $200) and are easy to install. You can expect to pay about $60 per month for cable Internet access, which makes it competitive with ISDN service. However, cable modems do have a few drawbacks:

➤ **Availability**   Your cable company might not offer Internet cable service.

➤ **Variable connection speeds**   Cable service is set up to serve a pool of users. The more users connected to one service station, the slower the connection. Although cable companies commonly advertise 8Mbps data transfer rates, the rate you'll experience will likely be around 1–2Mbps.

➤ **Upload problems**   Cable was developed to bring signals into homes, not carry them out. However, cable companies are developing two-way systems to eliminate this limitation. If your cable service handles only incoming signals, you'll need to install a standard modem, too.

When shopping for a cable connection, the primary consideration is how the cable service handles return signals. Most services use either *telephone-return* or *RF-return*. With RF-return, the cable modem transmits signals along the cable. With telephone-return, the modem sends signals along a standard modem connection. Before you purchase a modem, check with the cable service to determine the type of return system it uses.

Consult an Expert

Before you jump on the DSL bandwagon, do some research and ask your phone company to provide details on the cost, reliability, and performance boost you can expect from your DSL service. DSL is a relatively new technology and might fall a little short of the hype.

What About Satellite Connections?

Although a satellite service, such as DirecPC, offers speedy connections, it's tough to set up, the satellite connection is iffy at times, the service is relatively expensive, and you need a modem to carry outgoing signals. This isn't the best option for a new user.

Plugging Your Modem into the Phone Jack

Most computers are equipped with an internal modem. If your computer does not have a modem, you have two choices:

➤ Get an external modem, and (with the computer turned off) plug the modem into your computer's serial port (commonly labeled COM1 or COM2). When you restart your computer, Windows will lead you through the process of installing the modem's software.

➤ Hire a service technician or get help from a knowledgeable friend to install and set an internal modem. Although installing and setting up an internal modem is typically easy, you need to follow a long list of safety precautions to ensure that you don't damage any equipment. In addition, internal modems occasionally cause conflicts with other devices, and troubleshooting these conflicts can be a very complicated process.

After the modem is installed, connect it to the phone line. If you're setting up a standard modem, use a phone cord (with RJ-11 connectors) to connect the Line In or Telco jack on the modem and with the phone jack on the wall. If you're setting up an ISDN adapter, use an ISDN cable (with RJ-45 jacks) to connect the ISDN-U port or NT-1 port with the ISDN wall jack.

To share the phone line with a phone or fax machine, use another phone cord to connect the Phone jack on the modem to the phone or fax machine, as shown in Figure 16.1.

Figure 16.1

Connect a phone to your modem so you can place calls when you're not using your modem.

Side view of modem

You can plug a phone or fax machine into the Phone jack.

PHONE

Line In or Telco jack connects to the telephone line.

TELCO

○ MIC

○ LINE OUT

Dialing Out: Does It Work?

To make sure your computer acknowledges having a modem, use your modem to make your next phone call (assuming you have a phone connected to your modem). Click **Start**, **Programs**, **Accessories**, **Communications, Phone Dialer**. Type the phone number you want to dial, and click **Dial**. When someone answers, pick up the receiver on your phone and start talking.

Troubleshooting Your Modem Connection

If your computer and Windows do not acknowledge the fact that a modem is installed, you might have to do a little troubleshooting. Fortunately, the Windows Modem Troubleshooter can help. Take the following steps to run the Modem Troubleshooter:

1. Open the **Start** menu and click **Help**.
2. Click the **Contents** tab, if needed, to bring it to the front.
3. Click **Troubleshooting** (at the bottom of the Contents list).
4. Click **Windows 98 Troubleshooters** (or the equivalent command, depending on your version of Windows). The Windows help system displays a list of troubleshooters.
5. Click **Modem** to start the modem troubleshooter. In the right pane, the troubleshooter displays a list of questions, as shown in Figure 16.2.
6. Click the answer that best represents the problem.
7. Click **Next** and follow the Modem Troubleshooter's instructions to complete the troubleshooting process and correct the problem.

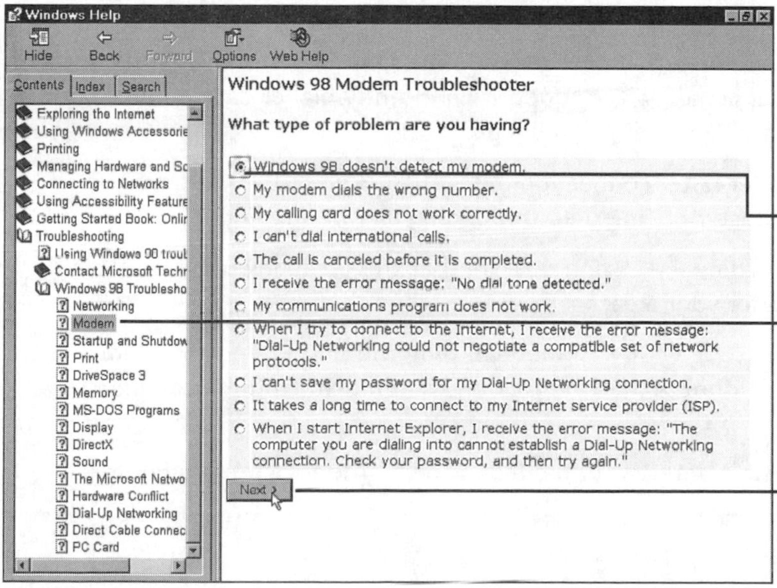

Figure 16.2

The Windows Modem Troubleshooter can help you track down and correct problems.

—— Click your problem.

—— Click **Modem**.

—— Click **Next**.

More Troubleshooters

Windows features several troubleshooters for tracking down everything from mouse problems to audio system failures. If, in Chapter 17, "Finding an Information FREEway," you have trouble connecting to the Internet, run the Networking Troubleshooter.

The Least You Need to Know

In the next chapter, you will use your modem to connect to an online service or to the Internet. But before you can do that, make sure you know the following modem basics:

➤ You can use a modem to connect to the Internet or a commercial online service, play multiplayer games over the phone lines, connect to a desktop computer from a remote location, or place free long-distance phone calls over the Internet.

➤ Although you can squeak by with a 28.8Kbps modem, a 56Kbps modem makes cruising the Web much more enjoyable.

➤ ISDN modems are preferred over standard modems because ISDN deals with digital-to-digital signals, which support significantly higher data transfer rates than standard analog-to-digital modems.

➤ DSL modems offer faster connections rates than even ISDN and have the included advantage of being used through regular phone lines.

➤ Call your cable company to find out whether the company provides cable modem service for your area.

➤ To use a phone along with your modem, plug the phone into the modem's Phone jack and connect the Line jack on the modem to the incoming phone line jack on the wall.

➤ If Windows doesn't detect your modem, run the Modem Troubleshooter.

Chapter 17

Finding an Information FREEway

In This Chapter

➤ Connecting to America Online and other commercial services

➤ Getting free training through free trial offers

➤ Canceling your subscription before you have to pay

➤ Connecting cheaply through Internet service providers

➤ Solving your own Internet connection problems

You have the required hardware for connecting to the digital world—a computer and a modem—but something's missing. Whom is your modem going to call? How can you use it to send email, check the weather forecast, and track your mutual funds?

To connect to the digital world, you need one more essential element—a commercial online service (such as America Online) or an Internet service provider (ISP). Both online services and ISPs provide you with a local phone number for dialing in to a special network that connects you with other users and services. Think of it as your doorway to the digital world.

So, how do online services and ISPs differ? Online services typically are more expensive and offer member-only features, such as exclusive chat rooms and discussion forums. With an online service, you use a program designed specifically to connect to and navigate the service. ISPs simply provide you with a connection to the Internet, typically for about $15–$20 per month. You use your own software to send and receive email and navigate the Internet. (Windows includes the software you need.)

Getting a Free Trial Offer to an Online Service

The best way to learn how to use an online service, exchange email, chat, and surf the Web is to do it. But when a commercial online service is charging you $2–$3 an hour to use the service, you can rack up a hefty bill by poking around. Fortunately, most online services provide free trial offers. Sign up for a service, use it to practice the basics, and then cancel it before the free trial period expires. I know it sounds unethical, but just think of it as being a savvy shopper.

Inside Tip

All-in-One

Commercial online services, such as America Online and CompuServe, provide you with a connection to the Internet in addition to members-only services.

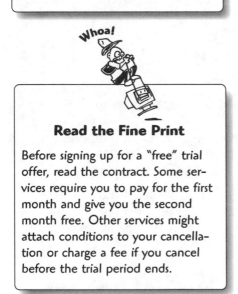

Whoa!

Read the Fine Print

Before signing up for a "free" trial offer, read the contract. Some services require you to pay for the first month and give you the second month free. Other services might attach conditions to your cancellation or charge a fee if you cancel before the trial period ends.

The following is a rundown of the four major commercial online services. (Keep in mind, the prices quoted here are current as of this writing but are subject to change—check with the service for price specifics.)

America Online   AOL offers several payment plans: $21.95/month for unlimited use ($239.40 or $19.95/month if you make a 1-year commitment), $9.95 for five hours per month (plus $2.95 for each additional hour), or $4.95/month for three hours (plus $2.50 for each additional hour). America Online is the most popular online service on the planet. It offers simple navigational tools, great services, and a friendly, hip social scene. Call 1-800-827-6364 for more information. If you have Web access through a friend, your local library, or work, you can get more information at **www.aol.com**.

CompuServe   Charges $9.95 for five hours per month, plus $2.95 for each additional hour, or $24.95 for unlimited use. Special services cost extra. CompuServe has traditionally been more technical and business oriented. Call 1-800-369-5544 (or visit **www.compuserve.com**) for more information.

Microsoft Network   MSN Internet Access is essentially an Internet service provider and offers little specialized content. The Unlimited plan costs $19.95 per month. Call 1-800-FREE-MSN (1-800-373-3676 or visit **www.msn.com**) for more information.

Prodigy Internet Gives you unlimited access for $19.95 per month ($189 or $15.75/month if you make a 1-year commitment). Prodigy also offers several other payment plans, including the Low Usage Plan ($9.95/month for 10 hours plus $1.50 for each additional hour). Prodigy Internet is more like an ISP than a commercial service, offering few members-only perks. Call 1-800-PRODIGY or visit **www.prodigy.com** for more information.

The next section shows you how to sign up for a subscription to these services. When you sign up as a new member, the service provides information about its free trial period.

Phone Bill Not Included

The rates listed here do not include phone charges. If the service does not have a local phone number for where you live, you may end up paying long-distance rates to connect. Some services offer 1–800 numbers, but typically charge a per-minute rate to use that number.

Signing Up for Your Membership

Check your Windows desktop for an icon named MSN or Online Services. The MSN icon is for The Microsoft Network. The Online Services icon contains additional icons for America Online, CompuServe, Prodigy, and AT&T WorldNet. Click one of these icons and follow the onscreen instructions to install the online service's program from the Windows CD, connect to the service, and sign up.

The installation program uses the modem to dial a toll-free number that lists local numbers. After you select a local number (and usually an alternate number, in case the first number is busy), the installation program disconnects from the toll-free connection and then reconnects you locally. Most services then ask you to supply the following information:

There's No Online Services Icon!

If the Online Services icon is not on the desktop, it may not be installed. Double-click the **Add/Remove Programs** icon in the Windows Control Panel, click the **Windows Setup** tab, make sure the **Online Services** check box is checked, and click **OK**.

➤ Your modem's COM port. To determine the COM port, double-click the **Modems** icon in the Control Panel, click your modem's name, and click **Properties**.

Disable Call Waiting

If you have call waiting, it will disconnect you if anyone calls when you're online. Before typing the phone number, type the code required to disable call waiting (in most cases, *70) followed by a couple of commas. The commas insert delay times, so the code can take effect before the program dials the phone number. (Check with your phone company to determine the code you must enter to disable call waiting, and ask if a service charge is added for each time you disable it.)

➤ Your modem's maximum speed. (Most services support up to 56K connections.)

➤ Any special dialing instructions, such as a number you must dial to connect to an outside line.

➤ Your name, address, and telephone number, as shown in Figure 17.1.

➤ A credit card number and expiration date. (Even if the service offers a free trial membership, you must enter a credit card number. If you don't feel safe entering your credit card number online, get the phone number of the service and set up your account over the phone.)

➤ The name (screen name) and password you want to use to log on to the service. (Write down your screen name and password, in case you forget them. Without this information, you are not able to connect.)

➤ An acceptance of the terms of service (TOS) or rules you must follow to continue to use the service. If you break the rules, the service may terminate your account. Read this so that you know what you're getting into.

Figure 17.1

To use a service, you must first register.

Enter the requested information.

156

Getting Help Online

Because online services differ, I can't give you specific instructions on how to navigate each service, send email messages, post notes on message boards, or chat online. The steps vary from one service to another.

However, all online services display a toolbar or other navigational tool with buttons or links that point to popular features. For example, in America Online, you click the **Read** button to access your electronic mail box. Click the **Internet** button to open a menu for accessing various Internet features, such as the Web, newsgroups (Internet message boards), or the Internet Yellow Pages.

In addition, all commercial services have their own help system, which typically consists of both online and offline help. Offline help is installed on your hard drive as part of the program and provides general instructions on how to use the service. Online help typically provides assistance for more specific issues, such as problems you encounter when trying to read email messages. Simply open the Help menu and choose the desired type of help. Figure 17.2 shows a typical online help screen in America Online.

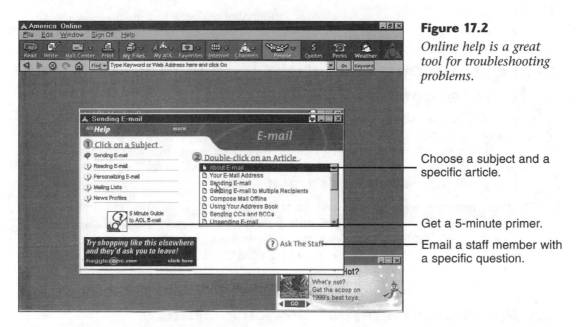

Figure 17.2

Online help is a great tool for troubleshooting problems.

Choose a subject and a specific article.

Get a 5-minute primer.

Email a staff member with a specific question.

The best way to learn how to use a service is to explore on your own and master the help system. If you run into problems and the help system doesn't have the answer, send your question to a technical support representative via email or ask your question in one of the member chat rooms. Most members are friendly and eager to help.

Canceling Your Membership

If you're not satisfied with your online service, don't just stop using the service. Unless you cancel your membership, your online service will dutifully charge the monthly fee to your credit card whether you use the service or not. If you choose to no longer use the service, be sure you cancel your membership before the next month's billing period begins.

They Changed the Phone Number!

If the phone number printed here does not work, check the online help system or the service's billing area for a customer service phone number.

Of course, you can't cancel your membership online. You need to call a customer service representative, so the person can grill you on why you want to dump the service. Here's a list of the customer service numbers for the major online services:

America Online: 1-888-265-8008

CompuServe: 1-800-394-1481

Prodigy: 1-800-213-0992

Microsoft Network: 1-800-373-3676

Finding Cheaper, Better Ways to Connect to the Internet

Commercial online services are great if you like to be a member of a virtual community or if you're just a little hesitant about exploring the digital world on your own. If you've become addicted to meeting new friends in America Online's chat rooms and have a well-established email address that all your friends and relatives use to contact you, you probably want to remain a member.

However, online services can be somewhat expensive and don't always provide fast, reliable Internet service. In addition, online services often have quirky email systems that make it difficult to exchange emails and attached files with nonmembers. If you're looking for a cheap way to establish a pure Internet connection, and you're not interested in any members-only perks, consider connecting through an ISP.

Locating a Local Internet Service Provider

To find an ISP, flip through the Yellow Pages—look under Internet Service Providers or Internet Online Service Providers. To find a good ISP, ask your friends, relatives, and colleagues for recommendations. Ask the following questions:

➤ How much does the service charge per month? Do you get unlimited connect time for one price?

➤ Was it easy to set up the connection?

➤ If you had trouble setting up the connection, did the company offer quality assistance?

➤ Do you ever have trouble connecting to the service? (Some ISPs oversell their service, making it difficult to connect during high-traffic hours.)

➤ Does the ISP provide a fast, reliable connection? (Again, ISPs who oversell their service might provide slow Internet connections or be quick to disconnect users during busy hours.)

➤ Has the ISP ever messed up your bill? I once had an ISP double-charge me for three months running and then threaten to cancel my account. Make sure the company has its act together.

If you don't have the Yellow Pages or any friends, relatives, or colleagues, skip ahead to the section called "Setting Up Your Internet Connection" later in this chapter. The Windows Internet Connection Wizard can help you track down an ISP.

What About Speed?

A fast, reliable Internet connection is most important, but tracking down a bottleneck can be difficult. At times, the entire Internet can slow down due to high traffic or multiple system failures. A bad phone connection or outdated telephone company equipment can restrict the data flow to your computer. Even your own computer, if it's bogged down trying to run too many programs, can make a fast connection seem slow.

Gathering the Information You Need to Connect

To set up your account, you need information and settings that tell your computer how to connect to the ISP's computer. Obtain the following information:

Username   This is the name that identifies you to the ISP's computer. It is typically an abbreviation of your first and last name. For example, Jill Eikenhorn might use jeikenhorn as her username. You can choose any name you like, as long as it is not already being used by another user.

Password   The ISP may let you select your own password or may assign you a password. Be sure to write down the password in case you forget it.

Connection Type   Most ISPs offer PPP (Point-to-Point Protocol), but ask to make sure. PPP is simply a "language" that two computers agree to speak in order to communicate over the Internet. An older protocol, called SLIP (Serial Line Internet Protocol), is a little slower and less reliable, but some ISPs still support it.

Domain Name Server   The domain name server is a computer that's set up to locate computers on the Internet. Each computer on the Internet has a unique number that identifies it, such as 197.72.34.74. Each computer also has a domain name, such as www.hollywood.com, which makes it easier for people to remember the computer's address. When you enter a domain name, the domain name server looks up the computer's number and locates it.

Domain Name   This is the domain name of your service provider's computer—for example, internet.com. You use the domain name in conjunction with your username as your email address—for example, jeikhorn@internet.com.

Page Not Found

If, when you try to open several different Web pages, you keep getting error messages indicating that the page doesn't exist or cannot be found, you may have the wrong DNS address. Some ISPs may even change the DNS address they use, although they typically notify you of any changes via email. If you run into problems, call your ISP's tech support line.

News Server   The news server enables you to connect to any of thousands of newsgroups on the Internet to read and post messages. Newsgroups are electronic bulletin boards for special interest groups. The news server name typically starts with news and is followed by the service provider's domain name—for example, news.internet.com.

Mail Server   The mail server is in charge of electronic mail. You need to specify two mail servers: POP (Post Office Protocol) for incoming mail, and SMTP (Simplified Mail Transfer Protocol) for mail you send. The POP server's name typically starts with pop and is followed by the service provider's domain name—for example, pop.internet.com. The SMTP server's name typically starts with smtp or mail and is followed by the service provider's domain name—for example, smtp.internet.com. (See Chapter 18, "Sending Email: Postage-Free, Same-Day Delivery," for details.)

Email Address   If you plan to receive email messages, you need an email address. Your address typically begins with your username followed by an at sign (@) and the domain name of your service provider—for example, jeikhorn@internet.com.

Setting Up Your Internet Connection

After you have all the information you need, you can run the Internet Connection Wizard and enter the connection settings. The wizard displays a series of screens prompting you to enter each piece of information. The wizard then creates a Dial-Up Networking icon you can click to establish your connection.

Although I would really like to give you step-by-step instructions for using the Internet Connection Wizard, the steps vary depending on which Internet Connection Wizard you are using; Microsoft keeps changing it. However, I can tell you how to start the wizard and tell you what to watch out for:

➤ To start the Internet Connection Wizard, click **The Internet**, **Internet Explorer**, or **Connect to the Internet** icon on your Windows desktop.

➤ If the previous step didn't work, the Connection Wizard may be hiding on your system. Check the **Start**, **Programs**, **Accessories**, **Internet Tools** menu for an option named **Get on the Internet**, or check the **Start**, **Programs**, **Internet Explorer** menu for an option called **Connection Wizard**.

➤ After the wizard starts, follow the onscreen instructions to set up your Internet account. The second screen (Setup Options) is the most important screen. If you already have an ISP, choose the option for using your existing ISP; otherwise, choose the option for locating a new ISP and setting up an account.

➤ If you need to find an ISP, the wizard asks for your area code and the first three digits of your phone number; it then downloads a list of ISPs available in your area, as shown in Figure 17.3. You need to register with the service and provide a credit card number. The wizard downloads the required connection settings for you, so you won't have to enter them manually.

Install Dial-Up Networking

To connect to the Internet, a Windows component called Dial-Up Networking must be installed. Open **My Computer** to see if the Dial-Up Networking icon is there. If it's missing, open the Windows Control Panel, double-click **Add/ Remove Programs**, click the **Windows Setup** tab, double-click **Communications**, and place a check mark next to **Dial-Up Networking**. Click **OK** twice and follow the onscreen instructions to install it.

Internet Connection Wizard

Step 1 of 3: Selecting an Internet service provider

Click Next to use Netcom Mindspring as your Internet service provider. If you would like to use another service provider select one from the list below, and then click Next.

Internet service providers:

- EarthLink
- JUNO
- MSN Internet Access
- Netcom Mindspring
- MindSpring
- Sprynet Mindspring
- America Online
- MCI WorldCom Internet
- AT&T WorldNet Service
- Concentric Network
- Prodigy Internet

Provider information:

MindSpring Netcom

Billing Rate	First 30 Days Free! Plans start at $6.95
Service	1-888-MSPRING (677-7464)
Modem Support	Up to 56k (v.90 technology)

"Best ISP" -PC World

< Back   Next >   Cancel

Figure 17.3
The Internet Connection Wizard can help you locate an ISP in your area.

Select an Internet service provider.

Click **Next**.

➤ If you already set up an account with a service provider in your area, you must manually enter the connection settings. This is no biggie; the wizard steps you through it. When asked whether you want to view the Advanced settings, however, click **Yes** so that you can check the settings.

➤ If asked to specify a logon procedure, leave **I Don't Need to Type Anything When Logging On** selected, even though your ISP requires you to enter a name and password. This option is for services that require you to manually log on using a terminal window or logon script. Most ISPs do not require this.

➤ Most ISPs automatically assign an IP (Internet Protocol) address to you when you log on, so don't choose to use a specific IP address unless your ISP gave you one.

➤ Most ISPs do provide a specific DNS Server address. Choose **Always Use the Following** and enter the DNS address in the **DNS Server** text box. If your ISP offers a secondary DNS, enter it so that you can still navigate if the first DNS is busy.

➤ The wizard also asks you to enter settings for connecting to the ISP's news and mail server. You can do this later or enter the settings now.

After running the Internet Connection Wizard, run My Computer and double-click the **Dial-Up Networking** icon. The Dial-Up Networking folder contains icons for any ISPs that you have set up. Right-drag the icon for your ISP to a blank area of the Windows desktop, release the mouse button, and click **Create Shortcut(s) Here**.

Panic Attack

There's No "Save Password" Option!

If you don't have the Save Password option, Client for Microsoft Networks is not installed. In the Control Panel, double-click the **Network** icon, click the **Add** button, and double-click **Client**. Click **Microsoft** and then double-click **Client for Microsoft Networks**. Make sure **Client for Microsoft Networks** is selected as the **Primary Network Logon** and click **OK**.

Testing Your Internet Connection

After you have an icon, you can double-click it to connect to the Internet. When you double-click the icon, a dialog box appears as shown in Figure 17.4, prompting you to type your username and password (supplied by your ISP).

Type your username and password. If desired, check the **Save Password** check box. This saves your username and password so you won't have to type it again the next time you logon. If you share your computer with someone else and you do not want that person using your Internet connection, leave the check box blank. Click the **Connect** button.

Enter your username.

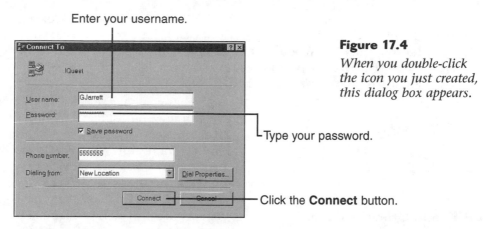

Figure 17.4
When you double-click the icon you just created, this dialog box appears.

Type your password.

Click the **Connect** button.

After you click the **Connect** button, Dial-Up Networking dials into your service provider's computer and displays messages indicating the progress—Dialing..., Checking username and password..., and Connecting.... Assuming that Dial-Up Networking could establish a connection, a dialog box appears indicating that you are now connected. You can now run Internet programs (explained in later chapters) to navigate the World Wide Web, send and receive email, and so on.

Can I Disconnect Now?

To disconnect, right-click the **Dial-Up Networking** icon on the right end of the taskbar and click **Disconnect**. (The icon looks like two tiny, overlapping computers.)

What Went Wrong: Internet Connection Troubleshooting

If your connection proceeds smoothly the first time, lucky you. Most first attempts fail for some reason or another. You might have forgotten to type your password, or your Dial-Up Networking connection may have a wrong setting. If the connection fails, check the following:

➤ Did you type your username and password correctly? (If you mistyped this information or if your ISP entered it incorrectly on the system, Dial-Up Networking typically displays a message indicating that the system did not accept your password.) Retype your username and password and try connecting again. (Passwords are typically case-sensitive, so type the password *exactly* as your service provider specifies.)

➤ Was the line busy? Again, Dial-Up Networking typically displays a message indicating that the line was busy. If several people are connected to the service, you may have to wait until someone signs off. Keep trying.

➤ Check your Dial-Up Adapter settings. Display the Windows Control Panel and double-click the Network icon. Click Dial-Up Adapter, and click the Properties button. Click the Bindings tab and make sure there is a check mark next to **TCP/IP—>Dial-Up Adapter**, as shown in Figure 17.5. (If NetBEUI or IPX/SPX are listed, make sure they are NOT checked.)

➤ Make sure you have selected the correct server type. In the Control Panel, double-click the **Dial-Up Networking** icon. Right-click the icon for connecting to your ISP, and choose **Properties**. Click the **Server Type** tab. Open the **Type of Dial-Up Server** drop-down list and choose the correct server type (specified by your service provider)—usually PPP.

➤ Did your modem even dial? Go to the Windows Control Panel and check your modem setup. Make sure that you've selected the correct modem and COM port.

➤ Do you have reliable phone lines? Unplug your modem from the phone jack and plug a phone into the jack. Do you get a dial tone? Does the line sound fuzzy? If you don't hear a dial tone, the jack is not working. If the line is fuzzy when you make a voice call, it has line noise, which may be enough to disconnect you.

TCP/IP and Other Protocols

TCP/IP stands for Transmission Control Protocol/Internet Protocol. More simply, TCP/IP is the language two computers use to communicate over the Internet. NetBEUI and IPX/SPX are two protocols commonly used for networks.

Figure 17.5

Make sure TCP/IP is linked to your Dial-Up Adapter.

Dial-Up Adapter Properties

Driver Type | Bindings | Advanced

Click the protocols that this adapter will use. Your computer must use the same protocols as other network computers you want to communicate with.

☑ 3Com TCAATDI Diagnostic TDI
☑ TCP/IP -> Dial-Up Adapter

OK   Cancel

The Least You Need to Know

A modem transforms your computer into one of the most powerful communications and information gathering tools on the planet. To get online and learn how to use this powerful resource, here's what you should do:

➤ Sign up for a free trial offer with America Online. Try to get 250 hours free.

➤ Use everything on America Online. Send a couple of email messages, check the Internet features, prowl the chat rooms, click buttons, open menus, and use the help system when you get in a jam.

➤ Keep track of the time you spent online and make sure you don't exceed the free trial limits. (To check your bill, press **Ctrl+K**, type **billing**, and click **Display Your Current Bill Summary**.)

➤ Just before the free trial period expires, call 1-888-265-8008 and cancel your membership (unless you have fallen in love with AOL and its online community).

➤ Find a local ISP and gather the information you need to establish a connection.

➤ Run the Internet Connection Wizard and set up a Dial-Up Connection for the ISP.

➤ Use Internet Explorer to connect to and navigate the Web and use Outlook Express for email, as explained in the following chapters.

Chapter 18

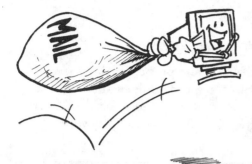

Sending Email: Postage-Free, Same-Day Delivery

In This Chapter

➤ Giving your email program directions to the post office

➤ Addressing and sending email messages

➤ Checking your electronic mailbox

➤ Jazzing up your messages with photos and fancy fonts

➤ Attaching files to outgoing messages

➤ Following proper email etiquette

How would you like to send a message to your friend and have it arrive in a matter of seconds instead of days? Send dozens of messages every day without paying a single cent in postage? Never again stare out your window waiting for the mail carrier?

Well, your dreams are about to come true. When you have a connection to the Internet and an email program, all of these benefits are yours. And in this chapter, you'll learn how to start taking advantage of them.

How Does This Email Thing Work?

Your online service or ISP has a *mail server* that acts as a post office. Whenever you send a message, the post office directs it to the specified destination. When someone sends you a message, the post office stores it in a special folder that acts as your mailbox. You then use an email program to retrieve and display your messages.

Running Your Email Program for the First Time

The hardest part about email is getting your email program to connect to your Internet service provider's email server. If you are using one of the major commercial online services, such as America Online or CompuServe, you can relax; the installation program took care of all the details for you. You simply click the email button and start using it.

However, if you connect through an ISP, you must use a separate email program (such as Outlook Express or Netscape Messenger) and enter settings that tell it how to connect to the mail server. Before you start your email program, make sure you have the following information from your ISP:

Email Address Your email address is usually all lowercase and starts with your first initial and last name (for example, jsmith@iway.com). However, if your name is John Smith (or Jill Smith), you might have to use something more unique, such as JohnHubertSmith@iway.com.

Outgoing Mail (SMTP) Short for Simple Mail Transfer Protocol, the SMTP server is the mailbox into which you drop your outgoing messages. It's actually your Internet service provider's computer. The address usually starts with "mail" or "smtp"(for example, mail.iway.com or smtp.iway.com).

Incoming Mail (POP3) Short for Post Office Protocol, the POP server is like your neighborhood post office. It receives incoming messages and places them in your personal mailbox. The address usually starts with "pop" (for example, pop.iway.com).

Account This one is tricky; it could be your username, the name you use to log in to your service provider (for example, jsmith), or something entirely different assigned to your account by your ISP.

Password Typically, you use the same password for logging on and for checking email. I can't help you here; you picked the password or had one assigned to you.

After you have the information, you must enter it into your email program. The following sections show you how to enter email connection settings in Outlook Express and Netscape Messenger.

Entering Email Settings in Outlook Express

Before you can enter connection settings, you must run Outlook Express. Click the **Outlook Express** icon on the Windows desktop or in the Quick Launch toolbar, or run the program from the **Start**, **Programs**, **Internet Explorer** menu.

When you first run Outlook Express, the Internet Connection Wizard starts and steps you through the process of entering the required information as shown in Figure 18.1. Just follow the onscreen instructions. If the Internet Connection Wizard does not start or you need to enter information for a different email account, open the **Tools** menu and choose **Accounts**. Click the **Add** button, choose **Mail**, and follow the onscreen instructions to enter the settings.

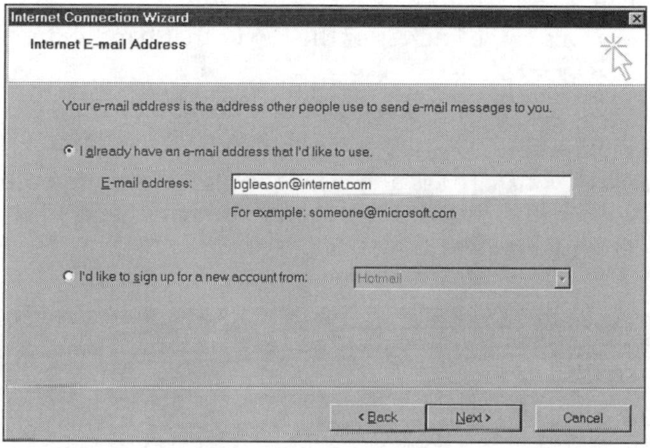

Figure 18.1

Before you can use Outlook Express, you must enter connection settings.

Entering Email Settings in Netscape Messenger

To enter connection settings in Netscape Messenger, first run the program. Click **Start**, **Programs**, **Netscape Communicator**, **Netscape Messenger**. After it's running, take the following steps to enter settings for your mail server:

1. Open the **Edit** menu and choose **Preferences**.
2. Click on the plus sign next to **Mail & Newsgroups** to display a list of categories.

169

3. Click **Identity**, and enter the following information in the Identity panel, as shown in Figure 18.2:

   Your name: This is your legal name or nickname (for example, Nyce&EZ).

   Email address: This is the address people will use to write to you or respond to your messages.

   Reply-to address: If you want people to reply to an email address other than the email address you entered above (for instance, if you have two email accounts), enter the preferred email address here.

   Organization: If you work for a company or run your own business, you can enter its name here.

   Signature File: A signature is a file you create (typically in a text editor) that includes additional information about you or a clever quote. You can skip this for now.

4. Click **Mail Servers**, and enter the following information in the Mail Servers panel:

   Mail server user name: This is the username you use to log on to your Internet account (for example, jsmith).

   Outgoing mail (SMTP) server: This is the address of the server in charge of handling outgoing mail.

   Incoming mail server: This is the address of the server that handles incoming email messages.

   Mail Server type: Choose the type of server used for incoming mail: POP or IMAP. Obtain this information from your service provider.

5. Click the **OK** button to save your settings and close the dialog box. If you have trouble connecting to your mail server later, perform these same steps to change settings or correct any typos you might have made.

Figure 18.2

Netscape Messenger makes it easy to enter the necessary settings.

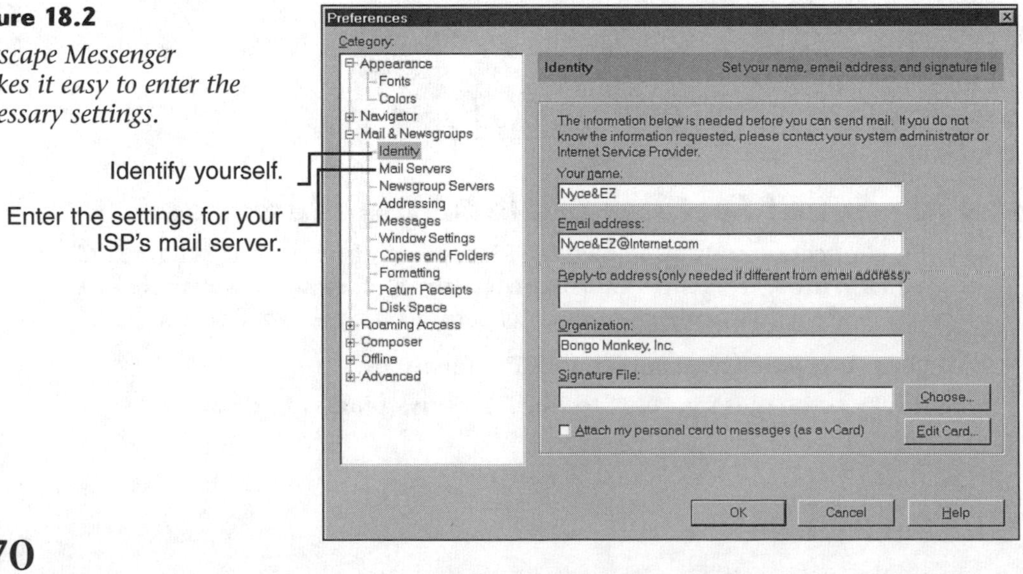

Identify yourself.

Enter the settings for your ISP's mail server.

Addressing an Outgoing Message

The procedure for sending messages over the Internet varies, depending on the email program or online service you're using. In most cases, you first enter a command for composing a new message. For example, in Outlook Express, you click the **New Message** or **New Mail** button. A window appears, prompting you to compose your message.

Click in the **To** box and type the person's email address and then click in the **Subject** box and type a brief description of the message (see Figure 18.3). Click in the large box near the bottom of the window and type your message. When you're ready to "mail" your message, click the **Send** button.

Some email programs immediately send the message. Other programs place the messages you send in a temporary outbox; you must then enter another Send command to actually send the messages. For example, in Outlook Express, you click the **Send and Receive** button. Outlook Express then sends all messages from the Outbox and checks for incoming messages.

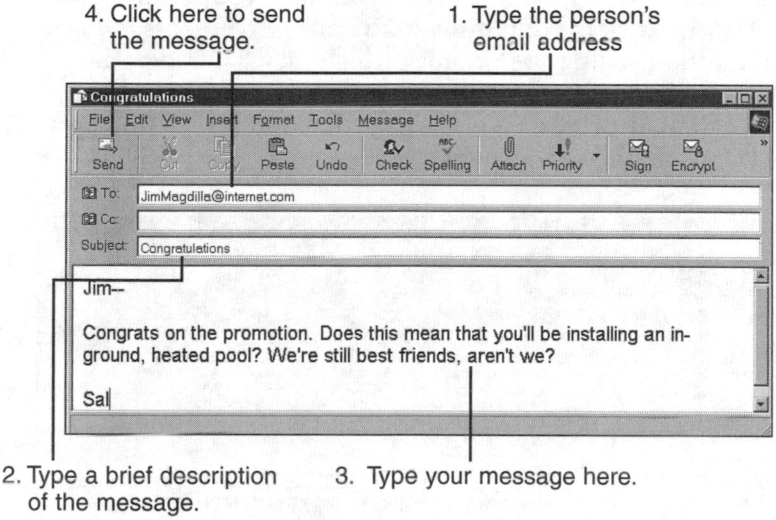

4. Click here to send the message.

1. Type the person's email address

Figure 18.3

Sending mail with a typical Internet email program (Outlook Express).

2. Type a brief description of the message.

3. Type your message here.

If you're sending messages from a commercial online service, such as CompuServe or America Online, you must specify that the message is going to someone outside of the service. For example, on CompuServe, you type **INTERNET:** before the email address. If you were sending a message from CompuServe to a member of America Online, the address might look something like this:

```
INTERNET:jsmith@aol.com
```

Check your online service's help system to determine if there's anything quirky about entering email addresses.

171

Inside Tip

Email Address Books

Most email programs, including Outlook Express and Netscape Messenger, include email address books. Instead of typing the person's email address, you simply select it from a list. To quickly display the address book, press **Ctrl+Shift+B** in Outlook Express or **Ctrl+Shift+2** in Messenger.

Checking Your Email Box

Whenever someone sends you an email message, it doesn't just pop up on your screen. The message sits on your service provider's mail server until you connect and retrieve your messages. There's no trick to connecting to the mail server... assuming you entered the correct connection settings. Most programs check for messages automatically on startup or display a button you can click to fetch your mail. The program retrieves your mail and then displays a list of message descriptions. To display a message, click or double-click its description as shown in Figure 18.4.

Figure 18.4

You can quickly display the contents of messages you receive.

Click the message description.

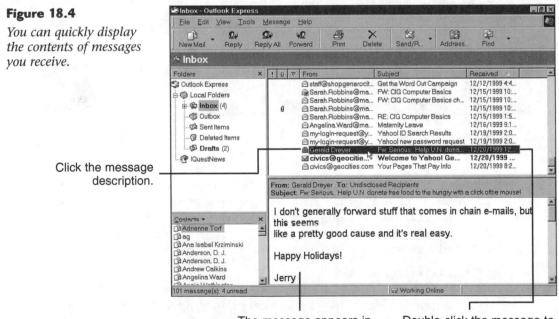

The message appears in the preview pane.

Double-click the message to display it in its own window.

Sending Replies

To reply to a message in most email programs, you select the message and then click the **Reply** or **Respond To** button. This opens a window that automatically inserts the person's email address and a description of the message. Many email programs also quote the contents of the previous message, so the recipient can easily follow the conversation. To indicate that text has been quoted, email programs typically add a right angle bracket (>) at the beginning of each quoted line. To respond, type your message in the message area, and then click the **Send** button.

Adding Photos and Other Cool Stuff

How would you like to add a photo to your message or jazz it up with some fancy fonts? Most email programs enable you to use special type styles and sizes, add backgrounds, insert pictures, and embellish your messages with other formatting options.

Both Netscape Messenger and Outlook Express offer a toolbar that contains buttons for the most common enhancements. In Outlook Express, shown in Figure 18.5, you can use the toolbar to make text bold or italic, add bulleted and numbered lists, and insert pictures, horizontal lines, links, and other objects. (If the toolbar does not appear, check the format menu for an HTML option. HTML stands for *Hypertext Markup Language*, the coding system used to format Web pages.)

Delete Most of the Quote

When replying to a long message, delete most of the quoted material from the message you received, leaving only one or two lines to establish the context. This makes the message travel faster and take up less disk space on the recipient's computer.

Drop the Fancy Stuff

When you send a message that has pictures, lines, and fancy fonts, the email program sends it as a Web page. The recipient's email program must support Web page formatting; otherwise, the message will appear to be packed with cryptic codes.

Make text bold,
italic, or underlined.

Create a bulleted or
numbered list.

Indent text.

Align text left,
right, or center.

Figure 18.5

*Many email programs
let you design fancy
messages.*

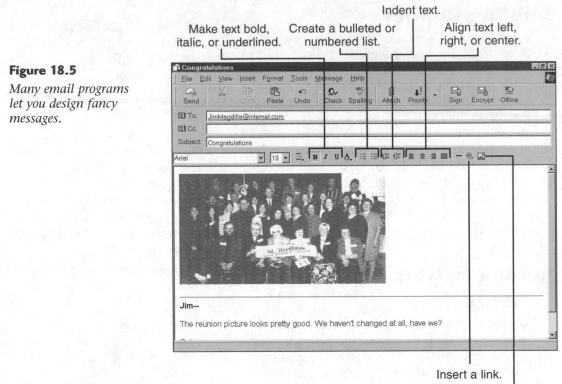

Insert a link.

Insert an image.

The buttons for inserting pictures and formatting text work the same way as in your word processing and desktop publishing programs. The only new thing here is the button for inserting links. To insert a link that points to a Web page, you drag over the text you want to appear as the link. You then click the button for inserting the link, type the address of the Web page you want it to point to, and click **OK**. You can also drag links from a Web page into the message area and plop them right down in the message area. (You'll learn more about links in Chapter 20, "Poking Around on the Web.")

Attaching Documents to Your Messages

You can fit most email messages on a Post-It note. A person typically rifles off a message or reply in less than a minute. However, there are times when you may wish to send something more substantial, perhaps an outline for a book, a graphic image of yourself, a copy of an article you found on the Web, or a document with its formatting intact.

Whatever the case, you can send files along with your messages by creating *attachments*. An attachment is a file in its original condition and format that you tack on to the message. For instance, if you have a résumé you created in Word, you can email it as an attachment to a prospective employer. That person could then open the résumé in Word and view or print it. Without attachments, you would need to copy the text of the résumé and paste it into your email message, losing any formatting you applied to the text and any graphics you inserted.

The process for attaching a file is fairly simple, but the steps vary depending on which email program you use. In most email programs, you perform the same steps you take for composing and addressing the message. You click a button (for example, **Attach** or **Insert File**). This displays a dialog box that lets you select the file you want to send. The dialog box looks just like the dialog box you use to open files. Change to the folder that contains the file you want to send and then double-click the file's name. When you are ready to send the message along with the attachment, simply click the **Send** button.

If you receive a message that contains an attached file, your email program will usually display some indication that a file is attached. For example, Outlook Express displays a paper clip icon. If you double-click on the message (to display it in its own window), an icon appears at the bottom of the window. You can double-click the icon to open the file, or right-click and choose **Save** to save the file to a separate folder on your hard drive.

In many cases, when someone forwards another message to you, the person's email program sends the forwarded message as an attachment. If the message has been forwarded several times, you might need to meander through a long line of attachments to view the original message.

Virus Concerns

If you receive a program file from someone you don't know, be careful about running the program; it might contain a virus. If you want to run the program file, be sure to check it first with an antivirus program.

What About Hotmail and Other Free Email Services?

You probably have heard of "free" email services, such as Hotmail, Yahoo!, and Juno, and wondered why anyone would need free email. Isn't all email free? Does your ISP charge extra for it? Of course, your email account is included with the service your ISP provides; your ISP does not charge extra for it. But there are several good reasons to explore these free email services:

➤ Free email is typically Web-based, allowing you to send messages and check your mail on the Web. If you travel, you can manage your email from anywhere in the world using any computer that's connected to the Internet. You don't need a computer that has your email account settings on it.

➤ Free email lets everyone in your home or business have his or her own email account. When Junior starts corresponding with members from the Aryan

Nation, he'll want his privacy, and he can have it with his own email program. Well, maybe that's not the best example, but you get the idea.

➤ Free email gives you another email address for registering "anonymously" for free stuff. Whenever you register for contests, shareware, and other freebies on the Internet, you must enter your email address. Use your free email account to register, so companies can send junk mail to that address, and keep your real email address private.

To get a free email account, connect to any of the following sites, register, and follow the instructions at the site to start using your free email account: Hotmail (`www.hotmail.com`), Juno (`www.juno.com`), Yahoo! (`mail.yahoo.com`), address.com (`www.address.com`), or Excite (`mail.excite.com`). To find more free email services, Yahoo!, and Juno, use your favorite Web search page to look for "free email."

Email Shorthand and Emoticons

If you want to look as though you're an email veteran, pepper your messages with any of the following *emoticons* (pronounced "ee-mow-tick-cons"). You can use these symbols to show your pleasure or displeasure with a particular comment, to take the edge off a comment that you think might be misinterpreted, and to express your moods.

`:)` or `:-)`	I'm happy, or it's good to see you, or I'm smiling as I'm saying this. You can often use this to show that you're joking.
`:D` or `:-D`	I'm really happy or laughing.
`;)` or `;-)`	Winking
`:(` or `:-(`	Unhappy. You hurt me, you big brute.
`;(` or `;-(`	Crying
`:¦` or `:-¦`	I don't really care.
`:/` or `:-/`	Skeptical
`:#` or `:-#`	My lips are sealed. I can keep a secret.
`:>` or `:->`	Devilish grin
`;^)`	Smirking
`%-)`	I've been at this too long.
`:p` or `:-p`	Sticking my tongue out
`<g>`	Grinning. Usually takes the edge off whatever you just said.

<vbg>	Very Big Grin
<l>	Laughing
<lol>	Laughing Out Loud
<i>	Ironic
<s>	Sighing
<jk>	Just kidding. (These are my initials, too.)
<>	No comment

In addition to the language of emoticons, Internet chat and email messages are commonly seasoned with a fair share of abbreviations. The following is a sample of some of the abbreviations you'll encounter and be expected to know:

AFAIK	As Far As I Know
BRB	Be Right Back
BTW	By The Way
CUL8R	See You Later
F2F	Face To Face (usually in reference to meeting somebody in person)
FAQ	Frequently Asked Questions. Many sites post a list of questions that many users ask, along with answers to those questions. They call this list a FAQ.
FOTCL	Falling Off The Chair Laughing
FTF	Another version of Face To Face
FYA	For Your Amusement
FYI	For Your Information
HHOK	Ha Ha Only Kidding
IMO	In My Opinion
IMHO	In My Humble Opinion
IOW	In Other Words
KISS	Keep It Simple, Stupid
LOL	Laughing Out Loud
MOTOS	Member Of The Opposite Sex
OIC	Oh, I See
PONA	Person Of No Account

177

ROTF	Rolling On The Floor (presumably in laughter)
SO	Significant Other
TIC	Tongue In Cheek
TTFN	Ta Ta For Now

Email No-No's

To avoid getting yourself into trouble by unintentionally sending an insulting email message, you might want to consider the proper protocol for composing email messages. The most important rule is to NEVER EVER TYPE IN ALL UPPERCASE CHARACTERS. This is the equivalent of shouting, and people become edgy when they see this text on their screen. Likewise, take it easy on the exclamation points!!!

Secondly, avoid confrontations in email. When you disagree with somebody, a personal visit or a phone call is usually more tactful than a long letter that painfully describes how stupid and inconsiderate the other person is being. Of course, if you're breaking off a relationship, sometimes email is the best way to do it.

If you are in marketing or sales, avoid sending out unsolicited ads and other missives. Few people appreciate such advertising. In fact, few people appreciate receiving anything that's unsolicited, cute, "funny," or otherwise inapplicable to their business or personal life. In short, don't forward every little cute or funny email message, "true" story, chain letter, or joke you receive.

Finally, avoid forwarding warnings about the latest viruses and other threats to human happiness. Most of these warnings are hoaxes, and when you forward a hoax, you're just playing into the hands of the hoaxers. If you think the warning is serious, check the source to verify the information before you forward the warning to everyone in your address book.

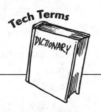

Flame Wars

When you strongly disagree with someone on the Internet, it's tempting to *flame* the person with a stinging, sarcastic message. It's even more tempting to respond to a flaming message with your own barb. The flame war that results is usually a waste of time and makes both people look bad. And another thing, don't bombard your enemy's email account with a billion messages in an attempt to make the person's email server crash. Even if it works, it's not very nice.

The Least You Need to Know

Assuming you entered the correct settings for connecting to the mail server, you should be able to send and receive email messages without running into any problems. Just keep the following information in mind:

➤ To set up a new email account in Outlook Express, open the **Tools** menu, choose **Accounts,** click the **Add** button, choose **Mail**, and follow the onscreen instructions.

➤ To access the email settings in Netscape Messenger, open the **Edit** menu, click **Preferences**, and click **Mail & Newsgroups**.

➤ To create a new email message, click the **Compose** or **New Message** button or its equivalent in your email program.

➤ Incoming email messages are often stored in the Inbox. Simply click the **Inbox** folder and then click the desired message to display its contents.

➤ To reply to a message, select the message and then click the **Reply** button.

➤ To attach a document to an outgoing message, click the button for attaching a file and then select the desired document file.

➤ If you receive a message that has a file attached to it, right-click the file's name and click the **Save** command.

➤ DON'T TYPE A MESSAGE USING ALL UPPERCASE CHARACTERS.

Chapter 19

Chatting with Friends, Relatives, and Complete Strangers

In This Chapter

➤ Experiencing the lively banter in chat rooms

➤ Sneaking a peek at a chatter's identity

➤ Chatting in private rooms

➤ Contacting friends and relatives with instant messages

➤ Adding other dimensions with audio and video

Every couple of months, I come across a news story about a couple who met in an online chat room and decided to get married. The woman usually sounds as dumb as a brick, and the guy typically looks like some shifty character who probably has three other wives and a dozen kids waiting for their child support checks. I could be wrong, but the negative speculation is a lot more interesting than the gushy story they put in the news.

Be that as it may, online chat does provide a fun and inexpensive way to meet people and "talk" with friends, relatives, colleagues, and complete strangers. In the right chat room, you can even make new business contacts and find a new job! When you're in a chat room, you simply type and send a message, and it immediately pops up on the screen of every person in the chat room. When anyone else in the chat room sends a message, it pops up on your screen. This makes for a frenetic conversation that can be fun to watch and partake in.

This chapter shows you how to use various chat tools in commercial online programs and on the Internet. Here, you learn how to converse in chat rooms, check out a person's profile (identity), use instant message programs to chat privately with friends and relatives, and use the audio and video features of your computer to place video "phone" calls on the Internet.

Hanging Out in Chat Rooms

America Online and CompuServe have their own, exclusive chat rooms, where members gather during all hours of the day and night to share interests, argue politics, discuss movies, flirt with one another, and explore various topics. If you subscribe to one of these online services, you can enter any of the standard chat rooms and start conversing, or just sit back and watch the messages scroll by.

To enter a chat room on America Online, first sign on and then cancel the ads that invariably pop up on your screen. This brings you to the Welcome window. Click the **People** button in the America Online toolbar (near the top of the window) and click **Find a Chat**. Double-click the desired chat category in the list on the left, and then double-click the desired chat room on the right. (The number next to each chat room indicates the number of people currently in the room.) America Online displays a chat window, as shown in Figure 19.1.

Before you start chatting, read the messages to get a feel for the content and tone of the room. When you're ready to jump in, type your message and press **Enter** or click the **Send** button. To leave the chat room, simply close its window. You can then select a different room from the Find a Chat window. In the following sections, you learn how to use more cool chat tools in America Online.

Figure 19.1

The chat window contains the controls you need to start chatting.

Messages from all chatters appear here.

Type your message here and press **Enter**.

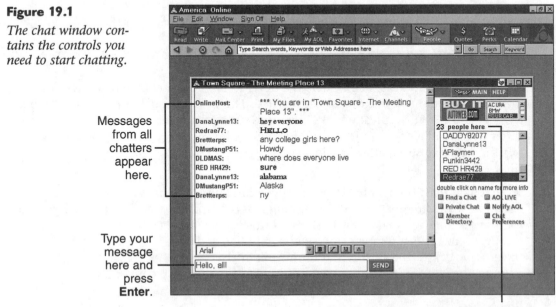

List of chatters

Checking Out the People Who Are Checking Out You

Every member of America Online has the opportunity to create a *profile* that lists the person's age, marital status, geographical location, hobbies, and other pertinent information. In most cases, the profile information is either overly cryptic or an outright lie, so you can't rely on it. However, the lies people tell usually reveal something about them, and they provide a key to understanding the individual.

To check out a person's profile, double-click the person's name in the list of chatters displayed on the right side of the window, and then click the **Get Profile** button. This displays the profile information that the person entered, as shown in Figure 19.2.

This Isn't the Room I Picked!

America Online chat rooms are limited to 23 members. If a room is full, America Online automatically bumps you into a room like the one you selected. For instance, if you chose The Flirts Nook, and it's full, America Online might bump you into The Flirts Nook 1.

```
┌─ Member Profile ──────────────────────── _ □ ✕ ─┐
│ Profile for:                              FREE    │
│                                           AOL!    │
│ Manemanx                                          │
│ ┌────────────────────────────────────────────┐▲ │
│ │Member Name:    Joe                          │  │
│ │Location:       Aruba, Carribean             │  │
│ │Birthdate:      01/25/60                      │  │
│ │Sex:            Male                          │  │
│ │Hobbies:        hang gliding, surfing, mountain climbing, skydiving│ │
│ │Computers:      Pentium III                   │  │
│ │Occupation:     Self-made millionaire         │  │
│ │Personal Quote: Seize me                      │  │
│ │                                             │▼ │
│ └────────────────────────────────────────────┘  │
│ ┌Locate┐ ┌E-Mail┐ ┌Create a Home Pag┐ ┌Online Greeting┐ ┌Notify AOL┐ ┌Help & Info┐│
└───────────────────────────────────────────────────┘
```

Figure 19.2

As my profile reveals, I'm as exciting as I think I am.

To check and edit your own profile, click the **My AOL** button in the America Online toolbar and click **My Member Profile**. Read the warning box that tells you that whatever information you enter is publicly accessible, and click **OK**. Enter your personal information (or whatever you want people to think about you) and click the **Update** button.

Sending Private Messages

If you strike up a conversation with someone who has completely captured your interest, you might want to grab a table for two in the corner and have your own private conversation. How do you do it?

Don't Be Too Open

Although most America Online members are fairly nice folks, there are plenty of creeps online. Don't give out personal information, such as your last name, phone number, address, or passwords. Some people may pose as customer service reps and request this information. Don't believe them.

Well, you have two options. The easiest way is to send the person an IM or Instant Message. An IM appears only on your screen and the screen of the recipient. To send an IM, double-click the person's name in the list of chatters on the right, and then click the **Send Message** button. Type your message and click the **Send** button. The Send Instant Message window remains on your screen, displaying a running dialog between you and your friend, but you both remain in the public chat room.

If you would like to leave the public chat room or want to chat in private with two or more other people, create your own private room. Under the list of chatters, click the **Private Chat** button. Type a name for your chat room and click **Go Chat**. You must then send an IM to your friend to tell the person the name of your private chat room. (To quickly display the Send Instant Message window, press **Ctrl+I**.) Private rooms are great if you and your pals are trying to have a serious discussion and some moron keeps interrupting and hassling you; simply create a private room and keep the jerk off the invitation list.

Making Your Own Public Chat Room

Are you the consummate host or hostess? Do you love throwing parties and mingling with your guests? Do you live for the thrill of greeting people and making them feel welcome? If you answered "Yes" to these questions, or are just plain bored with the chat rooms AOL offers, consider creating your own public chat room. Here's what you do:

Someone Invited Me to a Private Chat Room

If someone invites you to a private chat room, the person must tell you the name of the room. To go to the room, click the **Private Chat** button, type the name of the room, and click **Go Chat**.

1. Click the **People** button in the America Online toolbar and click **Start Your Own Chat**. America Online displays a dialog box asking if you want to create a public or private room.

2. Click the **Member Chat** button to create a public room. America Online now asks you to pick a category for the room, as shown in Figure 19.3.

3. In the chat category list (on the left), double-click the desired category name.

4. Click in the text box under "3" and type the desired name for your room.

5. Click **Go Chat** and then sit back and twiddle your thumbs until people start arriving.

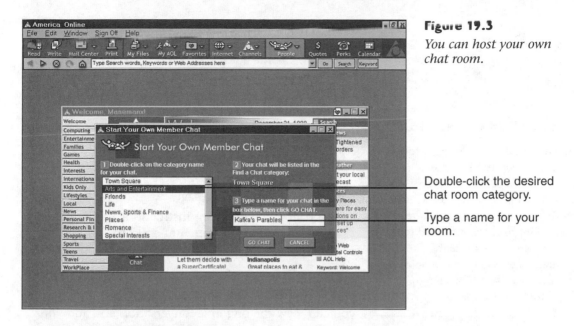

Figure 19.3
You can host your own chat room.

Double-click the desired chat room category.

Type a name for your room.

Chatting It Up on the Internet

There's no doubt about it, chat sells. People flock to online chat rooms where they can be anyone they want to be, travel incognito, and carry on in the relative safety of virtual worlds.

Although America Online first popularized chat rooms, many Internet companies have finally figured out that chat sells and have developed their own chat rooms, where anyone with an Internet connection and a Web browser can converse. The following sections show you where to find these chat services on the Web.

Hey, My Room Is Gone!

When the last person leaves a chat room, America Online automatically closes down the room and deletes it from the service. Talk about cleaning up after the party!

Chatting It Up at Yahoo!

Yahoo! has always been considered a premier Internet search site. Now, Yahoo! has injected its power and simplicity into the Internet chat arena. To access Yahoo!'s Chat rooms, first run your Web browser and use it to register for Yahoo! Chat. The following steps show how to use Internet Explorer (a Web browser installed on most PCs) to connect to Yahoo! and register for its chat rooms:

1. Double-click the **Internet Explorer** icon on the Windows desktop or click **Launch Internet Explorer Browser** in the Quick Launch toolbar.

What's All This "Web" Stuff?

The Web is a feature of the Internet that allows you to view interactive, multimedia pages using a Web browser. It's pretty easy to use, and the following sections provide the detailed instructions you need to access Internet chat rooms. However, if you need more details about using a Web browser, skip ahead to the next chapter.

2. Drag over the entry in the Address box near the top of the Window and type **www.Yahoo.com** This is the address of Yahoo!'s home page (its opening Web page).

3. Press **Enter**. Internet Explorer opens and displays Yahoo!'s home page.

4. Click the **Chat** link near the top of the page. (A *link* is an icon, picture, or highlighted text that points to another Web page.) When you click the link, your Web browser automatically opens the corresponding page.

5. Follow the onscreen instructions to complete the registration form and enter the desired chat room.

After you pick a chat room, Yahoo! automatically takes you to that room and displays a chat window, where you can view the ongoing conversation and add your own comments (see Figure 19.4).

Figure 19.4

Yahoo! brings chat rooms to the Web.

Messages from all chatters appear here.

Yahoo! Chat toolbar

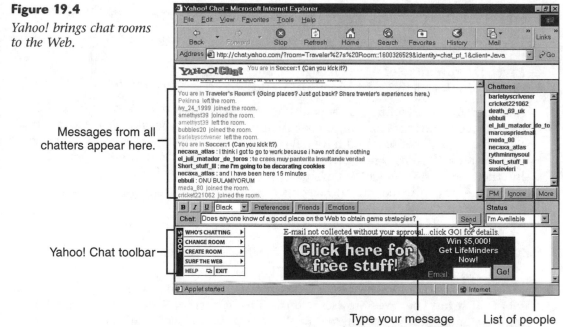

Type your message here and press **Enter**.

List of people in the chat room

186

After you are in a chat room, you can start chatting. The ongoing discussion is displayed in the large frame in the upper left. To send a message to the other chatters, click inside the chat text box just below the ongoing discussion, type your message, and press **Enter**. When you tire of this simple banter, try the following:

➤ Click the **Emotions** button and double-click an emotion (bow, agree, smile, or some other gesture) to send a text description of it.

➤ Right-click the name of someone in the room. This displays a dialog box, which enables you to find out more about the person, send the person a private message or a file, add the person to a list of friends, or ignore the person (prevent the person's messages from appearing on your screen).

➤ In the lower-left corner of the window is a list of tools. Click a tool to change to a different chat room, find out who's online, create your own room (public or private), edit your identity, get help, or exit. (You can edit your identity to provide additional information about yourself. Other chatters then see this information if they check your profile.)

Inside Tip

Finding Other Web Chat Sites

Although Yahoo! is on the cutting edge of Web chat, there are some other Web chat services that you can try out. Check out the following sites:
`www.flirt.com`
`www.chatting.com`
`wwbchat.com`

Keeping in Touch with Friends and Family

Relatively recently, developers have come up with a very innovative communications feature for the Web that allows people to create their own online community centers, family circles, or special interest groups to keep in touch. For example, if you have a large extended family, you can create a family circle and have all of your family members (at least those who have Internet access) join the circle. Members can then post messages, digitized photos, announcements, and calendar dates in a special area where everyone in the family can check them out. Many of these "community" centers also allow you to set up a members-only chat room and exchange electronic greeting cards and virtual gifts.

One of the best online community centers I know is eCircles, which you can find at `www.ecircles.com`. When you first go to eCircles, click the **Get Started!** link and register, as shown in Figure 19.5. You can then create your own eCircles or join existing circles, invite others to join, create your own online photo albums, enter important dates, post messages, and much more.

187

Figure 19.5

You must register for eCircles before you can join or create your own online community.

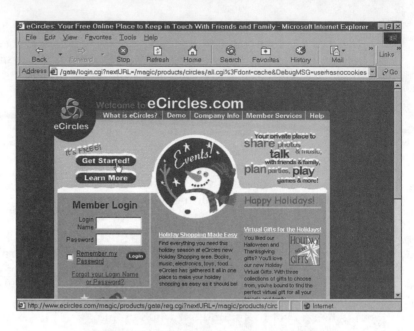

Other Community Centers

Although eCircles is one of the best places to set up your club or family circle, there are other places on the Web. Check out the following addresses:

www.excite.com/communities
www.friendfactory.com
www.wildabout.com

Chatting Privately with Friends and Relatives on the Internet

Hanging out with strangers can be interesting, but if you'd like to chat with friends and relatives, spotting them in crowded chat rooms can be a bit difficult. To help you track down individuals on the Internet, you can use an Instant Message program. You simply add the names and tracking information (typically an email address) of each person you may want to contact, and the program lets you know when the person is online. Assuming your friends and relatives run the same program (and are online), a dialog box pops up on your screen indicating that the person is available. You can then start your own private chat with that person.

Where do you get such a program? You can pick up America Online's Instant Messenger at **www.aol.com**, grab a copy of Yahoo! Messenger (formerly known as Yahoo! Pager) at **messenger.yahoo.com**, or snatch MSN Messenger Service from Microsoft at **messenger.msn.com**.

What About Audio and Video?

You probably have heard about Internet phone programs that enable you to place toll-free, long distance calls over the Internet using your sound card and speakers. These programs typically use a special server to enable two computers to exchange audio signals.

Now, I could tell you how to set up and use Microsoft NetMeeting (included with Internet Explorer) to place a call over the Internet, but there are easier ways to converse over the Internet without dealing with the complexities of Internet phone programs:

➤ Use Yahoo! Messenger, as explained in the previous section. At the time I was writing this book, Yahoo! Messenger featured voice support, and I bet that by the time this book hits the shelves most other instant message programs will offer voice support.

➤ Get your friends or relatives to join eCircle or a similar online community. When you choose the option for chatting, you are given the choice of text or voice chat. Choose voice chat to carry on an audio discussion.

To experience a high-quality audio connection over the Internet, your computer must be equipped with a full-duplex sound card (which can play and record at the same time), a fairly decent microphone, and a pair of speakers.

Video conferencing requires additional equipment and a dedicated Internet phone program, such as Microsoft NetMeeting or CUSeeMe. Your computer must be equipped with a video capture card (some newer display cards support video input) and a digital camera. Even if your computer is properly equipped, don't get your hopes up. Over a 56Kbps connection, the video is typically fuzzy and jerky and may even slow down the audio portion of your conversation.

Inside Tip

Sending Online Greeting Cards

If you're really cheap, instead of designing and printing your own invitations and greeting cards, send virtual cards online. There are hundreds of Web sites where you can create and send your own greeting cards via email. Just connect to **www.yahoo.com** and search for **virtual greeting cards**. Here are a few sites to get you started:
www.mygreetingcard.com
www.pcgreetings.com
www.netgreeting.com

The Least You Need to Know

Now that you know how to chat, you can join the millions of chat addicts who spend several hours a day popping in and out of chat rooms looking for a fix. As you skip from chat room to chat room, keep the following basics in mind:

➤ America Online and Yahoo! are two of the many places to find hordes of eager chatters.

➤ To chat on America Online, click the **People** button, click **Chat Now**, and start typing.

➤ To "talk" in a chat room, type your message in the message text box and press **Enter** or click the **Send** button.

➤ To send another America Online member a private message, press **Ctrl+I** to send an Instant Message.

➤ You can create a virtual meeting place or community center on the Web at eCircles (`www.ecircles.com`).

➤ You can send private messages to your friends and family members over the Internet using a special message program.

➤ The easiest way to carry on voice conversations over the Internet is to use Yahoo! Messenger or select the voice chat option on the Web.

Chapter 20

OOOooH...

Poking Around on the Web

In This Chapter

➤ Launching your Web browser on its virgin voyage

➤ Opening specific Web pages by entering addresses

➤ Skipping from one Web page to another with links

➤ Finding stuff on the Web

➤ Bookmarking Web pages for quick return trips

➤ Understanding cookies (pros and cons)

The single most exciting part of the Internet is the World Wide Web (or Web for short), a loose collection of interconnected *documents* stored on computers all over the world. What makes these documents unique is that each page contains a *link* to one or more other documents stored on the same computer or on a different computer (down the block, across the country, or overseas). You can hop around from document to document, from continent to continent, by clicking these links.

And when I say "documents," I'm not talking about some dusty old scrolls or text-heavy pages torn from books. Web documents contain pictures, sounds, video clips, animations, and even interactive programs. When you click a multimedia link, your modem pulls the file into your computer, where the Web browser or another program plays the file. As you'll see in this chapter, the Web has plenty to offer, no matter what your interests—music, movies, finances, science, literature, travel, astrology, body piercing, shopping—you name it.

Not Just Any Web Browser

Your ISP may offer you its own, custom Web browser, which is typically a waste of programming code. These custom browsers are usually customized to feed you more advertising from the ISP and are typically more difficult to navigate than popular browsers, such as Internet Explorer and Netscape Navigator. Stick with the popular browsers for now.

There's No Opening Page!

If you're not connected to the Internet when you start your browser, it might display a message indicating that it cannot find or load the page. Open **My Computer**, double-click **Dial-Up Networking**, and double-click the icon for connecting to your ISP.

First, You Need a Web Browser

To navigate the Web, you need a special program called a *Web browser*, which works through your service provider to pull documents up on your screen. You can choose from any of several Web browsers, including the two most popular browsers, Netscape Navigator and Internet Explorer. In addition to opening Web pages, these browsers contain advanced tools for navigating the Web, finding pages that interest you, and marking the pages you may want to revisit.

Windows comes with Internet Explorer, which should already be installed on your computer. To keep things simple, we'll use Internet Explorer in our examples. However, if you're using a different browser supplied by your service provider, don't fret. Most browsers offer the same basic features and similar navigation tools. Be flexible, and you'll be surfing the Web in no time.

Steering Your Browser in the Right Direction

To run your Web browser, click or double-click its icon on the desktop or choose it from the **Start**, **Programs** menu. If you're using Internet Explorer, click the icon named **The Internet** or **Internet Explorer** on the Windows desktop.

When your browser starts, it immediately opens a page that's set up as its starting page. For example, Internet Explorer opens Microsoft's home page. You can start to wander the Web simply by clicking links (typically, blue, underlined text; buttons; or graphic site maps). Click the **Back** button to flip to a previous page, or click **Forward** to skip ahead to a page that you've visited but backed up from (see Figure 20.1).

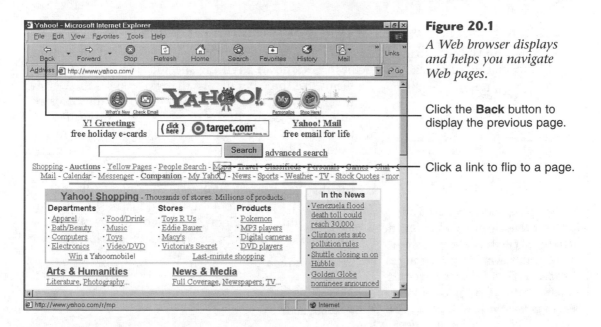

Figure 20.1

A Web browser displays and helps you navigate Web pages.

Click the **Back** button to display the previous page.

Click a link to flip to a page.

If you click a link and your browser displays a message that it can't find the page or that access has been denied, don't freak out. Just click the **Back** button and try the link again. If that doesn't open the page, try back later. In some cases, the Web page creator (*Web master*) might have mistyped the page address that the link points to or may have moved or deleted the page. On the ever-changing Web, this happens all the time. Be patient, be flexible, and don't be alarmed.

A Word About Web Page Addresses

Every page on the Web has an address that defines its location, such as **www.si.edu** for the Smithsonian Institution or **www.walmart.com** for Wal-Mart. The next time you watch TV or flip through a magazine, listen and keep your eyes peeled for Web page addresses. Not only do these addresses look funny in print, but they sound funny, too; for instance, **www.walmart.com** is pronounced "dubbayou-dubbayou-dubbayou-dot-walmart-dot-kahm."

Web page addresses are formally called URLs (uniform resource locators) and they allow you to open specific pages. You enter the address in your Web browser, usually in a text box called Go To or Address, near the top of the window, and your Web browser pulls up the page.

All you really have to know about a URL is that if you want to use one, type the URL exactly as you see it. Type the periods as shown, use forward slashes, and follow the capitalization of the URL. If you make any typos, a message appears indicating that the page doesn't exist or the browser loads the wrong page.

193

Finding Stuff with Popular Search Tools

Sure, the Web has loads of information and billions of pages, but this vast amount of information can make it difficult to track down anything specific. The Web often seems like some big library that gave up on the Dewey Decimal system and piled all of its books and magazines in the center of the library. How do you sift through this mass of information to find what you need?

URLs Dissected

All Web page addresses start with http://. Newsgroup sites start with news://. FTP sites (where you can get files) start with ftp://. You get the idea. HTTP (short for Hypertext Transfer Protocol) is the coding system used to format Web pages. The rest of the address reads from right to left. For example, in the URL http://www.whitehouse.gov, .gov stands for government, whitehouse stands for White House, and www stands for World Wide Web. Addresses that end in .edu are for pages at educational institutions. Addresses that end in .com are for commercial institutions. You can omit the http:// when entering Web page addresses, but omitting ftp:// or news:// causes the browser to attempt to connect to a Web site.

Use an Internet search tool. You simply connect to a site that has a search tool, type a couple words that specify what you're looking for, and click the **Search** button (or its equivalent). The following are the addresses of some popular search sites on the Web:

www.yahoo.com

www.lycos.com

www.go.com

www.altavista.com

www.excite.com

Most Web browsers have a Search button that connects you to various Internet search tools. For example, if you click **Search** in Internet Explorer, you connect to Microsoft's search page, which offers links to a half dozen search tools. The cool thing about the Search button is that it opens a separate pane that displays the search results. You can then click links in the left pane to open pages in the right pane without having to click the **Back** button to return to the search results (see Figure 20.2).

You can also use special search tools to find long-lost relatives and friends on the Internet. These search tools are like electronic telephone directories that can help you find mailing addresses, phone numbers, and even email addresses. To search for people, check out the following sites:

> **people.yahoo.com**
>
> **www.bigfoot.com**
>
> **www.whowhere.lycos.com**
>
> **www.infospace.com**

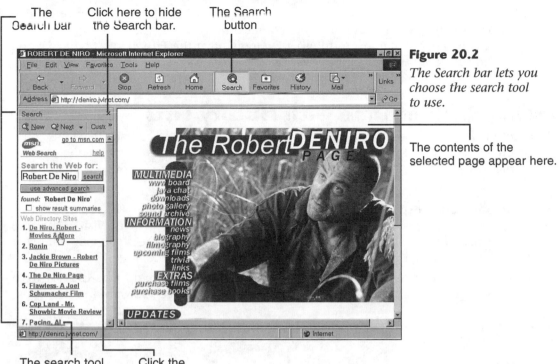

Figure 20.2

The Search bar lets you choose the search tool to use.

The contents of the selected page appear here.

The search tool displays a list of promising sites.

Click the desired link.

Opening Multiple Browser Windows

You're hot on the trail of a fabulous Web site when you encounter a site that catches your eye. Do you stop and explore the site, forsaking the path to your original destination or do you forge ahead and take the risk of never being able to return to the site?

Neither. Your browser offers some better options:

➤ Bookmark the page and quickly return to it later by selecting it from a menu. See "Marking Your Favorite Web Pages for Quick Return Trips" later in this chapter.

➤ Complete your journey to your original destination and then, later, use the history list to return to the site that caught your eye. See the next section, "Going Back in Time with History Lists."

Don't Open Too Many Windows

Every program window you open consumes valuable system resources. When resources run low, your computer gets slow. Keep only one to four windows open at a time.

➤ Open a new browser window, use it to complete your journey to your original destination, and then return to the other window when you have time. To open a new browser window in Internet Explorer, open the **File** menu, point to **New**, and click **Window** (or press **Ctrl+N**).

Going Back in Time with History Lists

Although the Back and Forward buttons will eventually take you back to where you were, they don't get you there in a hurry or keep track of pages you visited yesterday or last week. For faster return trips and a more comprehensive log of your Web journeys, check out the history list.

➤ In Internet Explorer, click the **History** button to display the History bar on the left side of the window. Click the day or week during which you visited the Web site and then click the Web site's name to view a list of pages you viewed at that site. To open a page, click its name, as shown in Figure 20.3.

➤ In Navigator, open the **Window** menu and click **History** or press **Ctrl+H** to view the history list. Double-click the name of the page you want to revisit.

Figure 20.3

Use the history list to retrace your steps.

Click the day or week icon.

Click the Web site's name.

Click the page you want to revisit.

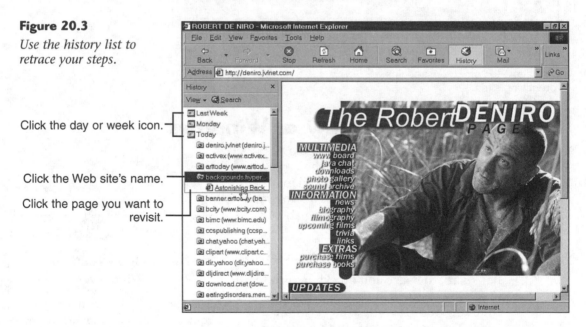

Marking Your Favorite Web Pages for Quick Return Trips

As you wander the Web, you pull up pages that you know you want to return to in the future. When you happen upon such a page, flag it by creating a *bookmark* or marking the page as a *favorite*. This adds the page's name to the Bookmark menu (in Navigator) or Favorites menu (in Internet Explorer). The next time you wish to pull up the page, you simply select it from your customized menu.

To mark a page, simply right-click a blank area of the page and select **Add Bookmark** (in Navigator) or **Add to Favorites** (in Internet Explorer).

In Internet Explorer, when you choose to add a page to the Favorites menu, the Add Favorite dialog box appears, asking if you only want to add the page to your Favorites menu or have Internet Explorer automatically download updates (*subscribe* to the page). If you choose to subscribe, Internet Explorer connects to the Internet at the scheduled times (typically when Internet traffic is light) and downloads the latest version of the page. When you choose to open the page, Internet Explorer quickly loads it from the cache rather than from the Web.

Whoa!

Covering Your Tracks

If you share your computer with someone, you might not want that person to know where you've been on the Web. To cover your tracks, clear the history list. In Internet Explorer, choose **Tools, Internet Options** or **View, Internet Options** (in earlier versions of Internet Explorer) and then click the **Clear History** button. In Navigator, choose **Edit, Preferences,** and click the **Clear History** button.

After you have added a page to the Bookmarks or Favorites menu, you can quickly open the page by opening the menu and clicking the name of the page.

Changing the Starting Web Page

Whenever you fire up your browser, it opens with the same page every time. If you have your own favorite page you'd like your browser to load on startup, just let your browser know:

Computer Cheats

Make a Shortcut for the Page

Right-click a blank area of the page and click **Create Shortcut**. This places a shortcut icon for the page on your desktop.

➤ In Internet Explorer, open the page you want to view on startup. Choose **Tools, Internet Options** or **View, Internet Options**. On the General tab, under Home Page, click **Use Current**, and then click **OK**.

➤ In Netscape Navigator, open the page you want to view on startup. Choose **Edit, Preferences**. Under Navigator Starts With, make sure **Home Page** is selected. Under Home Page, click **Use Current Page**, and then click **OK**.

Can Cookies Hurt Me?

When you visit some Web sites, they automatically send an electronic passport, called a *cookie*, to your computer. As you browse the site, use its tools, or order products, the site "stamps" your passport to keep track of your interests, passwords, and any products you ordered. Whenever you revisit the site, the site can grab the cookie and immediately identify you. Think of it as living in a small town where everyone knows your business.

Because cookies are used to track your Web habits, they give many people the heebie-jeebies and inspire allusions to Orwell's *1984*. Admittedly, cookies work behind the scenes to spy on you, but most cookies are designed to enhance your Web browsing experience and allow companies to target advertisements to your tastes (rather than pitching products that you probably wouldn't be interested in anyway).

In short, cookies are either good or bad depending on how they're used and how you view them. If you love to shop on the Internet, cookies are a necessary evil, because they act as your shopping basket, keeping track of the items you ordered. On the other hand, if you're the kind of person who gets nervous around security cameras, cookies may bother you.

So, can you refuse a cookie when a site tries to send you one? Of course—you have the option of blocking all cookies or having your browser prompt for your okay before accepting a cookie. Here's what you do:

➤ In Internet Explorer, choose **Tools**, **Internet Options** or **View**, **Internet Options**. Click the **Security** tab. Click the **Custom Level** button. Scroll down to Cookies and turn on the **Disable** option for both Cookies options. (Or turn on Prompt to have Internet Explorer ask for your confirmation before accepting a cookie.)

➤ In Netscape Navigator, choose **Edit**, **Preferences**. In the Category list, click **Advanced**. Click **Disable Cookies** or **Warn Me Before Accepting a Cookie**, and then click **OK**.

Learn More About Cookies

For additional details about cookies, check out **www.cookiecentral.com**.

If you've done plenty of Web surfing with the cookies feature enabled, you probably have several cookies on your computer. To get rid of cookies in Internet Explorer, use My Computer to change to the Windows/Cookies folder, press **Ctrl+A**, press the **Delete** key, and click **OK**. To delete Navigator cookies, use the **Start**, **Find**, **Files or Folders** command to search for a file on your hard disk named Cookies.txt. Click it, press the **Delete** key, and click **OK**.

The Least You Need to Know

Until you open your first Web page, the Web may seem intimidating. But if you know how to type an address and click links, you've pretty much mastered the Web. As you continue your exploration of the Web, keep the following factoids in mind:

➤ To start Internet Explorer or Netscape Navigator, double-click its icon on the Windows desktop.

➤ Links typically appear as buttons, icons, or specially highlighted text.

➤ Click a link to open the page that the link points to.

➤ If you know a Web page's address, type it in your browser's Address or Go To text box and press **Enter**.

➤ To search for a topic or site on the Web, use a search engine, such as **www.yahoo.com**, **www.lycos.com**, **www.go.com**, or **www.hotbot.com**, and enter one or two words to describe what you're looking for.

➤ To bookmark a page, right-click a blank area of the page and select **Add Bookmark** (in Navigator) or **Add to Favorites** (in Internet Explorer).

➤ If you're worried about cookies, disable the cookie feature in your Web browser.

Chapter 21

Shopping, Investing, Traveling, and Other Cool Web Stuff

In This Chapter

➤ Get up-to-the-minute news, weather, and sports online

➤ Go shopping at the biggest mall on the planet

➤ Buy and sell stocks through an online broker

➤ Check out some cool vacation spots

➤ Bone up on your movie trivia

Although the Internet hasn't changed anything we humans do, it has completely revolutionized the *way* we do everything. People still watch the news and read magazines and newspapers, but more and more folks are getting their news, weather, and sports on the Web. Investors still earn and lose millions of dollars on their stocks and bonds, but now they can do it faster online. People still have affairs, but now they can ignite their passions in online chat rooms.

In short, the Web offers features that enable you to perform the same tasks you performed in the past only more conveniently and (typically) at less expense. This chapter shows you how to take advantage of some of the Web's more practical, real-life applications.

Keeping Up with News, Weather, and Current Events

TV stations are capable of broadcasting the news as it happens. You can watch live speeches, trials, and debates; view late-breaking reports from Washington; and watch

Doppler radar track a storm as it moves through your town. The only trouble is that you're at the mercy of what the broadcasters want to show you. You need to wait for the news to come on and then wait for the reporters to get around to relating the information you want.

On the Web, news is slightly delayed. It takes a while for someone to format a story and place it on the Web. Even "live" video clips on the Web are delayed by the time it takes your modem to receive the data. However, the Web provides a self-directed approach to the news, so you don't have to sit through commercial breaks or wait for the story to air. You view only the information that interests you when you want it. In addition, Web news sites typically cover a story more thoroughly than on TV. Think of Web news as the ideal cross between a newspaper and TV news—it's fast and can provide audio and video coverage like TV, but it's thorough and scannable like a newspaper.

The following sections tell you where to find the best news, weather, and sports "channels" on the Web.

Checking Out Web Newsstands

Virtually every TV station and news publication has a Web site where you can find not only the major news stories, but also biographical information, health alerts, book and movie reviews, political analysis, travel information, and much more. Check out the following popular news sites:

➤ CNN at `www.cnn.com`. Even if you don't have cable TV, you can check out this award-winning news service online (see Figure 21.1).

➤ ABC News at `www.abcnews.go.com`. If you missed the evening news, check out the ABC News site to view the latest stories. You'll also find links to the other ABC news shows, including *20/20* and *Nightline*.

➤ CBS News at `www.cbs.com`. This address takes you to the CBS home page, where you must click the CBS News link. Here, you find brief clips of the top stories along with links for various news categories including National, Politics, SciTech, and Showbiz.

➤ MSNBC News at `www.nbc.com/msnbc/news/`. Although this site displays the standard "top stories" you find at most news sites, it's laid out a little differently, displaying a list of features from every NBC news show: *The Today Show*, *NBC Nightly News*, *Dateline NBC*, and *Meet the Press*.

➤ Associated Press at `www.ap.org`. Go to the source and get the news from the place where the press gets its news: The Associated Press. When you get to the AP home site, click **The Wire** link and then select your local news site from one of the available lists.

➤ Yahoo!'s Daily News at `dailynews.yahoo.com`. Although Yahoo! is a little light on the news, it does provide an excellent starting point for your search. Here, you find plenty of links to other news sites that offer more thorough coverage.

If you've poked around at the news sites and can't find the information you're looking for, use your favorite Internet search tool to search for the topic by name. Just browsing? Then go to Yahoo! and click the **News & Media** link on the opening page. You'll find links to thousands of news sites on the Web.

Figure 21.1
CNN offers the most thorough news coverage on the Web.

Getting the Latest Weather Reports

Sure, you can get a weather report at any of the sites mentioned in the previous section, but why settle for second-rate weather forecasts when the best weather station in the world is on the Web? Check out the Weather Channel at `www.weather.com`.

The Weather Channel's opening page displays snippets from the big weather stories along with any national weather alerts. For a specific local forecast, enter the name of the city or town or a zip code for the area in the Local Weather text box and press **Enter**. The local forecast appears, as shown in Figure 21.2.

Computer Cheats

Guess the Address

If you're ever unsure where an organization's Web site is located (or whether the organization even has a Web site), try guessing at its address. For example, for *USA Today*, you might enter `www.usatoday.com`. You'll probably hit the right site more than 50% of the time.

Figure 21.2

The Weather Channel can display local forecasts for any area in the world.

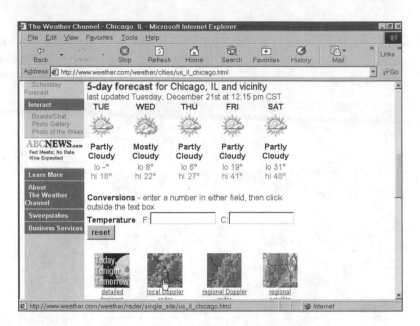

You can find hundreds of weather sites on the Web, including the National Weather Service (**www.nws.noaa.gov**) and EarthWatch Weather on Command (**www.earthwatch.com**). To find a more complete listing of sites, use any Internet search tool to search for sites.

Have Local Forecasts Mailed to You

Go to Weather by E-mail at **www.weatherbyemail.com**, and search for your local weather forecast. When the site displays your forecast, it also displays a link for subscribing to the forecast. Click the link and fill out the required form to have the forecast emailed to you daily.

Sports Fans Only

If you have cable TV, you can always find some sporting event to keep you entertained. But if you're flipping through stations and all you can find is the national Table Tennis championships, you might want to take a break and check out a site for your favorite sport.

Given the current popularity of sports, you would expect to find plenty of sports sites on the Web, and the Web does not disappoint. Every sport you can think of, from archery to wrestling and everything in between, has at least one Web site devoted exclusively to it. In addition, all of the major sports organizations and broadcasters have their own Web sites. Here are a few of my favorites:

➤ ESPN, at **espn.go.com**, is a great place to go for a rundown of scores as well as in-depth coverage of sporting events and behind-the-scenes interviews with your favorite players and coaches.

➤ CNN/SI, at **www.cnnsi.com**, is the Web home of *Sports Illustrated*. Although some of the articles at this site are mere teasers for the printed magazine, this site is packed with scores, team rankings, player statistics, and game analyses. You can even play fantasy sports and see how your teams stack up against fellow sports enthusiasts.

➤ NFL, at **www.nfl.com**, is the official home of the National Football League. Do you have a favorite NFL team? Click its insignia at the top of the page to view the official team information, win/loss record, and statistics for your favorite players. (Go to **www.nba.com** for professional basketball, **www.majorleaguebaseball.com** for baseball, or **www.nhl.com** for hockey.)

➤ CBS Sportsline, at **www.sportsline.com**, is the CBS sports center, where you can find coverage of major professional and college sports. Sportsline offers a robust collection of photos and the latest point spreads (not that I'm saying gambling is okay).

➤ Nando Times Sports, at **www.nandotimes.com/sports/**, is one of the best-established sports sites on the Web, offering quality sports reporting without the frills. Nando is also a great place to pick up the daily TV schedule for sporting events.

Mail-Order Paradise: Shopping on the Web

After businesses caught sight of the Internet, they began to realize the incredible opportunities it offered for advertising, marketing, and selling products directly to consumers. As more people purchased computers and started exploring online services and the Internet, businesses rushed to the Web to establish a presence, and many individuals created their own storefronts on the Web.

And boy, is business booming on the Web! Go to nearly any site, and an ad will pop up on your screen. Open any Internet search page, and you'll find thousands of links to retail stores, mail-order companies, manufacturers, online mega-malls, bookstores, music stores, and even mom-and-pop specialty shops. I'm not about to list all the great places to shop on the Web, because I'm sure you can find what you're looking for with your favorite search tool. However, before you do any serious shopping, you should be aware of the following shopping basics:

➤ When you find the desired product, you typically click a link for ordering it or placing it in your shopping basket. You can then click a link to keep shopping or to check out.

➤ Before you enter any personal information or credit card number, make sure you are at a legitimate site and that the form you are about to fill out is secure. Internet Explorer displays a blue lock icon at the bottom of the window to indicate that a form is secure. If the form's page address starts with https:// instead of http://, it is stored on a secure server.

➤ When you're ready to place your order, you must fill out an order form, such as the one shown in Figure 21.3. You'll be asked to select a payment method and enter billing and shipping data. Just pretend that you're entering information in a dialog box, and you'll do just fine.

➤ After you place your order, the site may display a confirmation page or send you a statement via email. Be sure to print out the statement—it typically contains a confirmation or order number that you can use to follow up on your order in case anything goes wrong.

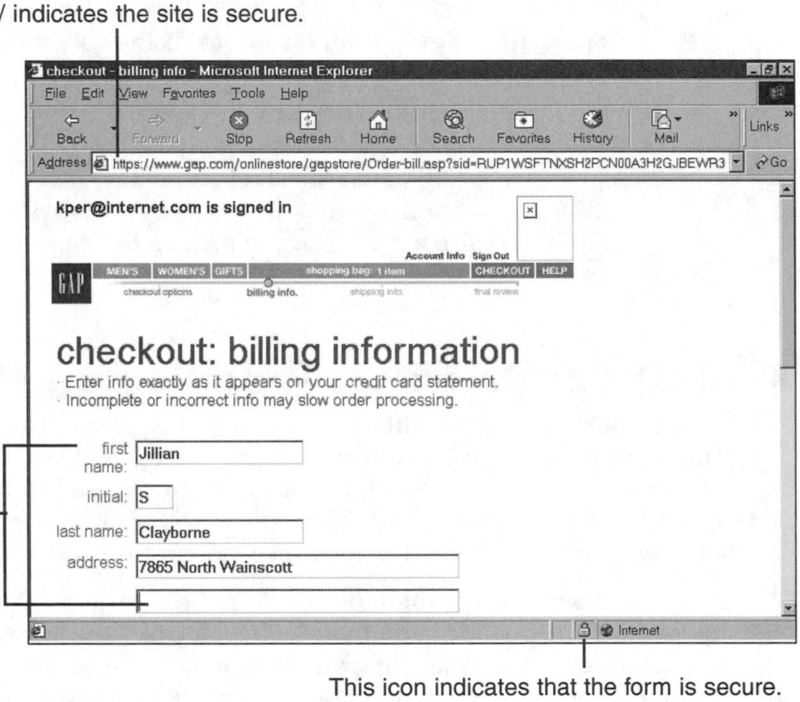

https:// indicates the site is secure.

Figure 21.3

Complete the online order form to place your order.

Type the requested information.

This icon indicates that the form is secure.

Becoming Your Own Stockbroker

Before state lotteries, bingo nights, and local casinos started becoming so popular, the stock market was the only game in town for legalized gambling. But even with the growing availability of lotteries and other betting venues, the stock market remains one of the most popular gambling institutions in the nation. And now, if you have Internet access and a little extra money, you, too, can place a bet on your favorite corporation.

Several Web-based stock trading companies allow you to buy and sell stocks online. You simply set up an account with the company and mail in a check to cover your future transactions. After your account is set up, you can buy and sell stocks using the money in your account. These services typically charge a base fee per transaction (for instance, $20 per transaction for up to 1,000 shares). Most services also provide tools for tracking your investments and researching companies.

To see how this online investing thing works, check out the following online stock brokerages:

➤ E*TRADE, at **www.etrade.com**, is one of the most popular stock brokerage firms on the Web, providing the tools you need to research companies, track your investments, and learn more about investing. You can open an account with a minimum of $1,000. Transactions cost $20 per 1,000 shares plus $.02/share for all shares over 1,000.

➤ AmeriTrade, at **www.ameritrade.com**, is one of the least expensive brokerages, offering a flat fee of $8 for most transactions. Ameritrade also provides plenty of tools and data for researching and tracking investments.

➤ DLJ Direct, at **www.dljdirect.com**, is one of my favorite places to check on my stocks and mutual funds. In fact, I set up DLJ Direct as my home page, as shown in Figure 21.4. I've never purchased stocks through DLJ Direct, but its services are competitive with the previous two brokerages mentioned here. DLJ Direct charges a little more per transaction than E*TRADE, but it provides more thorough information than either E*TRADE or Ameritrade.

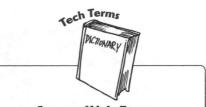

Secure Web Forms

When you enter data using a secure Web form, your browser scrambles the data before sending it. When the Web server receives the scrambled data, it decodes it. This significantly reduces the possibility that someone can intercept the data en route to its destination and read it.

Shameless Disclaimer

To protect myself from lawyers and other whiners, I must say that I don't recommend using any of these online stock brokerages, purchasing stocks online, or even purchasing stocks offline. In short, I'm not responsible for anything you do with your money, your spouse's money, or the money in your kids' piggy banks.

➤ Charles Schwab, at **www.schwab.com**, is a more full-service brokerage. As such, it charges more than any of the other online brokerages described here—$30 per 1,000 shares plus $.03/share for all shares over 1,000. When you're first learning the ropes, getting professional advice may be worth the extra cost.

Figure 21.4

Online brokerages provide the information you need to invest wisely.

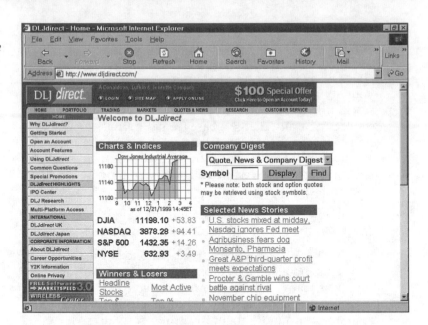

Plane Fares

Inside Tip

Several sites, including Yahoo!, provide free quotes for airline tickets. You simply enter the dates on which you plan to travel and the departure and arrival locations, and the site displays a list of fares, typically from lowest to highest.

Planning Your Next Vacation

Whether you already have a vacation destination in mind or need a few ideas on where to go, the Web has plenty of tools for planning your vacation, buying tickets, and making reservations. If you want to go through a travel agent, you can find several travel agencies online. If you would rather plan the trip yourself, you can find thousands of links for travel bureaus, airlines, motels, campsites, tourist centers, and everything else you can imagine.

One of the best places to start planning your vacation is at Yahoo! (www.yahoo.com). On Yahoo!'s opening page, scroll down to the Recreation & Sports category and click the **Travel** link. Scroll down the page to view a list of travel subcategories, as shown in Figure 21.5, and follow the trail of links to obtain the desired travel information.

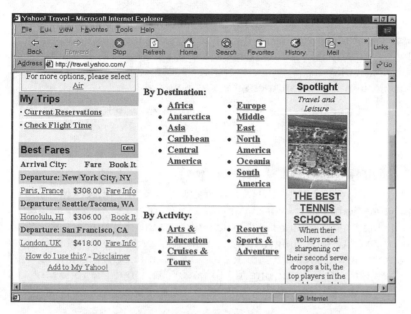

For Movie Buffs Only

Whether you're at a party swapping movie trivia or at home trying to decide which movie to rent, a thorough, up-to-date movie database can come in handy. With a movie database, you can obtain a complete list of movies in which your favorite actor or actress appeared, quickly determine who directed a particular movie, or scan plots to decide which movie you want to rent.

One of the most thorough movie databases on the Web is the Internet Movie Database at **us.imdb.com**. The opening page displays a form that lets you search for movies based on the movie's title or on the people involved in its creation (the actors, actresses, directors, and so on). Simply type a person's last name or a portion of the movie's title and click the **Go!** button to start your search. Follow the trail of links to narrow your search and find the desired information.

Although the Internet Movie Database is one of the best places to go to answer trivia questions and research the careers of your favorite stars and directors, the Internet offers much more for film buffs. Most major movie studios have their own Web sites (for instance, Paramount at **www.paramount.com**) where they

Inside Tip

Don't Forget the Chat Rooms

Twenty-four hours a day, seven days a week, you can find movie chat rooms where fans meet to discuss movie facts and trade trivia questions. If you're looking for some friendly banter about the movies you like best, check out the chat rooms.

typically showcase new and future releases. Video rental stores (such as Blockbuster at **www.blockbuster.com**) have their own sites, which typically display a list of upcoming video releases along with any promotional deals. Magazines, such as *New Yorker* and *Time*, have movie reviews. Many popular actors and actresses have their own "official" Web sites. You can even find shrines set up by devoted fans.

Use your favorite search tool to explore the Movies categories or search for a specific movie, director, actor, actress, movie studio, or other movie-related topic.

Creating Your Own Music Library

If you thought the transition from LPs to CDs was revolutionary, the effect the Internet has had on the music industry will make your head spin. As you would guess, every major label (and most minor labels) have their own Web sites where you can find out about your favorite recording artists, view video clips, and listen to sample audio clips. You can even find Web sites for lesser-known, independent artists, who use the Web to distribute their music directly to fans. Check out the following groovy sites:

Tech Terms

I Want My MP3

MP is short for MPEG, which is short for Moving Picture Experts Group, an organization that develops standards for compressing audio and video files. The MP3 standard improves file compression by stripping out data in audio signals that humans cannot hear anyway.

➤ Internet Underground Music Archive, at **www.iuma.com**, is just what its name describes, a music library where you can listen to bands you won't hear on the radio or see on MTV. If you're a musician yourself, you can create your own Web site and use it to chase your dream of signing that big record deal—or just have someone other than the neighbors listen to your tunes.

➤ SONICNET, at **www.sonicnet.com**, is an online music network where you can get the latest news, music charts, reviews, and lists of events. SONICNET features in-depth coverage of the music industry and allows you to search for individual artists by name.

➤ CDNOW, at **www.cdnow.com**, is a great place to pick up bargains on your favorite CDs and get some background information on your favorite artists.

➤ RollingStone.com, at **rollingstone.tunes.com**, is the electronic version of the popular *Rolling Stone* magazine. Here, you'll find plenty of reviews, industry news, and interviews. And if you have your own MP3 clip, you can submit it to the editors for inclusion in their Top 10 list.

Most music sites have audio clips you can download and play. You simply click the link to play the clip, and your computer downloads (copies) the audio file from the Web site and starts to play it. If your computer doesn't have the program required to play the clip, your Web browser displays a dialog box asking if you want to download and install the player. Simply give your okay and follow the instructions.

Getting Technical Support for Your Computer

Nearly every computer hardware and software company has its own Web site where you can purchase products directly and find technical support for products you own. If your printer is not feeding paper properly, you're having trouble installing your sound card, you keep receiving cryptic error messages in your favorite program, or you have some other computer-related problem, you can usually find the solution on the Internet.

In addition, computer and software companies often upgrade their software and post both updates and fixes (called *patches*) on their Web sites for downloading. If you are having problems with a device, such as a printer or modem, you should check the manufacturer's Web site for updated drivers. If you run into problems with a program, check the software company's Web site for a patch—a program file that you install to correct the problem.

The following table provides Web page addresses of popular software and hardware manufacturers to help you in your search. Most of the home pages listed have a link for connecting to the support page. If a page does not have a link to the support page, use its search tool to locate the page. You might also see a link labeled FAQ (Frequently Asked Questions), Common Questions, or Top Issues. This link can take you to a page that lists the most common problems other users are having and answers from the company.

Table 21.1   Computer Hardware and Software Web Sites

Company	Web Page Address
Acer	www.acer.com
Borland	www.borland.com
Broderbund	www.broderbund.com
Brother	www.brother.com
Canon	www.ccsi.canon.com
Compaq	www.compaq.com
Corel	www.corel.com
Creative Labs	www.soundblaster.com
Dell	www.dell.com
Epson	www.epson.com
Fujitsu	www.fujitsu.com
Gateway	www.gw2k.com

continues

Table 21.1 Computer Hardware and Software Web Sites Continued

Company	Web Page Address
Hayes	www.hayes.com
Hewlett-Packard	www.hp.com
Hitachi	www.hitachipc.com
IBM	www.ibm.com
Intel	www.intel.com
Iomega	www.iomega.com
Lotus	www.lotus.com
Micron Electronics	www.micronpc.com
Microsoft	www.microsoft.com
Motorola	www.mot.com
NEC	www.nec.com
Packard Bell	www.packardbell.com
Panasonic	www.panasonic.com
Sony	www.sony.com
Toshiba	www.toshiba.com
3COM (U.S. Robotics)	www.3com.com

Figure 21.6

Check out the FAQ or Top Issues link for answers to common questions.

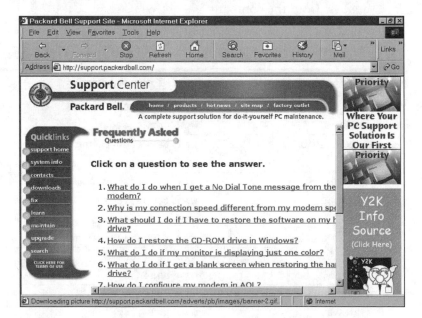

If the manufacturer you're looking for is not listed in this table, don't give up. Connect to your favorite Web search page and search for the manufacturer by name or search for the problem you're having. You should also seek help from online computer magazines. Here are some excellent resources:

Check the Manual

Although manufacturers like to keep the tech support phone number a secret, they want you to know their Web page address so that you can check out their other products. The Web site's technical support areas also cut down on calls to tech support.

➤ *ZDNet*, at **www.zdnet.com**, is the home of several quality computer magazines, including *PC Computing, Windows Sources,* and *ComputerLife*. Here you find articles on general computing, hardware and software reviews, tips, and answers to specific questions.

➤ *c\net*, at **www.cnet.com**, is a great place if you need technical support for Internet problems. It's also a great place to check out gaming information and obtain shareware programs. Although you don't find as much information about general computing issues as you find at ZDNet, the information you do find is very useful.

➤ *Windows Magazine*, at **www.winmag.com**, is an excellent place to find answers to your Windows questions, learn about the latest improvements, and check out software reviews.

The Least You Need to Know

Life on the Internet is no substitute for life in the real world, but the Internet can enhance your life and make you perform real-life tasks more efficiently. As you begin to incorporate Internet tools into your daily life, keep the following in mind:

➤ Thousands of Web sites are devoted to covering news, weather, and sports.

➤ Before you hand your credit card number over to a company, make sure the company is legitimate and that the site is secure.

➤ You can research investments and buy and sell stocks on the Web for a fraction of the cost you would pay a stockbroker.

➤ One of the best places to start planning your next vacation is on Yahoo!'s Travel page.

➤ Want to know the names of all movies in which Robert De Niro appeared? Check out the Internet Movie Database at `us.imdb.com`.

➤ Most music Web sites are packed with links for downloading and playing audio and video clips.

➤ Virtually every computer and software company has a Web site where you can obtain technical support for products.

Chapter 22

Publishing Your Own Web Page in 10 Minutes or Less

In This Chapter

➤ Understanding how the Web works

➤ Sneaking a peek at the codes behind Web pages

➤ Slapping together your own cool Web page

➤ Using the Web to make money

➤ Finding free enhancements for your Web page

You've wandered the Web. Perhaps you've sent out a few electronic greeting cards, played some audio and video clips, and even ordered products online. You can use search tools to track down information about the most obscure topics, and you can monitor the progress of all of your stocks and mutual funds.

But now you want more. You want to establish a presence on the Web, publish your own stories or poems, place pictures of yourself or your family online, show off your creativity, and communicate your ideas to the world.

Where do you start? How do you create a Web page from scratch? How do you insert photos and links? How do you add a background? And after you've created the page, what steps must you take to place the page on the Web for all to see?

This chapter shows you a quick and easy way to whip up your first Web page right online, without having to learn a special program or deal with any cryptic Web page formatting codes. And because you create the page online, you don't have to worry about *publishing* your Web page when you're done.

What Makes a Web Page So Special?

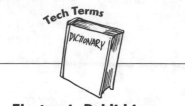

Tech Terms

Electronic Publishing

Publishing a Web page doesn't require anything as complicated as setting up a printing press or binding books. You simply copy the Web page and all related files (photos, audio clips, graphics) to a folder on a Web server. When you create a Web page online, you needn't publish the page, because the Web page creation site does that for you.

Behind every Web page is a text document that includes codes for formatting the text, inserting pictures and other media files, and displaying links that point to other pages. This system of codes (*tags*) is called *HTML* (short for Hypertext Markup Language).

Most codes are *paired*. The first code in the pair turns on the formatting, and the second code turns it off. For example, to type a heading such as "Apple Dumplin's Home Page," you would use the heading codes like this:

```
<h1>Apple Dumplin's Home Page</h1>
```

The <h1> code tells the Web browser to display any text that follows the code as a level one heading. The </h1> code tells the Web browser to turn off the level one heading format and return to displaying text as normal. Unpaired codes act as commands; for instance, the <p> code starts a new paragraph.

Web browsers use HTML codes to determine how to display text, graphics, links, and other objects on a page. Because the browser is in charge of interpreting the codes, different browsers may display the same page somewhat differently. For example, one browser may display links as blue, underlined text, whereas another browser displays links as green and bold.

Inside Tip

HTML Overrides

Even if a browser is set up to display all level one headings a particular way, HTML codes can override the browser's setting and give the heading a different look. (For example, they may make the heading appear in a different color or font.)

Forget About HTML

A basic introduction to HTML is helpful in understanding how the Web works, troubleshooting Web page formatting problems, and customizing Web pages with fancy enhancements, but you don't need a doctorate in HTML to create your first Web page. Many companies have developed specialized programs that make the process of creating a Web page as easy as designing and printing a greeting card.

You can use programs such as Web Studio, Front Page Express, Netscape Composer, and HotDog to create and format Web pages on your computer and then upload (copy) the pages from your computer to a Web server (typically your ISP's Web server). Or you can create and format your Web pages right on the Web simply by specifying your preferences and using forms to enter your text. The next section shows you just how easy it is to create and publish your own Web page online at Yahoo! GeoCities.

Making a Personal Web Page Right on the Web

When it comes to publishing your own Web page, you have simple needs—a single Web page that lets you share your interests with others and express yourself to the world. For someone with such simple needs, the Web offers free *hosting* services, such as Yahoo! GeoCities. These services offer tools for building your Web page online along with access to a Web server where you can publish your page.

So, let's get on with it and publish a simple Web page at Yahoo! GeoCities:

1. Run your Web browser and go to **geocities.yahoo.com**.

2. Follow the series of links required to sign up as a new user. (Because Web sites are notorious for changing steps and commands, specific instructions would only confuse you. You have to wing it— trust me.)

3. Fill out the required form, read the legal agreement(s), and jump through whatever hoops you need to jump through to get your free membership. This gives you an ID (member name) and password so you can sign in.

4. Use your ID and password to sign in to Yahoo! GeoCities. Your browser loads the Yahoo! GeoCities welcome page, as shown in Figure 22.1.

5. Click the link for building a new Web page. The site displays a list of neighborhoods grouped by category: Arts & Literature, Family, Travel, and so on.

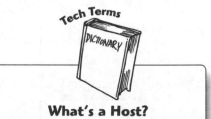

Tech Terms

What's a Host?

A Web host is a server on which you can store your Web page and all files related to it, such as photos and other graphics. Think of it as a neighborhood in which you can build your home. Your ISP may provide free hosting services (typically with a limit of 5 megabytes), but you typically need to create the Web page yourself and then upload it to the Web server.

Figure 22.1

Yahoo! GeoCities welcomes you.

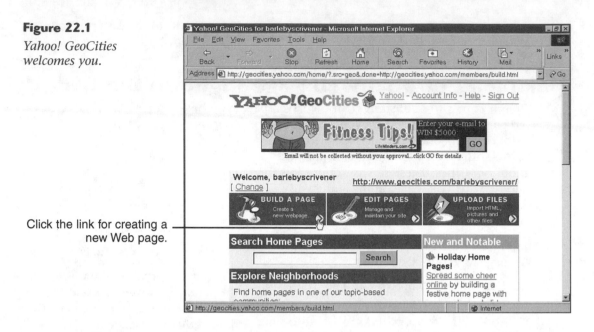

Click the link for creating a new Web page.

6. Click the link for the neighborhood in which you want to build your Web page. Yahoo! GeoCities displays a form asking you to describe the content of your page.

7. Enter the requested information and choose the options that best describe the page you want to create, and then click the **Submit** button. Yahoo! GeoCities displays your member information and the address of your Web page. (You might want to print this page for future reference.)

Use a Yahoo! Wizard

Yahoo! Wizards display a series of forms you fill out to enter your page preferences and any text you want to appear on your page. To start with a wizard rather than a template, click the **Yahoo! Wizards** link and follow the onscreen instructions.

8. Click the **Build Your Page Now!** link. Yahoo! GeoCities displays a list of predesigned Web page templates you can use to get started.

9. Click one of the Page Builder templates. Yahoo! GeoCities displays a preview of the template, as shown in Figure 22.2. (If the template doesn't appeal to you, click the **Back** button and choose another.)

10. Click **Launch PageBuilder** to download and start the Yahoo! PageBuilder program and load the template on your computer. After several minutes, PageBuilder appears and displays the selected template.

11. To change existing text, click a text box twice and then drag over the existing text and type your own text.

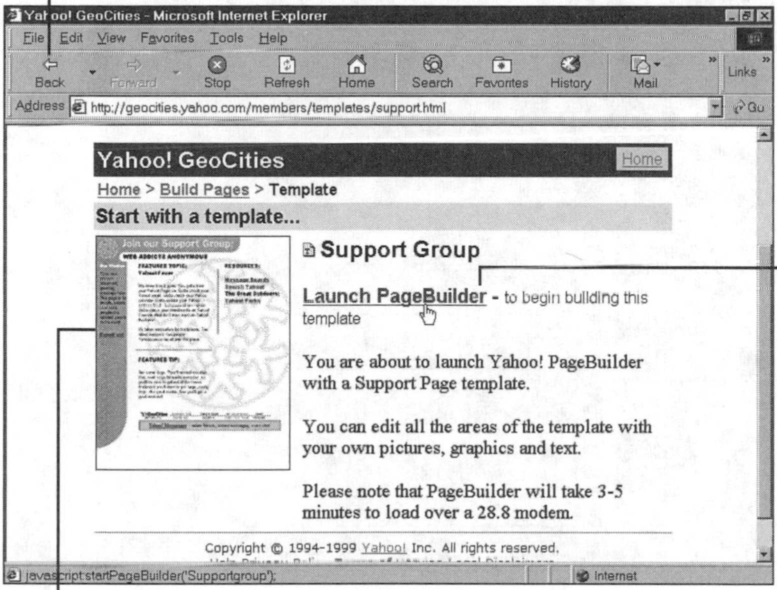

Click the **Back** button to pick a different template.

Figure 22.2

Preview the template before making your final selection.

Click **Launch PageBuilder** to get started.

Template preview

12. To transform text into a link, drag over the text and click the **Link URL** button (the one with the chain link on it). Type the address of the page you want the link to point to and click **OK**.

13. To insert a picture, make sure no text is selected, and then click the **Pictures** button. The Select Picture dialog box appears, as shown in Figure 22.3.

14. Open the **Collection** list, choose the type of picture you want to use, and then click the desired picture in the **Picture List**.

15. Under Optional Picture Properties, enter any of the following properties for the picture:

    Link to a Location uses the picture as a link. Users can click the picture to load a Web page that the picture points to. In the **Link to a Location Text Box**, type the address of the target page.

    Screen Tip displays a text description of the picture or provides a brief instruction, such as "Click me for financial advice." Simply type the desired text in the text box.

    Mouse-Over Picture lets you choose another picture you want to pop up when the user rests his or her mouse pointer on the picture. Click the **Choose** button and select the desired picture.

Figure 22.3

PageBuilder comes with a set of clip art images you can place on your Web page.

Select a clip art collection.

Select an image.

Enter any additional preferences.

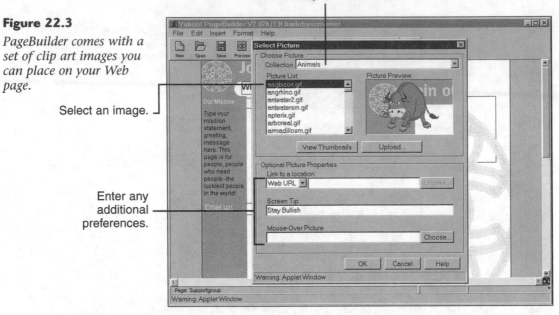

16. Click the **OK** button. The picture appears on your page. You can drag the picture to move it or drag one of its handles to resize it.

17. To save your page to the Web, click the **Save** button.

18. Type a page name or click the name of one of the files in the **Files Available** list.

19. Click the **Save** button. A dialog box appears, indicating that PageBuilder is in the process of saving the page. Assuming all goes as planned, PageBuilder asks whether you want to view your page; click **Yes**. PageBuilder loads the page into your Web browser.

You can change your page at any time. Just go to Yahoo! GeoCities at **geocities.yahoo.com**, sign in, and click the link for opening an existing page. The Open Page dialog box appears, listing the pages at your site. Click the page you want to edit and click **OK**.

Panic Attack

Can't Save Page

If any key elements on your page overlap, PageBuilder displays an alert indicating that you must first move some objects. Drag any of the red, crosshatched areas off one another to eliminate the overlap and try again.

Placing Your Business on the Web

Of course, you didn't build that Web page to make money or pitch a pyramid scheme to your friends or relatives, but you can use your Web page to generate income and set up your own business or online storefront.

If you already have a page at Yahoo! GeoCities, one of the easiest ways to generate income from your page is to sign up for the Pages That Pay program. With this program, you insert advertisements and links for ordering products on your page. When someone orders the product through your page, you receive a sales commission from the manufacturer or dealer. You don't have to mess with creating order forms, tracking orders, or shipping products. You're just the middleman.

For those who have more complex business needs (those who manufacture or ship their own products or provide a service), you may need more sophisticated Web-based business tools than Yahoo! GeoCities has to offer. You will need access to a secure Web server, a form for customers to use to place orders, and an online database that can receive and organize orders and track shipping information. In short, you need a more business-oriented Web hosting service. Check out the following sites:

➤ Netopia, at **www.nvo.com**, costs $19.95 per month for about the same service you get at Yahoo! GeoCities for free. However, Netopia has more of a business slant and access to software for taking credit card orders over the Web. Of course, this comes at a price—$800 just for the electronic bank account and software.

➤ Yahoo! Small Business, at **smallbusiness.yahoo.com**, costs $25.95 per month for your own online store. Although not as robust as Netopia, Yahoo! Small Business provides the basic tools you need to set up shop on the Web. For 70 bucks, you can even get your own custom Web site address.

➤ B-City, at **www7.bcity.com**, is a free Web site hosting service for businesses, entrepreneurs, and nonprofit organizations. Its no-frills approach is refreshing, and you can't beat the price.

Buyer Beware

When shopping for a Web host, compare costs and features carefully. Check the amount of disk space you get and whether the service charges you extra every time someone visits your site. Also ask whether there are any sales commissions involved.

You can find hundreds of Web sites hosting services on the Web that vary greatly in price and service. Use your favorite Web search tool to look for **web hosting** or **free web page**. (Most services have free trial offers that they advertise as "free." These sites typically are free only for 10–30 days and may include hidden costs for "special" business features, such as order forms.)

Finding Cool Stuff to Put on Your Page

You can decorate your Web page with everything from floral print backgrounds to cartoon clip art. You can even add clocks, counters that mark the number of times people have visited your page, video clips, audio clips, and even small programs that allow visitors to perform calculations or play games.

Where do you find all this stuff? On the Web, of course. Check out the following Web sites for some cool, free stuff you can use to enhance and enliven your Web site:

➤ CLIPART.COM, at **www.clipart.com**, is one of the best places to go for Web graphics, photos, and animations. As Figure 22.4 shows, you'll find dozens of free and shareware (try before you buy) clip art and animation libraries.

Figure 22.4

Download shareware and freeware clip art libraries.

➤ ArtToday, at **www.arttoday.com**, offers a free membership that gives you access to more than 40,000 Web page graphics. Of course, that's just a teaser—full membership (for $29.95/year) gives you the good stuff, access to more than 1.4 million Web page images.

➤ c|net, at **download.cnet.com**, provides plenty of free programs, ActiveX controls and Java applets (small programs you can place on your page), clip art, and audio and video clips. You'll need to poke around a little to find what you're looking for.

➤ Free-Backgrounds.com, at **www.free-backgrounds.com**, specializes in custom background designs with new backgrounds added every day. However, this is also a great place to pick up free clip art and animated graphics.

Grab Stuff off Existing Web Pages

If you see something you like on a Web page, write to the Web page author via email (if the person has his or her email address on the page) and ask for permission to use the object. You can drag most clip art images, icons, and other objects right off a page displayed in your browser and drop them onto your page displayed in your Web page editor.

The Least You Need To Know

It has never been easier to establish a presence on the Web and use the Web to express yourself and earn money. As you build and enhance your Web site, keep the following information close at hand:

➤ HTML (Hypertext Markup Language) is a system of codes used to format Web pages.

➤ You don't need to master HTML in order to create your own attractive Web pages.

➤ To create and publish a simple Web page online, go to Yahoo! GeoCities at **geocities.yahoo.com**.

➤ After you have created a page in PageBuilder, click the **Save** button to place your page on the Web.

➤ To edit your Yahoo! GeoCities Web page, sign in at **geocities.yahoo.com** and click the link for changing an existing page.

➤ For a more robust set of Web-based business tools, check out Netopia at **www.nvo.com**.

➤ For gobs of Web page clip art, go to **www.clipart.com**.

Part 5
Managing Your Finances

With the right software, you can transform your computer into your own personal accountant and financial advisor. It can help you develop a monthly budget, pay bills, reconcile your checking account, and even analyze loans and investments.

This part shows you how to use the most powerful (and popular) personal finance program on the market—Quicken—to take control of your finances. Here, you learn how to set up checking, savings, and credit card accounts; print checks; reconcile your accounts; create a realistic budget; calculate loan payments and investment returns; and even pay your bills electronically!

Chapter 23

Putting Your Checkbook on Your Computer

In This Chapter

➤ Shopping for a personal finance program

➤ Setting up checking, savings, and credit card accounts

➤ Entering transactions in your electronic checkbook

➤ Automating your check writing with printed checks

➤ Reconciling your checkbook balance and bank statement

The whole concept of money was supposed to simplify things, to make it easier to exchange goods. Instead of trading a fox pelt for a lobster dinner, you could sell the pelt for a handful of coins and then plop them down at your local seafood restaurant to pay for your lobster dinner.

Somewhere in the history of human existence, cash-based economies got all fouled up. We now store our money in banks and use checks to get at it; we have chunks of money removed from our paychecks before we've even touched it; and we invest money in companies, hoping that we'll get even more money back.

To manage the complexities of our finances in these trying times, a personal finance program is essential. In this chapter, you learn how to pick a good personal finance program, set up your accounts, and use the program to manage your checking and savings accounts. Later chapters in this part show you how to use more advanced tools to budget your money, pay your bills electronically, and track investments online.

Choosing a Good Personal Finance Program

In the early days of personal finance programs, your choice was simple: Either you used Quicken to manage your finances or you used a pencil and a calculator. There were no other personal finance programs on the market. As Quicken grew more popular (and profitable), other companies, including Microsoft, developed their own personal finance programs, but they couldn't begin to compete with Quicken—until recently.

Just a couple years ago, Microsoft Money started to give Quicken a run for its…er…money. Now, Microsoft Money and Quicken are powerful competitors, each having its own unique strengths and weaknesses. Both programs offer basic tools for managing your accounts, budgeting, and paying bills; they both include a set of financial planning calculators; and they both have tools for tracking investments online.

Inside Tip

Follow the Crowd

When a program is popular, it's more likely that someone you know owns and uses the program and can help you learn to use it. Books on popular programs are also more readily available—look for *The Complete Idiot's Guide to Quicken 2000.*

So, which is better? That depends on the person you talk to or the review you read. Personally, I like Quicken, but I've been using Quicken for nearly 10 years, and I'm not about to transfer all of my accounts and transactions to Microsoft Money and relearn everything at the ripe old age of 40. If you're just starting out and received a free copy of Microsoft Money with your new computer, don't run out and buy Quicken—Microsoft Money is an excellent personal finance program.

This chapter and the remaining chapters in this part focus on Quicken, and use Quicken to illustrate the basic tasks you perform in a personal finance program. If you have Microsoft Money, use the steps and illustrations as an overview; although the steps might differ, the programs take a similar approach to most tasks.

Entering Account Information

Before you can write checks or record transactions, you must create an *account*, specifying its opening balance and other important information. Most personal finance programs, including Quicken, enable you to create the following account types:

➤ **Checking** Create a checking account to record written checks, deposits, withdrawals, and transfers.

➤ **Savings** Create a savings account to record deposits, withdrawals, and transfers.

➤ **Credit Card** Create a credit card account to record your credit card charges and payments you make when you receive your monthly statement.

➤ **Cash** Create a cash account to track your cash expenditures.

➤ **Asset** If you think you might want to determine your net worth sometime soon, you can create an asset account to track the value of big ticket items, such as your home, car, boat, and RV.

➤ **Liability** A liability is the flip side of an asset. Use a liability account to keep track of how much you still owe on those big-ticket possessions.

➤ **Investment** If you've joined the wave of individual investors, you can use investment accounts to keep track of stock, bond, and mutual fund transactions.

➤ **401(k)** If you're fortunate enough to have a 401(k) retirement plan through your employer, you can use a 401(k) account to track the amount of money you and your employer contribute to it with each paycheck.

➤ **Money Market** Create a money market account to track funds you have invested in a money market fund. A money market fund is similar to a savings account.

The following sections show you how to create an account in Quicken and then select an account to view or enter transactions.

What's a Transaction?

A *transaction* is any activity that affects the balance of an account either positively or negatively. In a checking account, a written check and a deposit are both transactions.

Creating an Account

You don't have to be a banker to create an account in your personal finance program. Both Quicken and Microsoft Money feature wizards that step you through the process. To run the Create New Account wizard in Quicken and use it to create an account, here's what you do:

1. Press **Ctrl+A** to display the Accounts window, listing all of the accounts you have created. Assuming this is your first account, the list should be blank.

2. In the **Account List** menu bar, click **New**. The Create New Account wizard pops up, as shown in Figure 23.1, prompting you to specify the desired account type.

3. Click the desired account type and click the **Next** button.

Figure 23.1

The Create New Account wizard steps you through the process.

Select the desired account type.

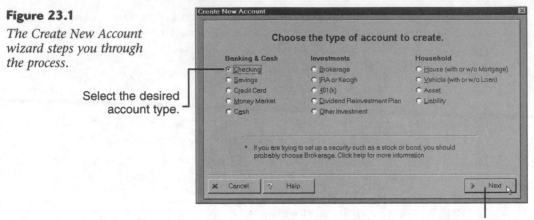

Click the **Next** button.

4. Type a name for the account in the **Account Name** text box and (if desired) type a description of the account in the **Description** text box. (In Quicken 2000, you can also choose a financial institution from the list of banks that support Quicken's online banking features.)

5. Click the **Next** button. For most accounts, the wizard asks whether you have the most recent statement for the account.

6. If asked whether you have the most recent statement for the account, click **Yes** or **No** to give your answer and then click the **Next** button.

7. If you clicked Yes in step 6, enter the statement date and the ending balance from the statement, and then click the **Next** button, as shown in Figure 23.2.

   If you clicked No in step 6, the wizard displays a message that it will create an account using today's date and a zero balance. Click the **Next** button.

Figure 23.2

Enter the date and balance of your most recent account statement.

Account Balance   Statement Date

8. Continue to answer the wizard's questions and enter the requested information. The steps vary depending on the account type you selected. When you reach the final dialog box, the wizard displays the Summary box with all the information you entered so far.

9. Edit the information, if necessary, and enter any additional information and preferences for the account. For example, you may want to link transactions for this account to tax schedules to simplify the process of filing your income tax return later.

10. Click the **Done** button. The wizard creates the account and displays its name, description, and current balance in the account list.

Computer Cheats

Quick-Start the Wizard

When you start Quicken, it displays the Quicken Home Page or My Finances. In the lower-right corner of the window is a link called "Create an account" with the word "Create" highlighted and underlined. Click **Create** to start the Create New Account wizard.

Selecting an Account

Obviously, before you can enter a transaction, you must select the appropriate account—checking, savings, credit card, or other account. Quicken provides several techniques for selecting accounts:

➤ Display the Account List (press **Ctrl+A**) and double-click the desired account.

➤ Display the Quicken Finances or Home Page (which appears when you first start Quicken) and click the link for the desired account under Accounts.

➤ Click the name of the desired account in the account list to the right of the active window (see Figure 23.3).

➤ In Quicken 99 and earlier versions, a row of buttons appears below the currently active account; click the button for the desired account.

Figure 23.3

Quicken lets you flip from one account to another.

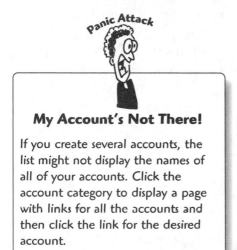

Click the name of the desired account.

Recording Transactions

Whenever you pay a bill, deposit your paycheck, or hit up the ATM machine for a wad of cash, you must record the transaction in Quicken just as you record transactions in your checkbook. The process for recording transactions varies depending on the account type. For all accounts, you must enter the transaction date, a description of the transaction, and the amount. Some accounts, such as checking accounts, require you to enter additional information (such as a check number). The following steps show you how to enter a transaction in a checking account register:

My Account's Not There!

If you create several accounts, the list might not display the names of all of your accounts. Click the account category to display a page with links for all the accounts and then click the link for the desired account.

1. Display your checking account register, as explained in the previous section. When you switch to an account, Quicken automatically inserts the current date for a new transaction and highlights the month.

2. If necessary, edit the date entry (see Figure 23.4).

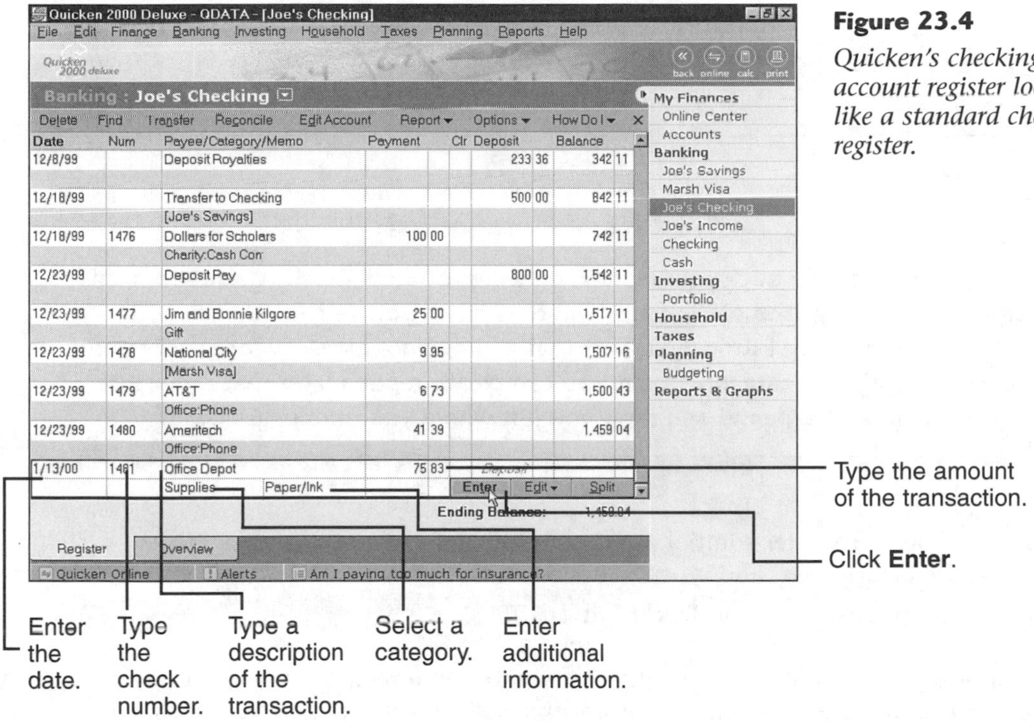

Figure 23.4

Quicken's checking account register looks like a standard checkbook register.

3. Tab to the **Num** field and type the check number. If the transaction is not for a check, you can leave the field blank or type or select a code to identify the transaction (for example, ATM for Automatic Teller Machine).

4. Tab to or click in the **Payee** box and type the name of the person or company to which the check is made out, or type a description of the deposit or withdrawal.

5. If the transaction is a withdrawal or payment, tab to or click in the **Payment** box and type the amount. If the transaction is a deposit, type the amount in the **Deposit** box.

6. (Optional) To assign the transaction to a category, open the Category list and select the desired category. (If the desired category is not listed, type a unique name in the **Category** box. When you save the transaction, Quicken will ask for additional information.)

Computer Cheats

Automated Numbering

When you start typing a check number, Quicken automatically inserts the next check number in the series. If Quicken is not inserting check numbers automatically, open the **Edit** menu (click **Edit** in the main menu bar, not the one just above the accounts window). Then, choose **Options**, **Register**; click the **QuickFill** tab; and select the setting for automatically completing field entries.

Do I Need Categories?

Categories help you track your money, showing you how much you've spent on groceries, clothing, and other goods and how much you've earned from your job and investments. I strongly suggest that you assign a category for every transaction. By assigning categories now, you can create reports later that summarize your income and expenses and show you just where your money is flowing.

7. (Optional) To enter additional information about the transaction, tab to or click in the **Memo** box, and type the desired text.

8. Press **Enter** or click the **Enter** button.

If you find yourself entering the same transaction on a regular basis (your paycheck deposit or mortgage payment, for instance), consider setting up the entry as a *recurring* (or *scheduled*) *transaction*. You simply tell Quicken the amount of the transaction and the frequency (weekly, every two weeks, every month), and Quicken automatically records the transaction for you. To set up a scheduled transaction, open the **Banking** menu and click **Scheduled Transaction List** (in Quicken 99, choose **Lists, Scheduled Transaction**), and then click the **New** button, click **OK**, and enter the requested information, as shown in Figure 23.5.

Choose the account and transaction type.

Figure 23.5

Quicken can enter transactions for you.

Deposits and transfers—

Specify the frequency of the payments.

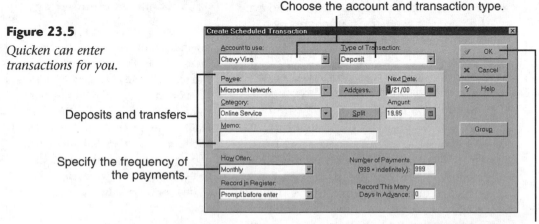

Click **OK** to save the scheduled transaction.

234

Printing Checks

Most people use Quicken to help them budget and keep their accounts balanced. They tote around a checkbook so they can write checks manually, and once a week or so they sit down and enter their transactions in Quicken. When they receive their monthly statement, they use Quicken to reconcile the statement with their own records. There's nothing wrong with using Quicken in such a limited way.

However, if you're looking to further reduce your workload, consider having Quicken "write" (print) the checks for you. All you need to do is type the name of the payee and the amount of the check. Quicken supplies the check number and spells out the amount based on the numerical entry you typed. When you're done "writing" the checks, you simply load blank checks into your printer and give Quicken the command to print the checks. The following steps show just how easy it is:

1. Open the **Banking** menu and click **Write Checks** (or press **Ctrl+W**). The Write Checks screen appears, as shown in Figure 23.6. (In Quicken 99, you choose **Features**, **Bills**, **Write Checks**.)

2. If desired, edit the date. (Quicken automatically enters the current date from your computer's clock.)

3. lick on the **Pay to the Order Of** line and type the person or company to whom you want to make the check payable.

4. Click on the line starting with the dollar sign ($) and type the payment amount.

5. Press the **Tab** key. Quicken automatically spells out the amount of the check.

6. If desired, type the payee's address, select a category, and type a memo (description) of the transaction.

7. Click the **Record Check** button. A new blank check appears, so you can write another check.

8. Repeat steps 2-7 until you have written all your checks.

9. Open the **File** menu and click **Print Checks**. The Select Checks to Print dialog box appears.

10. Enter your preferences for printing the checks. Especially important is the setting that specifies the number of checks you want printed on the first page. If the first page is a partial page of checks, make sure you specify that the page contains only one or two checks.

11. Click **OK**.

Quicken not only prints the checks for you but also records the transactions in your checking account register and calculates the new balance.

Figure 23.6

The Write Checks screen lets you type a check.

Type the date. Type the amount.

Type the payee's name.

Quicken writes out the amount.

If desired, type a memo and select a category.

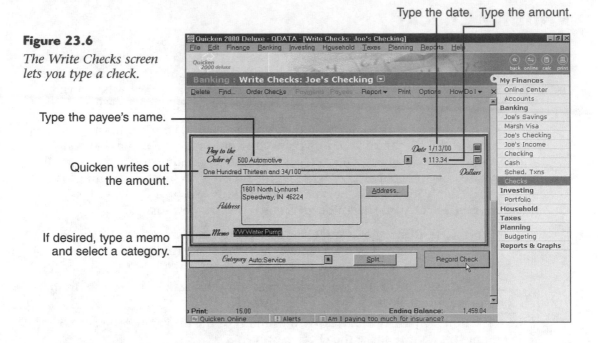

Reconciling Your Account and Bank Statement

Back in the old days, reconciling your checkbook balance with your monthly statement was an exercise in frustration. You calculated and recalculated until you started seeing double. With a personal finance program, such as Quicken, reconciling your checkbook is no longer an ordeal. You simply mark the checks that have cleared, mark the deposits that appear on the bank statement, and enter any service charges. Quicken performs the calculations and immediately determines whether your total matches the bank's total.

If you made a mistake by omitting a transaction or entering the wrong amount for a transaction, simply correct the transaction and return to the Reconciliation screen. Quicken automatically recalculates the totals for you.

To reconcile an account in Quicken, take the following steps:

1. Change to the account you want to reconcile.
2. Click **Reconcile** near the top of the account window. The Reconcile window appears, requesting information from your statement, such as the ending balance, service charges, and interest.
3. Enter the ending balance, as printed on your statement.
4. Enter the amount and date of any service charges, as printed on your statement.
5. Enter the amount and date of any interest you earned on the account, as printed on your statement.

6. Click **OK**. Quicken displays the Reconcile window, as shown in Figure 23.7, listing payments/checks and deposits.

7. Make sure the transactions you recorded match the transactions on the statement, and then click each transaction that matches an entry on the statement.

8. When you're done, check the number next to **Difference**. If the number is zero, you're in luck; click **Finished**. If the number is not zero, either you or your bank made an error. Find and fix the error, make any necessary corrections in the register, and then return to the Reconcile window and click **Finished**.

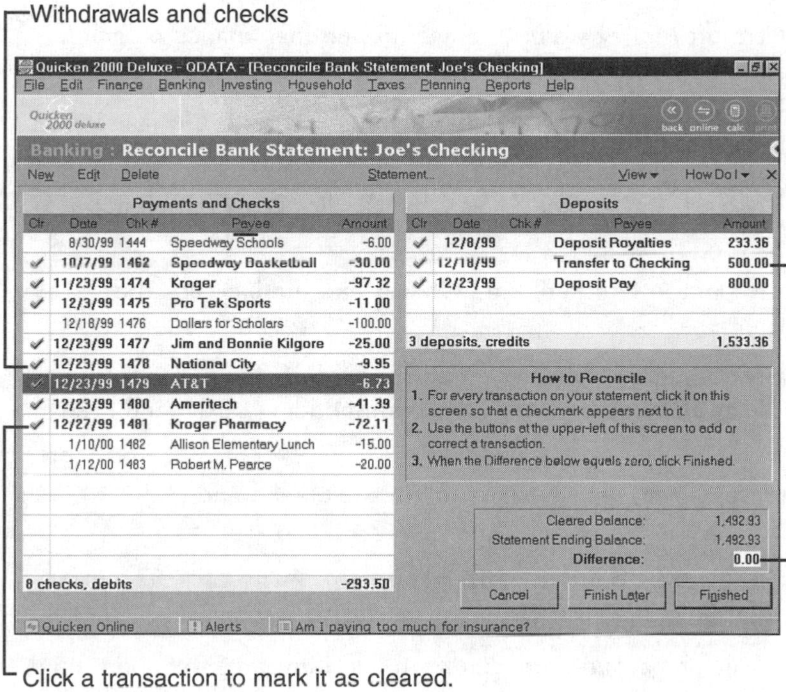

Withdrawals and checks

Figure 23.7

Click the cleared transactions in the Reconcile window.

Deposits and transfers

When you're done, the difference should be zero.

Click a transaction to mark it as cleared.

The Least You Need to Know

You can do much more with Quicken's accounts and transactions than this chapter can possibly cover. You can transfer cash from one account to another; have Quicken automatically deduct your taxes, insurance premiums, and 401(k) contributions from your paycheck (and keep track of them); and make Quicken automatically apply a credit card payment from your checking account to the balance in your credit card account. I encourage you to obtain a copy of Quicken or Microsoft Money, and learn how to take full advantage of these advanced features. Until then, just keep the following basics in mind:

➤ Quicken and Microsoft Money are both powerful personal finance programs. Either program will serve you well.

➤ Before you can enter transactions, you must create an account, specifying the starting date and current balance.

➤ To create a new account in Quicken, press **Ctrl+A**, click **New**, and follow the wizard's lead.

➤ To switch to an account in Quicken, press **Ctrl+A** and double-click the desired account.

➤ To record a transaction, enter the date, a transaction description, the amount of the transaction, and any other data in the corresponding boxes, and then click **Enter**.

➤ To write checks in Quicken, press **Ctrl+W**, fill in the blanks, and click **Record Check**.

➤ To print checks in Quicken, open the **File** menu, click **Print Checks**, enter the desired print settings, and click **OK**.

➤ To begin to reconcile an account, first display the account's register and then click **Reconcile** near the top of the register.

Chapter 24

Budgeting 101

In This Chapter

➤ Taking control of your finances before they take control of you

➤ Using a prefab budget template to get started

➤ Tweaking the budget template for your specific needs

➤ Adjusting the budget to make it more realistic

➤ Dabbling in financial planning with specialized calculators

Before you can take control of your personal finances, you must figure out where your money is coming from and where it's going. You can't decide whether car repairs are costing more than a new car payment unless you know how much you spend on car repairs each month. And you'll never have any money to invest unless you set realistic spending goals and stay within the limits. To take stock of your current financial status and start setting goals, draw up a budget.

But how do you draw up a budget? And, more importantly, how do you determine whether you're staying on track? You basically have three options:

➤ Hire a financial advisor to sit down with you and hash out all the details. The only problem with this plan is that the advisor is going to make you do all the legwork—gathering paycheck stubs, bills, credit card statements, bank statements, and other financial records.

➤ Do it yourself with a budget workbook from your friendly neighborhood office supply store. The drawback here is that you must record your actual income and expenses manually and use a calculator to figure the totals.

➤ Use your personal finance program to create a budget and track your income and expenses automatically.

Most personal finance programs, including Quicken and Microsoft Money, have the required budget tools. You simply enter the budgeted amounts for each category: income, food, rent, entertainment, clothing, and so on. As you enter transactions in your account registers and assign categories, the program keeps track of your income and expenses by category. To see whether you're on track, simply print a budget report. This chapter shows you just what to do.

Who Needs a Budget?

Do *you* need a budget? If you're calling the Money Store for a loan, you need a budget. If you get a paycheck loan to cover your bills, you need a budget. If you're arguing with your spouse over money, you need a budget. If the repo man is driving away in your new Cadillac, you need a budget.

Most people are not in such desperate financial straits and figure that a budget is just a waste of time. They think they just need to eat out less and keep their old clunker for a couple more years. These folks typically spend every dollar they earn and then wonder at the end of the month where their paycheck went. These same people refuse to create a budget because it would restrict their lifestyles.

Although a budget might seem like a restriction, it's actually very liberating. When you know where each dollar you earn is going and you can control your cash flow, you're in charge. You gain confidence that you have enough money to pay your bills and cover your expenses. And you know that with a few minor adjustments, you can even set aside some money for retirement, a new car, a real vacation, or your kids' education.

So, to answer the question we started with: We all need a budget.

Panic Attack

My Budget Shows Only One Month!

If your budget shows only the current month, open the **Options** menu (just above the budget window) and click **Display Months**.

Starting with a Budget Template

All personal finance programs, and even some spreadsheet programs, include a budget template that enables you to create a budget simply by filling in the blanks. The template typically consists of a grid of intersecting rows and columns. Each row is devoted to a single income or expense category, such as food, rent, or clothing. The columns list the 12 months of the year. To create a budget, you simply enter the amount you earn each month (for each income category) and the amount you spend each month (for each expense category).

To view the budget template in Quicken, open the **Planning** menu and click **Budgeting** (in Quicken 99, choose **Features**, **Planning**, **Budgets**). The budget template appears, as shown in Figure 24.1.

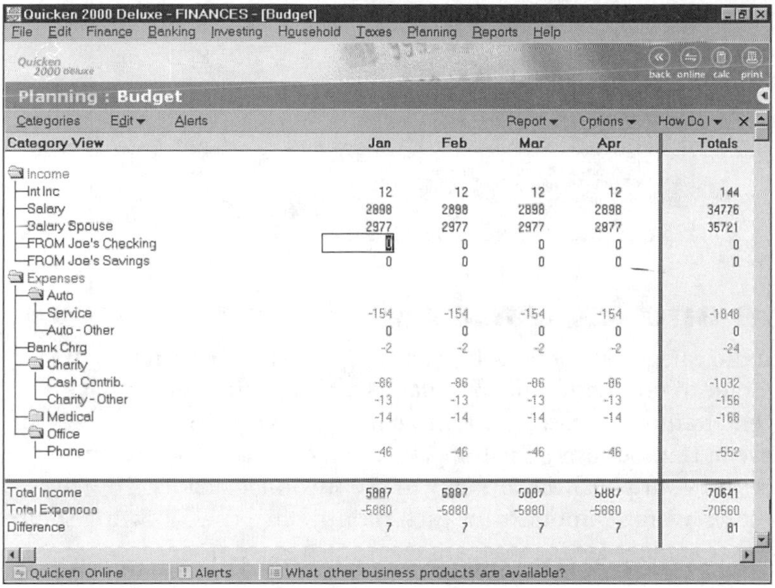

Figure 24.1

The budget template lets you enter monthly amounts for income and expense categories.

Tweaking Your Budget

As you can see in Figure 24.1, the budget template contains a comprehensive list of income and expense categories. Before you even think about entering numbers in the template, consider simplifying the budget by deleting some of the categories:

1. At the top of the Budget window, click **Categories**. The Select Categories to Include dialog box appears, displaying all available categories.

2. To remove a category from the budget, click its name to remove the check mark next to it (see Figure 24.2). To add the category back into the budget, click its name again.

3. Repeat step 2 until only those categories you want included in the budget are checked.

4. Click **OK**.

Computer Cheats

All or Nothing

If you want only a few categories in your budget, click **Clear All** and then select the desired categories. To exclude only a few categories, click **Mark All** and then click the names of the categories you want to exclude.

Figure 24.2

Quicken lets you customize the budget.

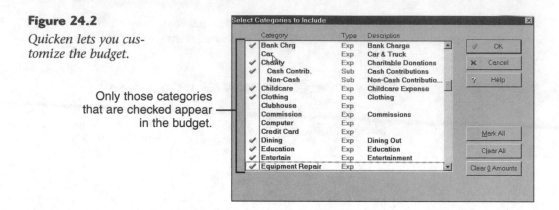

Only those categories
that are checked appear
in the budget.

Entering Income and Expenses

After you've established the categories for your budget, you can start entering income and expense amounts. You can enter amounts manually by typing them in or have Quicken automatically enter amounts based on transactions you've already entered. For instance, if you have several transactions showing paycheck deposits, you can have Quicken automatically enter your paycheck amount in the Income category. To have Quicken automatically enter average amounts for each month, take the following steps:

1. Open the **Edit** menu at the top of the Budget window and click **Autocreate**. The Automatically Create Budget window appears, as shown in Figure 24.3. Unless you specify otherwise, Quicken will use values from transactions entered for the previous calendar year.

2. To change the date range from which Quicken will obtain the budget data, type the desired dates in the **From** and **To** text boxes.

3. Under Amounts, open the **Round Values to Nearest** ___ list and click the desired value: $1, $10, or $100.

4. To have Quicken insert values based on actual income and expense amounts you have entered each month, click **Use Monthly Detail**. To have Quicken insert values that reflect the average income or expense amount for each month, click **Use Average for Period**.

5. To have Quicken include all categories that have any transactions, click **Include All Nonzero Transaction Amounts**. When Quicken creates a budget, it automatically omits any categories that have no transactions. It also omits any category that has a single transaction of less than $100 unless you turn on Include All Nonzero Transaction Amounts.

Monthly Detail or Average?

If you choose Monthly Detail, the budgeted amount for your heating bill rises in the winter and falls in the summer. With Use Average for Period, the budgeted amount remains the same throughout winter, spring, fall, and summer.

6. Click **OK**. Quicken creates your budget and inserts monthly income and expense amounts for each category based on transactions you have entered.

Enter the desired range of dates.

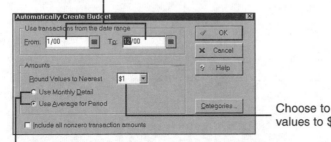

Figure 24.3

Quicken can automatically generate a budget based on past records.

Choose to round the values to $1, $10, or $100.

You can use actual values or averages.

Panic Attack

What's with All the Zeros?

You know you recorded your mortgage payments and the checks you wrote to pay your heating bills, but the budget dropped those categories or displayed a bunch of zeros. What's up? When entering transactions, it's easy to skip the step for selecting a category. Go back to your accounts (Checking, Savings, Credit, Cash) and make sure you have assigned a category to every transaction.

Making Adjustments

Now that your budget is complete, you can hang it on your refrigerator door and start saving money, right? Wrong. Before you use your budget, review it to make sure you can live with the numbers. If the monthly income value does not accurately reflect your current paycheck, you might need to adjust the amount. Likewise, if an expense seems too high or too low, you might need to enter a more realistic number.

Making changes to your budget is fairly easy. Use the Tab and arrow keys to highlight the desired value (or click the value) and then type the new value. To enter the same value for a category for every month, enter the value for January and then open the **Edit** menu, click **Fill Row Right**, and click **Yes**. To clone a column and use its values in all of the columns to the end of the year, click any value in the column you want to clone and then open the **Edit** menu, click **Fill Columns**, and click **Yes**.

Multiple Budgets

If you like the budget you have but want to play around with the numbers, create a new budget. Open the **Options** menu at the top of the Budget window and click **Other Budgets**. Click the **Create** button. Type a name for the budget, specify whether you want to create a copy of the current budget or auto-create a new budget, and click **OK**.

Using Your Budget to Stay on Track

The hardest part about budgeting is trying to stick to the budget. The first month, your car is running perfectly, so you get a little cocky and blow the auto repair money on a new suit. The next month, your car's transmission starts to slip, and the mechanic hands you a bill for five hundred bucks. To make it worse, he mentions how great your new suit looks.

Face it, unless you're Bill Gates or Donald Trump, you have to stick to your budget in good times and bad. If you have $150 set aside each month for car repairs, don't spend it on anything else. Eventually, you will need that money for a repair or to purchase a new car. If, after three months or so, you see that your budgeted amount is way too high and another category's budgeted amount is way too low, adjust the numbers to set more realistic goals, but don't stray from your budget.

Keeping Track of Your Cash Flow with Reports

A budget is useless unless you keep track of your actual income and expenses, evaluate your financial progress regularly, and make any necessary adjustments. If you budgeted $300 a week for food and find that you're spending in excess of $400, either the budgeted amount was unrealistic or you need to cut down on the imported beer and bonbons. But you cannot make the necessary changes unless you first take an honest look at the numbers.

Watch Your Cash

If you're like me, you like to pay with cash. That's fine, but be sure to create a cash account in Quicken. Save your receipts and enter your cash transactions just as loyally as you enter transactions for your checking and savings accounts. (And don't forget to assign each transaction to a category.)

Fortunately, Quicken can spit out the numbers for you in the form of a *budget report*, as shown in Figure 24.4. The budget report lists the income and expense categories and shows the difference between the amount you budgeted for each category and the actual amount recorded in your transactions. You can quickly scan the numbers in the Difference column to identify problem areas.

Categories

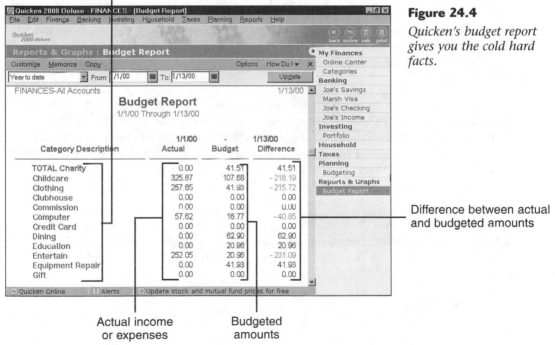

Figure 24.4

Quicken's budget report gives you the cold hard facts.

Actual income or expenses

Budgeted amounts

Difference between actual and budgeted amounts

To create a budget report, display your budget, and then open the **Report** menu and choose **Budget Report** (in Quicken 99, open the **Reports** menu, point to **Planning**, and click **Budget**). Open the **Report Dates** list, and click the desired period for the report (for example, Year to date, Current month, or Current quarter). Or, type the desired dates in the **From** and **To** text boxes. Click the **Create** button.

Customize Your Budget Reports

To customize your budget report, hold off on clicking the Create button and click the **Customize** button instead. This displays the Customize Budget Report dialog box, which enables you to exclude columns, handpick categories, and enter other preferences.

Planning Ahead with Financial Calculators

You're looking at a $17,000 car, and your bank is offering new car loans at 7.25%. How much is the monthly payment? If you invest $250 a month in a mutual fund and see an average annual return of 10%, how much money will you have in 30 years? At an inflation rate of 4% per year, how much will that money be worth? Would it pay to refinance your home? How much do you need to set aside for your kids' education?

Every personal finance program on the market, including Quicken, comes with a collection of financial calculators that can answer all of these questions and help you plan for the future. To display one of Quicken's financial calculators, open the **Planning** menu, point to **Financial Calculators**, and click the desired calculator: **Loan**, **Refinance**, **Savings**, **College**, or **Retirement**. (In Quicken 99, choose **Features**, **Planning**, **Financial Calculators** to access the calculators.)

When the calculator appears, simply fill in the blanks and click the **Calculate** button to get the answers you need. Figure 24.5 shows the Loan Calculator in action. By default, the Loan Calculator determines the payment amount per period based on the loan amount, interest rate, term, number of periods per year, and the compounding period.

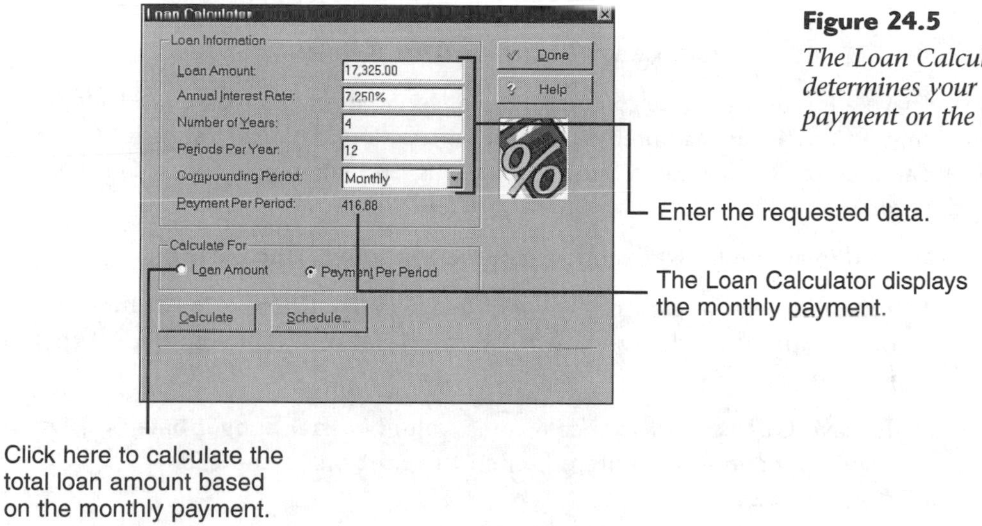

Figure 24.5

The Loan Calculator determines your monthly payment on the loan.

Enter the requested data.

The Loan Calculator displays the monthly payment.

Click here to calculate the total loan amount based on the monthly payment.

I Can Afford Only $250 per Month!

If you know how much you can afford to pay per month, work backward with the Loan Calculator. Under Calculate For, click **Loan Amount**. Then, enter the amount you can afford per month. The Loan Calculator determines the amount you can safely borrow at the specified interest rate and term.

The Least You Need to Know

If you have a job and are able to pay your bills, you're doing pretty well in today's economy. To do better than pretty well and to stop floundering in the seas of financial uncertainty, draw up a budget, stick to it, and know how to use Quicken's budget tools:

➤ To display the Budget window, choose **Planning**, **Budgeting**.

➤ To add or remove categories in your budget, click **Categories** at the top of the Budget window and mark the categories you want your budget to include.

➤ To have Quicken automatically insert values in your budget based on transactions you have entered, open the **Edit** menu and click **Autocreate**.

➤ To change a value in the budget, click it and type the desired value.

➤ To create a budget report for the current year, display your budget, open the **Report** menu, click **Budget Report** and click **Create**.

➤ To access one of Quicken's financial calculators, choose **Planning**, **Financial Calculators**, and click the desired calculator.

SELL! SELL!!

Chapter 25

Paying Bills and Tracking Investments Online

In This Chapter

➤ Doing all your banking with a modem

➤ Evaluating the cost versus convenience

➤ Opening an account with an online bank

➤ Paying bills without writing or printing checks

➤ Transferring funds from one account to another

➤ Day trading on the stock market with Quicken

Just as word processors eliminated the extra work associated with typewriters, online banking and investing are quickly reducing the busywork inherent in banking. With online banking, you no longer need to fill out a transfer request and then hand it to a teller to have it keyed into the system. You perform the transfer on your computer, and the bank immediately processes your request. You don't have to wait around for a printed receipt, because the transaction is already recorded on your computer.

Likewise, online investment programs and Web sites have streamlined the process of tracking and trading stocks by linking you directly to online brokers. You simply execute the transaction by using your personal finance program to tell the broker to buy or sell. You can even set up your personal finance program to track your investments and graph their performance.

This chapter takes you on a tour of online banking and investing, showing you how to use specialized tools in Quicken to access your accounts via modem and track the performance of your stocks and mutual funds.

Electronic Banking 101

Most banks have automated phone-activated tellers that you can use to transfer funds from one account to another, obtain current balances, list recent deposits and withdrawals, and even check on interest rates. These phone-activated tellers are great. You don't have to drive to the bank to transfer money, and you can perform transactions even when the bank is closed, but snaking your way through a long list of menu commands with a touch-tone phone isn't the most efficient way to access your accounts.

To make accounts even more accessible, many banks offer online banking services. Using your personal finance program or a specialized online banking program, you can access your account information 24 hours a day, 7 days a week, without leaving your home or office. You can even use the service to pay your bills electronically and send printed checks to individuals and companies not equipped to accept electronic payments. In addition, if your credit card company offers online access, you can download up-to-date transaction details from the company to avoid typing the transactions manually.

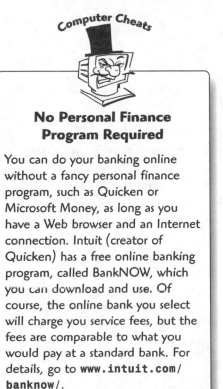

No Personal Finance Program Required

You can do your banking online without a fancy personal finance program, such as Quicken or Microsoft Money, as long as you have a Web browser and an Internet connection. Intuit (creator of Quicken) has a free online banking program, called BankNOW, which you can download and use. Of course, the online bank you select will charge you service fees, but the fees are comparable to what you would pay at a standard bank. For details, go to **www.intuit.com/ banknow/**.

That's what online banking is all about. It allows you to pay bills, transfer money, and get account information without filling out deposit slips and transfer requests and without writing or printing checks. And if you're fortunate enough to have an online banking service that supports your personal finance program, you can immediately transfer transaction details from your bank to your computer, ensuring that you have the most up-to-date and accurate information.

How Much Is *This* Going to Cost?

Online banking isn't free, but its cost is not out of line with the service fees that traditional banks charge. Many banks offer free-trial accounts for six to 12 months and may charge $5/month after the free-trial period. Some banks offer free online banking for as long as you use the account. If you choose to use the bill-paying feature, expect to pay more (an extra $12 or more per month plus per-check fees for any printed/mailed checks). Make sure you read the agreement and understand the service fees before you open an account.

Signing Up for Electronic Transactions

Before you can even think about doing your banking online, you must lay the groundwork in Quicken. This consists of entering settings that tell Quicken how to connect to the Internet on your computer, and applying for an online bank account. The following sections show you what to expect and lead you through the process.

Setting Up Your Internet Connection in Quicken

Assuming you created a dial-up networking icon for connecting to your Internet service provider (as explained in Chapter 17, "Finding an Information FREEway"), telling Quicken 2000 how to connect to the Internet is a snap:

1. Open the **Edit** menu and select **Internet Connection Setup**. The Internet Connection Setup dialog box appears.

2. Click **I Have an Existing Dial-Up Internet Connection** and click **Next**. The next dialog box displays a list of available dial-up networking connections on your computer, as shown in Figure 25.1.

3. Click the dial-up networking connection for your ISP and click **Next**. The Browser Preference warning pops up, indicating that you need a relatively recent Web browser to use Quicken's online features.

4. Read the warning and click **Next**. The Internet Connection Setup dialog box appears, displaying a list of Web browsers installed on your computer. (On most systems, only one browser appears in the list.)

5. Click the Web browser you want Quicken to use and click **Next**. The next dialog box asks if you want to send diagnostic data to Intuit.

6. Click **Yes, I Want to Send Diagnostic Data** and click **Next**. One last dialog box appears (I promise), showing the settings you've entered.

7. Click **Finish**. Quicken connects to the Internet, sends the diagnostic data, and (assuming all goes well) returns you to the Get Started with Online Financial Services Setup dialog box.

Tech Terms

What's a Bill-Pay Option?

A bill-pay option allows you to pay bills electronically without having to print and mail a check. You enter the transaction in your personal finance program, and the bank transfers the funds automatically to the payee as instructed by you. If the payee cannot accept electronic payments, the bank prints a check and mails it to the payee.

Panic Attack

Setting Up Quicken 99

These steps show how to set up a new online banking account in Quicken 2000. If you're using Quicken 99, choose **Online, Online Financial Services Setup**, and then follow the wizard's instructions.

Figure 25.1

The Internet Connection Setup wizard leads you through the setup process.

Click the Dial-Up Networking connection for your ISP.

Click Next.

> **Internet Connection Setup**
>
> **Which dial-up Internet connection do you want to use?**
>
> Use the following Internet connection:
>
> America Online 5.0 for Win95
> CS3 Connection
> Desktop
> IQuest
> Other
>
> Note: This list contains all detected Internet connections. If you have trouble using your connection, or your connection is not listed, select "Other".
>
> <<Back   Next>>   Cancel   Help

Applying for an Online Bank Account

Does your bank (or credit union) support online banking with Quicken? Probably not, but it doesn't hurt to call and ask. If you're lucky and your bank supports Quicken's online banking features, the bank will make you fill out an application or sign some legal forms to activate the online banking service. After receiving the required forms, your bank gives you some login information, including a PIN number. You can then enable your account in Quicken, as explained later in this section. In the following section, you learn how to find a bank that supports Quicken's online banking features and apply for a new online bank account.

Finding a Bank Supporting Quicken Online Features

If your bank or credit union does not support online banking or Quicken's online banking features, then you need to find a bank that does. Fortunately, Quicken can help you track down such a bank and register for an account. Take the following steps to apply for an account in Quicken 2000:

Panic Attack

Applying in Quicken 99

If you're using Quicken 99, open the **Online** menu and click **Online Financial Services Setup** to display the Online Financial Services dialog box, click **Apply Now**, and follow the onscreen instructions.

1. Open the **Finance** menu and click **Online Financial Institutions** List. The first time you select this option, the Customize Quicken 2000 Download dialog box appears.

2. Enter your preferences for connecting to the Internet through Quicken and click **OK**. (To display this dialog box later to adjust the settings, choose **Edit**, **Options**, **Internet Options**.) The Quicken 2000 for Windows dialog box appears, asking for your confirmation to connect.

3. Click **OK**. Quicken connects to the Internet and displays a list of financial institutions that support Quicken's online features.

4. To limit the list to institutions that support online banking (excluding credit card companies and online stock brokers), click **Banking Account Access** under Online Financial Services.

5. Scroll down the list under Financial Institution Directory and click the name of the bank that you think you might want to use. Information about the bank appears on the right, as shown in Figure 25.2.

Click **Banking Account Access**.

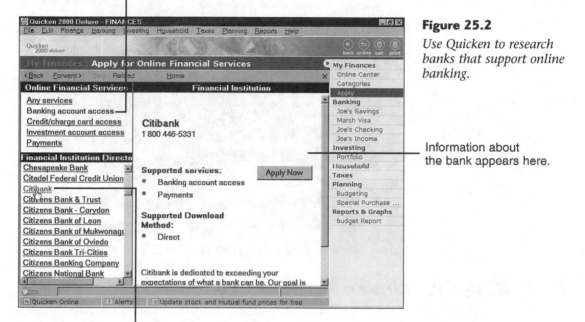

Figure 25.2

Use Quicken to research banks that support online banking.

Information about the bank appears here.

Click the desired bank.

6. Contact the bank or visit its Web site to obtain information about services and fees.

7. When you have found a bank you want to use, pull up the information page for it, as you did in step 5.

8. Click the **Apply Now** button or its equivalent, and follow the onscreen instructions to pull up the online registration form (see Figure 25.3) or information on how to apply over the phone. (Some banks do not support online applications at this time.)

9. Follow the onscreen instructions to apply for online banking. You might need to phone the bank to request an application and then mail in the application. (I know it seems archaic, but that's the way most banks do it.)

Assuming your application is approved, the bank provides you with login information including your PIN number. You must then enter this information in Quicken, as explained in the next section. (Of course, you need to deposit some money in your new account before you can pay any bills electronically, but I'll let you work that out with the bank.)

Figure 25.3

Some banks allow you to apply for an account online.

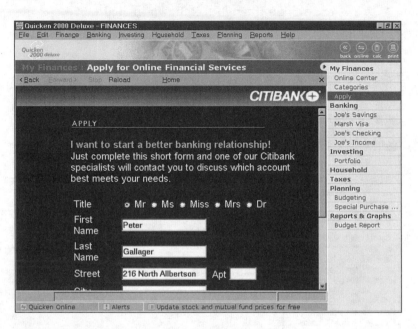

Activating Your Online Account in Quicken

Whether your current bank supports online banking or you opened an account with a new bank, the bank provides you with a secret code for accessing your account. To enter your secret code in Quicken, open the **Banking** menu and click **Online Banking Setup**. This starts the Online Account Setup wizard, which leads you step-by-step through the process of creating a new account or entering online connection information for one of your existing accounts. Follow the onscreen instructions and answer the questions to give Quicken the information it needs to access your online account.

Enabling Online Transactions for an Account

After you sign up for online banking and create a new account, you must edit the properties of the accounts to enable online banking. To edit an account's properties, take the following steps:

1. Press **Ctrl+A** to display the Accounts List.

2. Right-click the account you want to use for online banking and click **Edit**. The summary window for the selected account appears.

3. Click **Online Access** (just above the summary window). The Online Setup screen appears, displaying the three-step process to creating an online account.

4. Click **Enable Your Quicken Account**. The Select Financial Institution dialog box appears, as shown in Figure 25.4.

5. Select **Online Account Access** and **Online Payment** to turn on both options.

6. Click the **Next** button.

7. If the **Financial Institution** list appears, open it and select the online finacial institution you want to use for this account. (If you already specified a financial institution for this account, Quicken might display its name, not allowing you to change it at this time.)

8. Click in the **Routing Number** text box, enter the routing number as specified by the financial institution, and click **Next**.

9. Follow the instructions in the resulting series of dialog boxes to enter the requested information about your financial institution.

Figure 25.4

Make sure you turn on the online banking options for your account.

Turn on these options.

Paying Your Bills Electronically

With Quicken, paying bills electronically is a snap. You simply display the account register for your online bank account and enter the transaction information as you normally do. The only difference is that instead of entering a check number, you specify that you want to pay the bill electronically. Open the list in the Num column for the transaction and choose **Send Online Payment**, as shown in Figure 25.5.

As you enter online transactions, Quicken keeps track of those transactions but does not immediately process them. To process the transactions and actually send the online payments, open the

Panic Attack

No Online Payment Support?

Many banks let you check your balance and download transaction details, but do not allow you to pay bills online. In cases where online payment is unavailable, Quicken gives you the option of signing up for its online payment service.

Banking menu, click **Online Banking**, and click **Update/Send**. (In Quicken 99, choose **Online**, **Online Center**, click the **Payments** tab, and click **Update/Send**.) Follow the onscreen instructions to execute the transactions; for example, you might need to re-enter your PIN number.

Figure 25.5

Enter the transaction in your register just as you would enter a payment by check.

Choose to send an online payment.

Setting Up Automatic, Recurring Payments

Nowadays, most banks, credit unions, and other financial institutions support automatic withdrawals. If you have a car loan or a mortgage, you can call the lender and have your payments automatically withdrawn from your savings or checking account on a specified day each month. You might even have payments automatically withdrawn and deposited in a mutual fund or used to pay your utility bills (if you're on a budget plan with the utility company).

For companies that do not support automatic withdrawals, you can set up Quicken to automatically send payments on a specified date each month. You simply set up a *scheduled transaction*. Here's what you do:

1. Open the **Banking** menu and choose **Scheduled Transaction List** (or choose **Lists**, **Scheduled Transactions** in Quicken 99).

2. If the transaction you want to schedule is already in the list, right-click the transaction and click **Edit**.

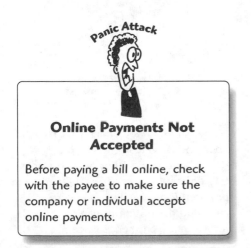

Panic Attack

Online Payments Not Accepted

Before paying a bill online, check with the payee to make sure the company or individual accepts online payments.

If the transaction is not in the list, click **New** just above the Scheduled Transaction List.

3. Open the **Account to Use** list and click the online account from which you want the bill paid.

4. Open the **Type of Transaction** list and click **Online Pmt**, as shown in Figure 25.6.

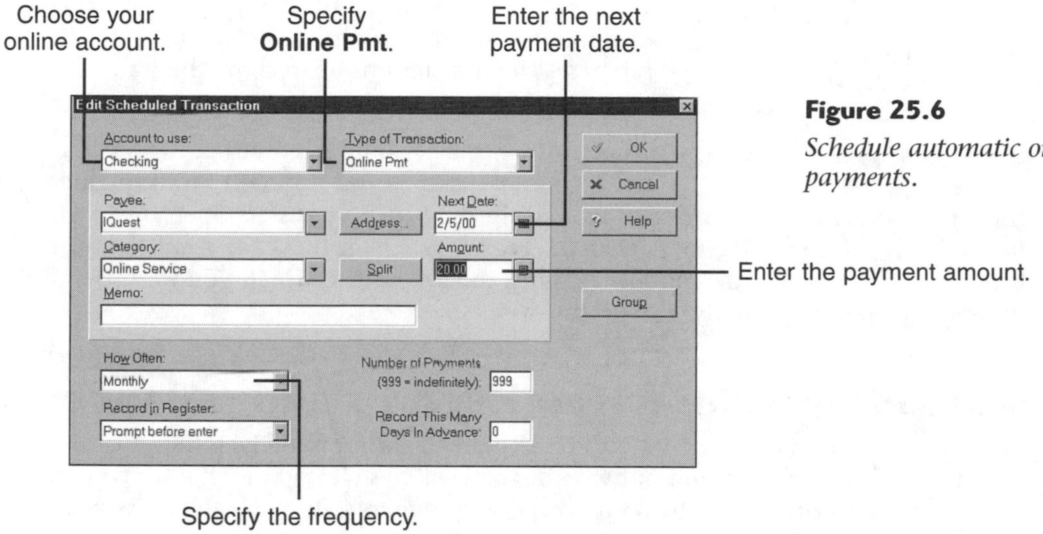

Choose your online account.

Specify **Online Pmt**.

Enter the next payment date.

Figure 25.6

Schedule automatic online payments.

Enter the payment amount.

Specify the frequency.

5. Click the button next to the **Next Date** box and select the next date to send a payment. (Send the payment a few days before it's due to give your bank time to process the payment.)

6. Click in the **Amount** box and type the payment amount.

7. Open the **How Often** list and click the desired frequency of the payments—for instance, monthly or yearly.

8. Enter any other preferences and click **OK**. The Set Up Online Payee dialog box appears, prompting you to enter information about the payee.

9. Enter the requested information, including the payee's address and account number and click **OK**. Another dialog box appears asking you to confirm the information you entered.

10. Click **Accept**. Quicken might display additional dialog boxes if it detects that the payment will cause a problem with your budget or balance. Respond to the dialog boxes as needed.

When the specified payment date rolls around, Quicken automatically transfers the payment amount from your account to the payee's account, as specified.

Not Just Online

You can set up scheduled transactions for depositing your paycheck and for printing checks. Their use is not limited to electronic payments.

Transferring Cash Between Accounts

Online banking completely revolutionizes the way you transfer money from one account to another. Instead of filling out a transfer request, waiting in line, and then having the teller process the request and print a receipt, you simply transfer funds from one account to the other in Quicken. Quicken processes the transfer online, records the transaction, and recalculates the account balance.

To perform a transfer online, enter the transfer in the account register as you normally would—enter the date, a description of the transfer, and the amount to transfer. Open the list in the Num column and choose **Online Transfer**. Open the **Xfer Acct** list (just below the transaction description) and click the account to which you want the money transferred. Click the **Enter** button.

Downloading Transaction Records and Balances

Traditionally, you have to wait around for the mail carrier to deliver your monthly statement before you can find out whether a check has cleared or whether your balance is correct. With online banking, you don't have to wait. You can access your account anytime, day or night, and download the latest record of your transactions and balances. To get the latest transaction details online with Quicken, take the following steps:

1. Open the **Banking** menu and click **Online Banking** (or choose **Online**, **Online Center** in Quicken 99).

2. Click the **Update/Send** button.

3. Make sure the **Download My Latest Online Transactions and Balances From...** option is checked. Quicken might prompt you to enter your PIN number if the bank requires you to enter it before performing the next step.

4. If prompted, enter your PIN number and any other login information required by your bank and click **Send**. (Some banks might not prompt you to enter your PIN number until you click **Send**.) Quicken downloads your transactions and updated balance and displays the Transaction Summary window.

5. Review the transactions to make sure they are correct and then click **OK**.

Tracking the Performance of Your Investments

In Chapter 21, "Shopping, Investing, Traveling, and Other Cool Web Stuff," you learned that you could open an account with an online stockbroker, such as E*TRADE or Charles Schwab, and trade stocks over the Internet.

So, why do you need Quicken to manage your investments? Because Quicken can download all of your investment data, consolidate it in a portfolio, help you analyze it, keep track of your capital gains and dividends for tax purposes, and even include the data in your reports.

Applying for an Online Investment Account

Before you can process investment transactions online with Quicken, you must open an account with an online investment service and then enter the login information for your account in Quicken. If you already opened an account after reading Chapter 21, you simply need to enter the login information.

The process for opening an account with an online broker is nearly identical to the process for opening an online bank account. Open the **Finance** menu and click **Online Financial Institutions List** (or in Quicken 99, choose **Online**, **Online Financial Services Setup**). Under Online Financial Services, click **Investment Account Access**. Click the service you want to use, click **Apply Now**, and follow the onscreen instructions. For details, see "Applying for an Online Banking Account," earlier in this chapter.

Investing Online

After you have set up your investment account in Quicken, you can begin your life as a day trader, buying and selling stocks, downloading the latest numbers, and analyzing your portfolio's performance. Of course, this chapter isn't long enough to provide step-by-step instructions for using Quicken's investment tools, but here's an overview of what you can do in Quicken 2000:

➤ **Buy and Sell Stocks and Mutual Funds**   Open the **Investing** menu and click **Investing Center**. Open the **Easy Actions** menu (just above the transaction list) and click **Buy/Sell Shares**. Follow the onscreen instructions to complete the purchase.

➤ **Track Your 401(k)**   Open the **Investing** menu, point to **Investing Activities**, and click **Track My 401(k)**. This starts the 401(k) Setup wizard, which leads you through the process of entering details about your company's 401(k) plan.

➤ **Update Your Investment Portfolio**   Go to Portfolio View by choosing **Investing**, **Portfolio View**. Click **Update**, select the type of information you want (for example, **Get Online Quotes** or **Get Asset Classes**), enter the requested information in the resulting dialog box, and click **OK**.

➤ **Research Investments**   Select **Investing**, **Investment Research**. This displays the Quicken Investment Research window, which helps you track down the financial information you need to make well-informed investments.

The commands for accessing the investment features in Quicken 99 are entirely different from those used in Quicken 2000. For instructions, check the help system.

Computer Cheats

Get Everything at Once

Quicken's One Step Update lets you download all of your online financial data at once, including bank transactions and investment share prices. Open the **Finance** menu and click **One Step Update**.

The Least You Need to Know

Although online banking and investing gives you more control over your finances and investments in the long run, learning to use online financial tools can seem overwhelming. Learn a little at a time and keep the following basics in mind:

➤ Online banking provides convenient access to your accounts 24 hours a day, 7 days a week.

➤ To set up your Internet connection in Quicken, choose **Edit, Internet Connection Setup**, and follow the onscreen instructions.

➤ To apply for and enable online accounts in Quicken, choose **Banking, Online Banking Setup**, and follow the onscreen instructions.

➤ To pay a bill electronically, enter the transaction in the account register as you normally would, but choose **Send Online Payment** from the Num list.

➤ To schedule a regular payment, choose **Banking, Scheduled Transaction List**, click **New**, and enter the requested information.

➤ To download transaction details from an online bank, choose **Banking, Online Banking**, and click the **Update/Send** button.

➤ You can find most of Quicken's online investment options on the **Finances** menu.

Part 6
Kids and Other Family Stuff

Although you might think that your food processor is the most versatile tool in your home, your computer has it beat. With the right software, your computer can moonlight as a powerful game machine, reference library, interactive tutor, electronic photo album, family tree maker, and much more.

The chapters in this part introduce you to the most popular home-based computer software. Here, you learn how to shop for games and educational software, safely introduce your children to the Internet, organize and print photographs, and even research your lineage and create your own family tree.

Chapter 26

Finding and Playing Cool Games

In This Chapter

➤ Picking the right games for your computer system

➤ Checking out some essential game gear

➤ Finding and downloading free games on the Web

➤ Buying cool games online

➤ Getting game reviews, codes, and tips on the Internet

Many people buy a computer under the pretext that it will help them work more efficiently; organize their lives; or improve communications with friends, relatives, and colleagues. Two weeks after they get the computer home, they're plugging in a joystick and installing arcade games. Two months later, their eyes are glazed over, their thumbs are twitching, and they can't speak in complete sentences. Computer games can transform even the most disciplined worker, the most responsible adult, into a dysfunctional game junkie.

This chapter sets you on the path to your own computer game addiction. Here, you learn how to find the best computer games on the market, beef up your system with the latest game gear, get free games off the Web, and learn gaming tricks from the masters.

Shopping for the Right Games

The term *computer game* has different meanings for different people. For some people, *computer game* conjures up the image of old standards, such as Solitaire or Tetris. Other people envision action games, such as Mech Warrior and Doom. And still others think of strategy games, such as SimCity. The fact is that a computer game is any program that people play for fun.

Because the market is flooded with all sorts of computer games, dealers typically categorize games to help customers find what they like. Before you start shopping, familiarize yourself with these categories:

➤ **Action/Fighting.** Whether you want to blast alien warships out of the sky or do a little kick-boxing, this category is the one for you. If you're in a software store, just look for a group of angry boys and you'll find the Action games.

➤ **Adventure.** In an adventure game, you set out on a journey to complete a mission, discover something valuable, or solve a mystery. Adventure games typically give you clues and allow you to pick up helpful tools along the way, such as flashlights or keys. The Adventure section is where the geeks usually hang out.

➤ **Sports.** This category is self-explanatory. Here you'll find games for playing football, baseball, basketball, golf, and any other popular sport whose athletes are overpaid. Sports is the category of choice for jocks and jock wannabees.

➤ **Driving/Simulation.** Whether you want to drive the NASCAR circuit or pretend you're an F-16 fighter pilot, you'll find plenty of games to put you behind the wheel. This category appeals to everyone—young or old, male or female, geek or jock—anyone who likes to be in the driver's seat.

➤ **Role-Playing.** Do you want to be somebody else? Take a momentary break from reality? Then, a role-playing game might be just the escape you need. You take on the role of one of the story's characters and then interact with other characters and your surroundings in an attempt to gain power. Of course, this may sound too much like reality.

➤ **Board Games.** If you grew up playing Monopoly, Risk, checkers, chess, or other board games, you'll be happy to know that there's a computer version for nearly every traditional board game on the market. Of course, there's no replacement for seeing the anguish on your opponent's face when he lands on a hotel-heavy Boardwalk, but with computer games, you never have trouble finding enough players.

➤ **Card Games.** Tired of Solitaire and FreeCell? If you are, maybe it's time to change games. Card game collections, such as Hoyle Card Games 2000, provide a robust selection of traditional card games, including Poker, Euchre, Gin Rummy, and even Old Maid.

➤ **Strategy.** Strategy games require thought and planning. You must be able to outthink your opponent and anticipate her every move. Although most strategy games are based on planning and executing attacks on the battlefield, some strategy games are rather peaceful. SimCity, for instance, elects you mayor and tests your ability to successfully govern a booming metropolis.

Additional Equipment You Might Need

First-time gamers can be pretty naïve. They spend hours tracking down the coolest action game around and completely overlook the fact that their computer is ill-equipped to run it. Can you imagine flying a spaceship with a mouse or blasting enemy warships with a keyboard? Of course not!

To fully enjoy top-of-the line action games or simulations, make sure your system is properly equipped:

➤ **SVGA Video.** Most monitors manufactured in the last three years are SVGA, so this shouldn't be a problem for you. Although many good games require only VGA, graphics-heavy action games demand better monitors and video cards. Some games require a special video card, such as the Voodoo video card, with additional video RAM.

➤ **3D Audio.** Sounds are unimportant for card games and some strategy games, but they can make or break an arcade game. If you're shopping for an arcade game, make sure the game supports the audio card installed in your computer. Some of the better computer games support 3D audio, which requires a special audio card along with speakers and a subwoofer.

➤ **Game Controller.** Some games don't support a joystick or other game controller. You must use the keyboard and mouse to navigate and blast the alien enemies. That's no fun. Get yourself a joystick or other game controller, and if you're shopping for an arcade game, make sure it supports a joystick.

Running Stubborn DOS Games in Windows

Many computer games are designed to run on the operating system that preceded Windows. This operating system, called DOS (pronounced "Dawss"), isn't quite as intuitive as the Windows desktop. When you start a computer that runs DOS, the DOS prompt appears on screen as C:\>. To run the game, you type the specified command at the prompt and press **Enter**.

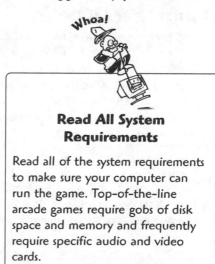

Read All System Requirements

Read all of the system requirements to make sure your computer can run the game. Top-of-the-line arcade games require gobs of disk space and memory and frequently require specific audio and video cards.

Get Help

Some game installations can play havoc with your computer, completely rewriting the startup files and potentially disabling Windows. Consider consulting with a knowledgeable friend before installing a DOS game under Windows.

Fortunately, you no longer need to know much about DOS to use a computer. You install a program and then click its icon or select it from a menu to run it. But when you're working with computer games, DOS is still boss. Many games still require you to run them under DOS. Although the game might run smoothly without your intervention, some games might cause problems or might not run at all under Windows. The following sections show you how to run games designed for DOS and make adjustments when you run into problems.

Running DOS Games and Other Programs

Windows is designed to run DOS games and other programs better than they run under DOS alone—in theory, anyway. To run the program, change to the disk and folder in which the program files are stored and double-click the icon for running the program. (The files that execute DOS programs are typically displayed with an icon that looks like a tiny blank window.) You can add the DOS program to the Programs menu or create a shortcut to it, as explained in Chapter 3, "Launching Your First Program."

Running a DOS Game That Won't Budge

If you have trouble running a DOS game from Windows, create a shortcut icon for the game: Drag the game's program icon from My Computer onto the desktop, release the mouse button, and click **Create Shortcut(s) Here**. Right-click the shortcut and click **Properties**. Click the **Program** tab and click the **Advanced** button. Choose **MS-DOS Mode**, as shown in Figure 26.1, and click **OK**. This gives the DOS game all available system resources. Click **OK** to save your changes. Double-click the shortcut icon to run the game.

If the game still does not run, right-click the shortcut icon and choose **Properties**. Click the **Programs** tab and click the **Advanced** button. Click **Specify a New MS-DOS Configuration**. Move the insertion point to the end of the **DEVICE=C:\ WINDOWS\HIMEM.SYS** line and press **Enter** to create a blank line. Type `DEVICE=C:\WINDOWS\EMM386.EXE RAM`, as shown in Figure 26.1. This provides expanded memory for running programs that require it. Click the **OK** button. When you return to the Properties dialog box, click **OK** to save your changes.

Make sure
MS-DOS
mode is
checked.

You can
add startup
commands
here.

Figure 26.1
*You can coax Windows
into running a stubborn
DOS game.*

Still won't run? Try running the game from
the DOS prompt, using one of these methods:

➤ Click the **Start** button, point to
Programs, and click **MS-DOS Prompt**.
Type **cd*folder*** (where *folder* is the name
of the folder in which the program's files
are stored) and press **Enter**. Type the
command for running the game (refer to
the game's documentation), and press
Enter.

➤ Click the **Start** button, choose **Shut
Down**, choose **Restart** in **MS-DOS
Mode**, and click **OK**. Run the program
from the DOS prompt as explained in
the previous item in this list.

➤ If that doesn't work, restart Windows. As
soon as your computer beeps, press and
release the **F8** key. This displays the Microsoft Windows 98 Startup Menu. Type
the number next to **Command Prompt Only**. Run the program from the
DOS prompt as explained in the first item in this list.

It Still Won't Run!!

Some games may require you to create a special floppy disk to use for
starting your computer. Whenever
you want to play the game, you
must insert the disk and restart your
computer. Contact the game developer's technical support department
for help.

Getting Free Games off the Web

For a dedicated gamer, the only thing better than a new computer game is a new, *free*
computer game. You can download all sorts of free games and trial versions off the
Web, assuming, of course, that you know where to look. Check out the following
Web sites for a great selection of free games:

➤ GameSpot, at **www.gamespot.com**, is an excellent place to get started. GameSpot features not only one of the best selections of free games, but also game codes, tips, and even a guide for downloading and installing games.

➤ HotGames.com, at **hotgames.com**, offers a wide selection of game demos along with tips and tricks for the most popular games.

➤ The Games Network, at **www.gamesnetwork.com**, is another excellent starting point for new and seasoned gamers. Here, you'll find game reviews, previews, tips, and a wide selection of game demos. This site also covers popular video game systems, including Nintendo64 and Dreamcast.

➤ Free Games Net, at **www.free-games-net.com**, offers free games in a wide variety of categories—from Action and Adventure to Simulation and Strategy (see Figure 26.2).

➤ Ziff-Davis, at **www.zdnet.com/downloads/games.html**, takes you to zdnet's download site, where you'll find links to all sorts of freeware and shareware, including games, utilities, Internet programs, and educational software. Click the **Games** link for a complete list of games organized by category.

➤ Gamer's Inn, at **www.gamersinn.com**, offers more than a collection of computer games. Here, you'll find an extensive list of free games, a message board where you can get help and trade tips, and a game room where you can test your skills against other gamers.

➤ GameGenie.com, at **www.gamex.net**, is a great place to go for reviews and demos of the most popular games. Click the **Cheats** link to access a collection of tips, tricks, and codes from the masters.

Figure 26.2

Free Games Net offers a wide selection of computer games.

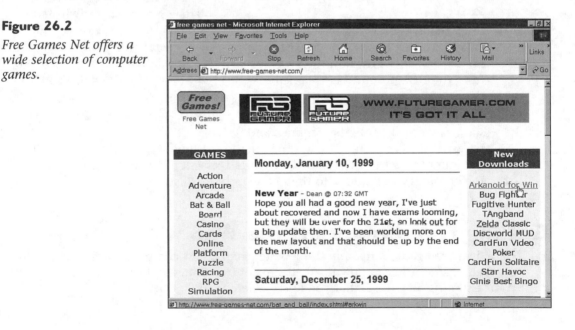

Many downloaded games are packaged as self-extracting, self-installing files. After downloading the file, you simply double-click its name in My Computer or Windows Explorer and follow the onscreen installation instructions.

Some downloaded games, however, arrive as compressed (zipped) files, which you must decompress before installation. These files typically have the ZIP filename extension. You use a decompression program, such as WinZip, which you can get at **www.winzip.com**.

When you install WinZip, the installation routine associates WinZip with ZIP files. This makes it easy to decompress ZIP files. In My Computer or Windows Explorer, double-click the ZIP file to open it in WinZip. This displays a list of the files contained in the ZIP file. When you use WinZip to extract files, keep the following points in mind:

➤ If the ZIP file contains files for installing a program, you do not need to extract the files. Simply double-click the Setup.exe or Install.exe file in the WinZip window. WinZip will automatically extract the necessary files and run the installation. If you extract the files first, you'll have to delete them after you install the program.

➤ It's a good idea to extract files to a separate folder, so they don't get mixed up with your other files.

➤ If you click the WinZip's Extract button before selecting a file, WinZip extracts all the files in the ZIP folder (which is what you usually want to do). If you select a file first, WinZip extracts only the selected file.

To extract files from a compressed file using WinZip, take the following steps:

1. In My Computer, click the icon for the ZIP file.
2. (Optional) To extract selected files, click a file and **Ctrl+click** any others you want to extract.
3. Click the **Extract** button.
4. Choose the disk and folder in which you want the extracted file(s) placed.
5. Click the **Extract** button.

Buying Games Online

Most of the "free" games you can download on the Web are trial versions (shareware). The developer might stipulate that you can play the game for free for 30 days and may even program in a routine that disables the game when the free trial period expires. To continue playing the game legally, you must purchase a copy.

You can purchase the most popular games at your local software store. For less popular or newly released games, shop on the Web. Check out the following online game and software dealers:

➤ gamestop at **www.gamestop.com**.

➤ Outpost.com at **www.outpost.com**.

➤ Beyond.com at **www.beyond.com/games.htm**.

➤ Buy-Rite Video Games at **www.buyrite1.com**.

➤ Buy.com at **www.buy.com/games**.

Finding Game Reviews and Tips

Inside Tip

Online Shopping Malls

You don't need to find a store that specializes in games. Most Web-based software retailers and mega-stores carry a wide selection of games.

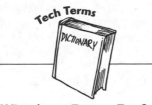

Tech Terms

What's an Easter Egg?

An Easter Egg is a hidden message, screen, or action in a game or other program that you initiate by pressing a keystrokes or buttons in a special sequence when a certain screen is displayed or by performing some weird series of steps you would never ever think of doing in real life.

Tired of getting clobbered by meaner opponents wielding better weapons? Having trouble dodging fireballs? Do you keep running out of ammo in the middle of a battle? Then, you probably need a few tips from the experts.

Fortunately, many of the same sites that offer game demos and shareware have links to game hints, cheats, strategies, and guides that can transform the greenest novice into a seasoned veteran. To start tracking down tips and tricks on the Web, revisit the sites you checked out in "Getting Free Games off the Web," early in this chapter. After you have exhausted those resources, check out the following Web sites dedicated to cheats:

➤ CheatStation, at **www.cheatstation.com**, features tips and tricks for playing more than 1,400 PC games and most games designed for popular game systems, including Nintendo64 and Dreamcast.

➤ Cheater's Guild, at **www.cheaters-guild.com**, offers a robust collection of tips organized by unique categories, such as Cheat Codes, Dirty Tricks, Easter Eggs, Hot Hints, and Level Codes.

➤ Future Games Network, at **www.fgn.com**, is one of the largest and most well-established gaming networks. In addition to offering thousands of reviews, previews, and game tips, this site features plenty of links to other quality game sites.

➤ IGN Guides, at **guides.ign.com**, is a great site to pick up detailed strategy guides for a variety of computer games. To download the free guides, you must register with IGN.

➤ GameStats, at **www.gamestats.com/tips**, not only provides a comprehensive list of tips and tricks from real players but also allows you to submit a tip or trick you have discovered while playing the game. At GameStats, you'll also find links to online forums where you can post questions, answers, and comments about your favorite games.

➤ Super Games, at **cheats.dreamhost.com**, features tips and tricks for playing games designed for a PC, Mac, Nintendo64, Dreamcast, or other platforms. Simply click the desired platform and then click the game's name.

Computer Cheats

Searching for Tips

Use your favorite Web search tool to search for "game tips," "game cheats," or "game hints." To find tips and tricks for a specific game, search for the game by name; for instance, to find tips for playing *Ultima*, search for "Ultima tips."

The Least You Need to Know

You don't need to know much to become a computer game junkie. Just buy a game that looks like fun and start playing. To get the most out of your gaming experience, however, you should know the following:

➤ The first step in choosing a computer game is to figure out which game category interests you: Action, Adventure, Sports, Strategy, and so on.

➤ Before you purchase a game, make sure your computer is properly equipped to run it.

➤ Many games require you to run the game from the DOS prompt.

➤ To display the DOS prompt in Windows 98, choose **Start**, **Programs**, **MS-DOS Prompt**.

➤ One of the best places to pick up free games and other programs is at zdnet's download site (**www.zdnet.com/downloads/games.html**).

➤ Most Web-based software retailers and other online merchants carry computer games and allow you to order games online.

➤ If you're having trouble playing (or winning) a game, you might be able to find a strategy guide, tips, tricks, and hints on the Web.

Chapter 27

Tapping the Power of Educational Software

In This Chapter

➤ Building your own computerized reference library

➤ Teaching your children reading, writing, and arithmetic

➤ Taking piano lessons with your computer

➤ Learning a foreign language from your computer

➤ Painting, drawing, and doing other creative activities

Face it, a computer can't make you smart. It can't pour knowledge or wisdom into your head. It can't stamp multiplication tables on your brain cells. It can't infuse your mind with an understanding of quantum physics. And it sure can't help you experience the pains and pleasures of real life.

What a computer can do (when equipped with the right software) is present a subject in an engaging format, complete with text, graphics, sounds, animation, and video. It can drill a student tirelessly to help the student retain facts, equations, and rules. It can illustrate complex concepts. And it can test the student, provide immediate feedback, and help the student determine which material he or she needs to review.

This chapter takes you on a tour of the educational software and shows you how to use your computer as a tool for research and learning.

Researching Topics with Multimedia Encyclopedias

How would you like a 26-volume set of encyclopedias on a single disc? An encyclopedia that can play snippets of Mozart's symphonies, shows full-color pictures of world leaders and exotic animals, and displays video clips of famous speeches and historical events? How would you like to search the entire set of encyclopedias by typing a single word or phrase? And how would you like to save more than a thousand dollars on a complete set of encyclopedias?

Sound too good to be true? It's not. For less than a hundred bucks, you can purchase an entire set of encyclopedias on CD or DVD that gives you all the benefits described previously.

Figure 27.1 shows Microsoft's Encarta in action. Here, I'm looking up an article about Wolfgang Amadeus Mozart. I click **Find**, type **mozart**, and double-click the entry for **Mozart, Wolfgang Amadeus**. This displays an article about Mozart's life along with an outline of the article, a multimedia kiosk for playing audio clips and viewing pictures, and a link for viewing a timeline chart.

Dirt Cheap

At the time I was writing this book, you could get the entire 32–volume Britannica encyclopedia set with text, pictures, and maps plus the Merriam–Webster Collegiate Dictionary for $59.95 (after a $39.95 rebate). The printed version costs more than $1,200!

Type a description of the topic.   Click here to view the multimedia library.

Figure 27.1

An encyclopedia on disc gives you instant access to the information you need.

Click **Find**.

Double-click the topic's title.

Check out some Web sites.

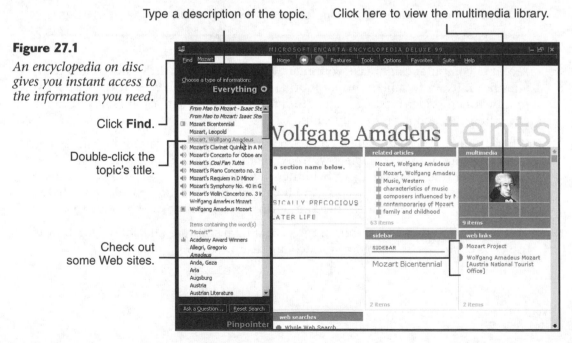

More Books for Your Reference Library

If you do any writing for school, business, or pleasure, you probably use several reference books to develop your work. You might use a dictionary to verify spellings and check meanings, a thesaurus to find synonyms, and a book of quotations to give yourself the appearance of being well-read.

Juggling these reference volumes and flipping pages to track down the information you want can be a daunting task and an inefficient way to find information. Consider placing a complete reference library on your computer. For example, Microsoft Bookshelf includes the following reference books:

Computer Cheats

Free Britannica

Late in 1999, Britannica published the complete text of its encyclopedia on the Web. Of course, the Web version is slower than the disc version and excludes pictures and multimedia clips, but for free, up-to-date information, you can't beat it. Check it out at **www.britannica.com**.

➤ *The American Heritage Dictionary*   Contains definitions of more than 66,000 words. To find a definition, you simply type the desired word and press **Enter**. No more flipping pages.

➤ *Roget's Electronic Thesaurus*   Need another word for lazy? Simply press **Alt+E**, type **lazy**, and press **Enter**. The thesaurus gives you a list of suggestions. You can then choose a word from the list to view the synonyms.

➤ *World Almanac and Book of Facts*   This electronic book contains a hodgepodge of information about the world, including census figures, U.S. economic data, employment figures, offbeat news stories, scientific achievements, and much more.

➤ *Bartlett's Familiar Quotations*   If you like snappy quotes and insights from famous poets, world leaders, and other visionaries, you'll love this book. In addition to offering the famous quotes from the printed version of the book, the CD-ROM version makes it easy to look up quotes either by author or by using a word from the quote.

➤ *Concise Columbia Book of Quotations*   This book offers 6,000 quotations that are appropriate for speeches and presentations. The quotations are organized by subject, so you can look up quotations for subjects such as war, city life, and even living together.

➤ *Concise Columbia Encyclopedia*   This encyclopedia is no match for Britannica or even Encarta, but it does have more than 15,000 pages covering historical topics, including everything from Greek mythology to the Iran-Iraq war.

Shopping at Specialty Shops

Several Web-based retailers specialize in educational software titles and typically offer better deals than the manufacturers. Check out The Education Catalog at `www.edutainco.com`, The Discovery Software Store at `software.discoveryschool.com`, SmarterKids.com at `www.smarterkids.com`, and Kids Lab at `www.kidslab.com`.

More Educational Tools from Mattel

Mattel has a wide selection of educational software, including the Carmen Sandiego series, ClueFinder's Math, Amazon Trail, All-Star Typing, Compton's Learning tools, and Dr. Seuss books. You can check out Mattel's complete selection of software at `www.shopmattel.com` or call 1-800-395-0277.

Learning to Read with Your Computer

One of the greatest pleasures of parenthood is to read to your children and watch them learn to read on their own. No program can replace the quality time you spend reading with your children and encouraging them through your own desire to read. However, the techniques and patience required to teach your child how to read properly may be a bit beyond your abilities. You just don't know what kind of exercises your child needs, and even when you do know, you might not have the patience to work through those exercises as often as needed. To help, purchase a reading readiness program for your child.

One of the most popular reading series on the market is the Reader Rabbit series from The Learning Company, a division of Mattel. In these reading programs, Reader Rabbit and friends demonstrate reading skills and teach basic phonics through engaging stories and games. The characters in the program provide plenty of positive feedback to reward and encourage beginning readers (see Figure 27.2).

Figure 27.2
With Reader Rabbit and friends, students learn to read while they play. (Screen shot courtesy of The Learning Company.)

Reinforcing Math Skills

Ever since my kids began their formal education, I've been getting more and more homework. I'm expected to help them study their spelling lists, quiz them on making change, help them trace their family lineage, and drill them on their multiplication tables. Don't get me wrong, I love performing science experiments in the microwave oven and showing them how to make money on Wall Street, but when it comes to the basics, I think they should figure out how to study on their own. Of course, I do feel a little guilty when I see devoted parents flip through flash cards, build award-winning science projects, and take credit for their kids' spelling bee awards.

To alleviate my guilt, I purchased my kid a copy of Math Blaster (from Knowledge Adventure) and sat her down in front of the computer. She immediately began blasting numbers, never realizing that she was learning basic math skills in the process. Flash cards could never have inspired her to "study" so diligently and work so tirelessly. Figure 27.3 gives you a glimpse of just how much fun it can be to learn math.

Figure 27.3

Math Blaster teaches math through arcade-style games. (Screen shot courtesy of Knowledge Adventure.)

Contact Knowledge Adventure

Knowledge Adventure's product line isn't limited to Math Blaster. It also includes the popular JumpStart series for preschool to sixth grade, Money Town, Reading Blaster, Spelling Blaster, Solar System Explorer, Typing Tutor, SmartStart Spanish, and much more. For product information, visit Knowledge Adventure's Web site at **www.knowledgeadventure.com** or call 1–800–545–7677.

Encouraging Your Child to Play with Language

Kids love to create and print their own publications. They can spend hours composing and illustrating their own comic books or writing stories about their pets. They love to make signs for their bedrooms, write letters to their friends, keep journals, and even publish their own newsletters. Kids don't see this "play" as work. The fun they're having completely blinds them to the fact that they're learning how to write and how to present their ideas and opinions to an audience.

To encourage kids to write and to play with language and illustrations, several companies have developed writing/desktop publishing programs just for kids. One such program, Microsoft's Creative Writer, is set up like a desktop publishing program. On startup, the program provides options for creating a greeting card, viewing project ideas, printing banners, starting with an idea, or creating a Web page. The child picks the desired option, enters a few preferences, and then sits back and watches the program slap together a roughed-out version of the publication. The child can then customize the publication with text, clip art, original drawings or paintings, borders, and other objects.

One of the coolest features of Creative Writer is that it can inspire creativity. The Splot Machine (a slot machine for words) displays random phrases that can kick-start a storyline (see Figure 27.4). If a child is more visually oriented, she may opt for the Story Starters—colorful graphics designed to get the creative juices flowing.

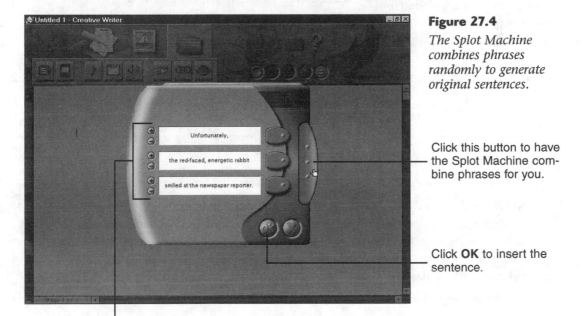

Figure 27.4

The Splot Machine combines phrases randomly to generate original sentences.

Click this button to have the Splot Machine combine phrases for you.

Click **OK** to insert the sentence.

Click these buttons to cycle through phrases.

Learning to Play the Piano

With the right software and some fancy add-on devices, your computer can moonlight as a piano teacher. JumpMusic's Piano Discovery System consists of a CD and MIDI keyboard that work together to teach students how to play popular piano tunes and read music. The keyboard (which you can purchase separately or as a part of the system) plugs into your computer's sound card. The software displays an onscreen keyboard that shows you which keys to press and in which sequence. You simply follow along to play the tune.

Check It Out for Free!

If you have an Internet connection, visit Microsoft Kids at **www. microsoft.com/kids** and check out Microsoft's line of educational software. Here, you can download a shareware copy of *Creative Writer* and check it out for yourself. Better yet, have your kids check it out.

To help you learn notes and chords, the Piano Discovery System takes an arcade-game approach, challenging you to shoot ducks by playing the proper notes and chords. Although the Piano Discovery System cannot replace a good piano teacher and formal lessons, it functions as a great supplemental tool for teaching specific tunes and drilling students on the basics.

Learning a Foreign Language

Most students struggle and many flounder in standard foreign language classes. They like to learn common phrases, but when it comes to studying long lists of vocabulary words and learning how to conjugate irregular verbs, they lose their motivation. It's just too much work and not enough fun.

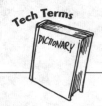

What's MIDI?

MIDI (pronounced "middy") is short for Musical Instrument Digital Interface. The musical industry developed the MIDI standard to ensure uniformity among music devices, such as sound cards, synthesizers, keyboards, and other instruments. A MIDI keyboard has a MIDI port that you can connect to a standard sound card using a MIDI cable.

Of course, there's no replacement for motivation and hard work, but foreign language software can add a little fun to the drudgery by making your lessons more interactive. *Learn to Speak Spanish*, for instance, features a talking dictionary to teach you proper pronunciation, conversation simulations, and speech recording and playback tools to help you compare your pronunciation with that of native speakers. The program also contains more than 100 exercises to help you learn vocabulary, reading, writing, and grammar. You can even create your own study plan and track your progress.

A more down-to-earth foreign language program from Knowledge Adventure is JumpStart Spanish (see Figure 27.5). For details about the "JumpStart" series and other language titles, go to **www.shopmattel.com** or **www.knowledgeadventure.com**, or use your favorite Web search tool to search for additional foreign language software.

Figure 27.5
JumpStart Spanish helps students learn vocabulary and other essentials in "real life" situations.

Bringing Out the Artist in Your Child

Now that our society has determined to specialize in science and math, language, music, and fine arts are quickly falling by the wayside. To help your child develop some artistic sensibilities, you must encourage your child on your own and provide the tools and opportunities for your child to develop his or her artistic talents.

Of course, crayons, paper, and water colors are still the staple diet of a developing artist, but for an artist to make a living nowadays, some basic training in computer graphics is essential. Fortunately, several software companies have developed graphics programs just for kids. Check out the following offerings:

➤ Art Dabbler, from MetaCreations (**www.metacreations.com** or 1-888-707-6382), features the drawing and painting tools you'll find in professional graphics programs, along with online art lessons, traceable drawings, animation tools, photo-editing tools, flip-book animations, and much more.

➤ Crayola Creativity Packs, from IBM (**www.ibm.com/pc/multimedia** or 1-800-321-7511), are a collection of software packages that encourage kids to color onscreen with computerized crayons. With Crayola Print Factory, for instance, kids can create banners, signs, greeting cards, reports, and other school-related publications.

➤ Flying Colors, from Magic Mouse Productions (**www.magicmouse.com** or 415-669-7010), consists of a library of more than 3,000 color stickers and backgrounds plus a complete set of professional paint tools. Kids can use the program to create their own paintings and greeting cards, signs, Web page graphics, and other publications (see Figure 27.6).

Read Reviews

Several services specialize in reviewing, rating, and recommending educational software. Check out Children's Software Review at **www.childrenssoftware.com**.

➤ ImaginAction, from Rose Studios (**www.rosestudios.com** or 1-888-543-7748), is more than just a paint program for kids. Here, kids must pay attention and use logic along with their artistic talents to understand spatial relations, shapes, and their functions in the real world.

➤ JumpStart Art Class, from Knowledge Adventure (**www.knowledgeadventure.com** or 1-800-542-4240), is an art/creativity program where kids enter a treehouse to experiment with various artistic media, including painting, collages, drawing, folk art, and crafts. JumpStart Art Class was due to hit the market during the writing of this book.

➤ You Can Draw!, from Cognitive Technologies (**www.cogtech.com** or 301-581-9652), uses interactive lessons to teach kids how to draw everyday objects. This computerized art class covers six topics: Gesture and Expression, Line, Shape, Value, Volume, and Perspective. The lessons engage students by using a good dose of animation, video, and audio.

Figure 27.6

Flying Colors helps bring out the artist in a child.

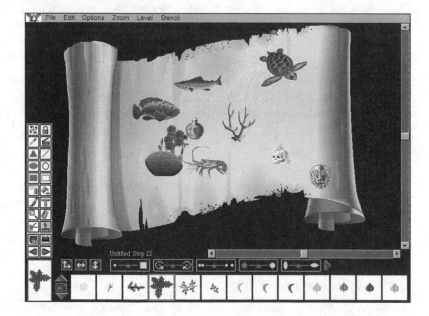

The Least You Need to Know

The software market is packed with so many educational software products that it's nearly impossible to keep track of them all. When you're shopping for educational software for your kids, your students, or yourself, keep the following basics in mind:

➤ To take advantage of your computer's power as a research tool, equip it with a good CD or DVD encyclopedia, dictionary, and other reference tools.

➤ Beginning readers can benefit from interactive reading programs, such as Reader Rabbit.

➤ Math programs, such as MathBlaster, are excellent for teaching students basic skills and concepts and for enforcing basic skills by using arcade-style drills.

➤ Writing programs designed for kids, such as Creative Writer, encourage students to play with language and communicate clearly with their own publications.

➤ With a MIDI keyboard and music lessons on CD (such as JumpMusic's Piano Discovery System), your computer can help you learn how to play your favorite tunes.

➤ If studying a foreign language seems like a drag, hire a foreign language tutor on CD, such as Learn to Speak Spanish.

➤ Although there's no replacement for paper, pencil, and watercolors, a good graphics art program, such as Art Dabbler, can help you learn basic techniques.

➤ For educational software reviews and ratings, check out Children's Software Review at `www.childrenssoftware.com`.

Chapter 28

Safely Introducing Your Child to the Internet

In This Chapter

➤ Ensuring your child understands the rules

➤ Spying on... er... supervising your kids

➤ Blocking undesirable Web content with a censoring program

➤ Playing computer games with other people online

➤ Visiting educational sites on the Web

➤ Avoiding deviants in chat rooms and via email

The Internet is a virtual city, packed with shopping malls, libraries, community centers, museums, newsstands, meeting rooms, and other positive offerings. But like any city, the Internet has its dark side—a section of town ruled by pornography, violence, bigotry, and theft.

As a society, we want our children to have the freedom to explore the Internet, but we have the responsibility to protect them from media and individuals who threaten their innocence. We want our children to visit museums online, communicate with students in other parts of the world, take classes, visit political institutions, and research topics of interest. We don't want our kids or students pulling up porno pages, reading racist propaganda, or sitting in the Hot Tub chat room conversing with a bunch of old guys and gals who should know better. And we surely don't want our 11-year-olds corresponding via email with deviants two or three times their age.

This chapter acts as a parent/teacher guide to the Internet. Here, you learn ways to introduce children to the Internet, help them fully explore the positive features it has to offer, and prevent them from accessing undesirable content or falling prey to smooth-talking perverts.

Explaining the Rules of the Road

Most kids aren't rotten. They're confused, frustrated, careless, and selfish, but not intentionally bad. A child usually makes a wrong choice or breaks a rule either because the child doesn't understand the rule or faces no consequence for misbehaving. So, before you let your child or student fire up the Web browser, lay down the rules and explain the consequences. Here are a few rules to pass along to your kids:

➤ **Keep passwords secret.** Anyone who knows your username and password can use your account, racking up connect time charges, placing orders, and performing illegal activity in your name.

➤ **Don't enter any personal information online without permission from a parent or guardian.** Using your real name, address, or phone number in your profile gives stalkers the information they want. Registering for contests and "free" stuff can make your private information public.

➤ **Don't use the credit card.** Leaving your teenager alone on the Web with your credit card can be a disaster. The Web is the biggest shop-at-home network in the world.

➤ **Don't run or install any programs without permission.** Downloading and running programs from unreliable sources can introduce computer viruses. You and your kids should also be careful with any program files you receive via email.

Enforce the Rules

Use computer time as a reward for proper behavior. If your child fails to follow the rules, reduce or eliminate the time your child spends on the computer. Your kid might claim that the punishment is only harming his education. Don't buy it.

➤ **Don't view sites that you wouldn't view with parents or guardians next to you.** Later in this chapter, I show you how to block out undesirable content, but censoring programs can't block everything. Be sure your kids know that you expect them to use good judgment.

➤ **Don't chat or correspond with creeps.** Some creepy adults use the Internet to prey on kids. Have your kids notify you immediately of any suspicious individuals or messages. Tell your kids not to send photos of themselves to strangers or post their photos on their Web pages.

➤ **Don't meet anyone in person known only from online contact.** If your child wants to meet a friend from the Internet, have your child schedule a meeting in a public place and take you along.

In addition to laying down the rules, specify limits on Internet use, just as you would limit TV viewing. Specify the time of day your child can access the Internet and the amount of time he or she can spend at the keyboard. Although the computer and the Internet can be great tools for education and entertainment, they can also interfere with a child's education and social and physical development.

A Little Personal Supervision Goes a Long Way

When my kids started watching TV, I was pretty naive. I told my children to watch only those shows that they would feel comfortable watching with me or their mom. A couple days later, I walked into the den to catch my 13- and 10-year-old watching MTV's *Celebrity Death Match*. Of course, they saw nothing wrong with it.

As a parent, it's your obligation not to be stupid. Don't stick a computer in your kid's bedroom and then celebrate because you now have more quality time to spend with your spouse. The only reason your son isn't pestering you or picking on his kid sister is because he has found something much more sinister to do on the Internet.

Keep Your Password Secret

To be sure your kids can't surf the Internet without your permission, keep the password you use to connect to your ISP secret. Also, remove the check mark from the **Save Password** check box in the Connect To dialog box.

Place the computer in a quiet room that you can enter without looking like a spy. If you have young children, spend some time exploring the Internet with them and supervising their activity. Your kids might balk and think of you as a control freak, but that's your job.

Censoring the Internet

Over the years, people have debated the issue of whether the government should censor the Internet. As society wrestles with this issue, offensive material remains readily available. In the following sections, you learn what you can do on your end to prevent this material from reaching you or your children.

Using America Online's Parental Controls

Without some level of censorship, America Online can be the most dangerous place for kids to hang out. Kids can access chat rooms, such as The Flirts Nook and Chance Encounters, where chat topics are definitely adults only and where chatters are likely to receive instant messages directing them to the latest porno site on the Web.

Spying on the Kids

View the history list to see where your kids have been. In Internet Explorer, click the **History** button to display the History bar. Click the folder for the week or day you want to check. The History bar displays a list of sites visited during the selected week or day. Click the site folder to view a list of pages that were opened at the site, and then click the page name to view the page. (If your kids are wise to history lists, they might know how to clear the list.)

America Online's Parental Controls allow you to block access to the red light districts on America Online and the Internet. Take the following steps to create a screen name for one of your children and set limitations:

1. Sign on to America Online using your primary screen name. (You can add users to your account only by signing on with your primary screen name.)

2. In the button bar, click **My AOL** and click **Screen Names**. The AOL Screen Names dialog box appears, displaying a list of screen names for your account.

3. Click **Create a Screen Name**. The Create a Screen Name dialog box appears, displaying a brief description of screen names.

4. Click **Create Screen Name**. AOL prompts you to type a screen name.

5. Type the name your child wants to use and click **Continue**. AOL prompts you to type a password.

6. Type a password for your child to use when logging on (6-8 characters), press **Tab**, type the same password again, and click **Continue**. AOL prompts you to select a Parental Controls setting.

7. Click the desired setting, as shown in Figure 28.1 and click **Continue**. AOL prompts you to confirm or customize the settings.

8. Click **Customize Settings**, so you can check the settings. The Parental Controls dialog box appears, listing the various groups of settings: E-mail control, Chat control, IM control, and so on.

9. Click the green check box next to the control group you want to check or modify. A dialog box pops up, showing your options.

10. Enter your preferences and click **Save**. For example, if you chose E-Mail control in step 9, you can choose to block all email messages, receive messages only from AOL members, or create a list people from whom email messages are to be accepted. Whether you click **Save** or **Cancel**, a confirmation message appears.

11. Read the confirmation message and click **OK**. You are returned to the window for customizing parental controls.

12. Repeat steps 9–11 to check or customize any other controls and then click the **Close** (**X**) button to exit the window.

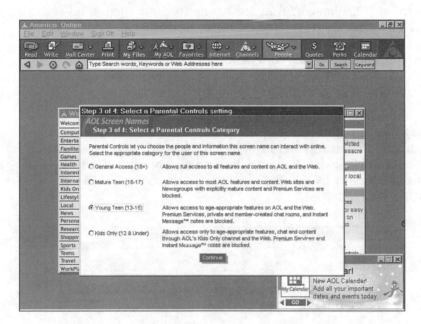

Figure 28.1
*Pick the desired age level and click **Continue**.*

I Already Created the Screen Name!

If you already created a screen name for your child without specifying restrictions, you can specify restrictions at any time. Click **My AOL** in the button bar and click **Parental Controls**. Click **Set Parental Controls** and then open the **Edit Controls For** list and click your child's screen name. At the bottom of the dialog box, click the button for the desired age group: General Access, Mature Teen, Young Teen, or Kids Only. You can then customize the settings if desired.

Censoring the Web with Internet Explorer

If you don't subscribe to America Online or some other commercial online service, you connect to the Internet through an ISP and are responsible for finding your own

289

tools for censoring content. The next section reviews some of the specialized censoring programs currently available. In the meantime, if you use Internet Explorer as your Web browser, you can use its built-in Content Advisor to filter out undesirable content.

To censor sites with Internet Explorer, activate the Ratings feature. Open the **View** or **Tools** menu, click **Internet Options**, and click the **Content** tab. Under Ratings or Content Advisor, click the **Enable** button and click **OK**. The Create Supervisor Password dialog box appears. Type a password in both text boxes that you will remember, but that your kids will have a tough time guessing. Click **OK** as many times as needed to save your changes and close the dialog boxes.

Now, don't set the kiddies in front of the screen just yet. Test your setup first. Try going to **www.playboy.com**. If you see some hot babes in various stages of undress, the Content Advisor is disabled. Close Internet Explorer, run it again, and then try going to the nudie page. You should see the Content Advisor dialog box, as shown in Figure 28.2, displaying a list of reasons why you have been denied access to this site (as if you didn't know). Click **OK**.

Figure 28.2

The Content Advisor won't let you view the peep show.

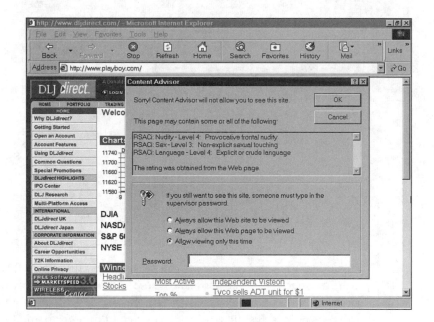

Using Censoring Software

If your Web browser does not have a built-in censor or you want more control over the content and features that your children can access, purchase a specialized censoring program. Following is a list of some of the better censoring programs along with addresses for the Web pages where you can find out more about them and download shareware versions:

➤ **Cyber Patrol** (at **www.cyberpatrol.com**)
The most popular censoring program
on the market, Cyber Patrol uses a list of
forbidden words to block access to objectionable material or a list of child-friendly
words to block access to all Web pages
except those that contain one of the specified words. Passwords enable you to set
access levels for different users, and Cyber
Patrol can keep track of the amount of
time each user spends on the Internet.
The one drawback of Cyber Patrol is that
it doesn't keep track of the sites that your
kids try to visit.

➤ **CYBERsitter** (at **www.solidoak.com**)
Another fine censoring program,
CYBERsitter is a little less strict than Cyber
Patrol, but is easier to use and configure.
CYBERsitter has a unique filtering system
that judges words in context, so it won't
block access to inoffensive sites, such as the
Anne Sexton home page.

➤ **Cyber Snoop** (at **www.pearlsw.com**)
Not the best content-blocker in the group,
Cyber Snoop's claim to fame is that it can
create a comprehensive log of a user's
Internet activity. The best way to use Cyber
Snoop is to install it and tell your kids that
Cyber Snoop is recording everything they
do on the Internet. You might not even
have to buy the program—the threat
might be deterrent enough.

➤ **Net Nanny** (at **www.netnanny.com**)
Net Nanny is unique in that it can punish
the user for typing URLs of offensive sites
or for typing any word on the "no-no" list.
If a user types a prohibited word or URL, Net Nanny can shut down the application and record the offense, forcing your child to come up with an excuse. To
make the most of Net Nanny, however, you're going to have to spend a bit of
time configuring it; it's not the most intuitive program of the bunch.

Inside Tip

Relax the Ratings

Unless you change the Content
Advisor's settings, it'll block every
unrated page on the Web—just
about every page you try to pull
up. To relax the ratings, open
the **View** or **Tools** menu, click
Internet Options, and click
the **Content** tab. Click **Settings**,
enter your password, and enter your
preferences.

Whoa!

Your Job's Not Over Yet

No censoring program is perfect.
Some objectionable content can
slip through the cracks, and the
program can block access to unob-
jectionable sites. Use the censoring
program only when you are unable
to personally supervise your kids.

Playing Games Online

Most kids need little encouragement to start exploring the Internet, but some kids might need a little push to get started. If your child seems reluctant to set out on his or her first journey, try introducing your child to some online games. Yahoo! offers several two-player and multiplayer games to encourage kids and adults alike to spend a little more time on the Web and generate a little human contact.

To get started, use your Web browser to go to **games.yahoo.com** and click the **Gameroom** link if it is not already selected (see Figure 28.3). This displays a list of board games, card games, and other games you can play with other people at Yahoo! Click the link for the desired game. You must then log in (if you already registered with Yahoo!) or register to obtain a screen name and password. Follow the onscreen instructions.

Figure 28.3

Check out Yahoo!'s Game Room.

Be sure **Gameroom** is selected.

Click the desired game.

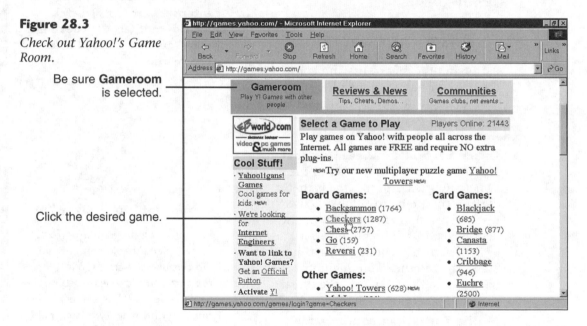

After you sign in, Yahoo! attempts to send you the Java applet you need for playing the game. If your Web browser displays a dialog box asking you to confirm the download operation, give your okay to install the applet. Yahoo! then displays a list of game rooms where people are already playing the game you selected. To enter a game room, click its name. Yahoo! places you in a game room where several game "tables" are set up. Scroll down the list of tables until you find one that interests you. Then, click **Watch** to watch a game in progress or **JOIN** to sit down at a game table and play (see Figure 28.4).

Click **Play Now** to start a new game.

Click **Create Table** to create your own table.

Figure 28.4

In Yahoo!'s game rooms, you can sit and watch or join in the fun.

Scroll down the list of tables.

Click **JOIN** to play against an opponent.

Click **Watch** to act as a spectator.

If no open tables are available, you can click the **Create Table** button to create your own table or click **Play Now** to start playing a game. If you click **Play Now**, and an open "chair" is available at another table, you're automatically placed at the table and can start playing. Otherwise, a game table appears with two or more Sit buttons. Click one of the **Sit** buttons to sit down at the table and wait for an opponent to join you. As soon as someone chooses to join the game at your table (and be your opponent), you can start playing.

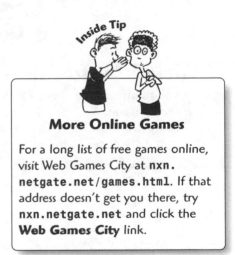

Inside Tip

More Online Games

For a long list of free games online, visit Web Games City at **nxn. netgate.net/games.html**. If that address doesn't get you there, try **nxn.netgate.net** and click the **Web Games City** link.

Visiting the White House

Most kids have their own agenda for using the Web. They want to play games, download the latest music clips, and do a little shopping. Adults, on the other hand, expect the kids to check out educational sites and build their knowledge base. So, how do you steer kids in the right direction? Try pointing your kids to sites designed specifically for them, such as The White House for Kids.

Using your Web browser, you can visit the White House online at **www.whitehouse.gov**. Although you won't be able to make reservations to sleep in the Lincoln bedroom, you

293

can view pictures of the President, Vice President, and First Lady; read the Citizens Handbook; access official White House documents; and learn more about the various federal agencies. Near the bottom of the page is a link called White House for Kids that's a little more kid-friendly, as shown in Figure 28.5.

Figure 28.5

White House for Kids introduces children to United States government.

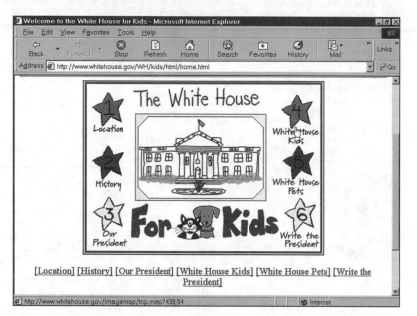

Visiting Museums and Libraries

You might not be able to fly your kids to the Louvre to see the *Mona Lisa* or drive to Washington, D.C. to visit the Smithsonian Institution, but you can do the next best thing: Visit the most famous museums and libraries online and access the best educational resources online. Here's a short list of Web-site addresses to get you started:

That's .gov, NOT .com!

Be sure you enter that White House Web site address as `www.whitehouse.gov`. If you enter `.com` instead of `.gov` by mistake, you'll be kicking yourself for not installing Cyber Patrol!

➤ `www.louvre.fr` takes you to the most famous art museum in the world—France's Le Louvre.

➤ `www.moma.org` opens the doors to the most famous modern art museum in the world—New York's Museum of Modern Art.

➤ `www.si.edu` carries you to the Smithsonian Institution's home page, where you'll find plenty of links to exhibits and special programs.

➤ `www.memphis.edu/egypt/main.html` connects you to the University of Memphis Institute of Egyptian Art and Archeology, where you can learn about ancient Egyptian history, take a tour of Egypt online, and find additional links to related sites.

➤ www.adlerplanetarium.org shifts your focus to the skies to study celestial bodies and astronomical figures from the Adler Planetarium in Chicago.

➤ www.msichicago.org displays the Museum of Science and Industry's most popular exhibits online. Take the submarine tour, do a little coal mining, or check out an online version of the International Space Station without ever leaving your home.

➤ www.loc.gov gives you a free ticket to the Library of Congress, the world's largest library. Here, you can find an electronic version of the library's card catalog, hundreds of digitized photos, and a hefty collection of online journals, newspapers, and other publications.

➤ www.lights.com/webcats/ gives you access to an index of libraries throughout the United States that allow you to search for books, audio tapes, video tapes, CDs, and other media online. Check it out—search for your local library.

Computer Cheats

Find Every Museum on the Web

For a comprehensive list of museums on the Web, check out wwar.com/museums.html.

Of course, this is an extremely short list of what's available on the Web. You can find thousands of museums and libraries throughout the world that have placed their most famous exhibits, collections, virtual tours, and interactive educational programs online. Use your favorite Web search tool to find additional sites.

Helping Your Child Find a Pen Pal

The best way to learn about the world and experience other cultures is to travel. The second best way is to correspond with someone who lives in a different part of the country or in a foreign land. In addition to giving a child a different view of the world, having a pen pal encourages a child to use online resources and research tools to learn more about foreign lands and cultures.

Teachers have always encouraged their students to correspond with pen pals, but finding and connecting with a pen pal traditionally has been a long and complicated process. Email and the Web have simplified the process considerably. Now, a student can use the Web to locate a pen pal in a matter of minutes and immediately send an email message to his or her pal. To find a pen pal, check out the following sites:

➤ epals.com, at www.epals.com, owns bragging rights for having the largest network of pen pals—more than 900,000 students from more than 13,000 classrooms representing three different languages (English, French, and Spanish).

➤ KeyPals, at www.mightymedia.com/keypals/, can't compete with epals.com when it comes to numbers, but it does provide another fairly safe and secure environment for connecting students and classrooms in different countries.

KeyPals screens messages for obscene content and lets students keep their email address private.

➤ Kids' Space Connection Penpal Box, at **www.ks-connection.com/penpal/penpal.html**, offers the easiest way to find a pen pal. You simply click the Penpal box for the desired age group to view a list of kids looking for a pen pal and then click the kid's email address to send a message. (I suggest that you steer your kids or students clear of this site and any site similar to it, because such sites have no safeguards in place.)

The Least You Need to Know

When raising children, you have two goals—protect them from harm and provide the resources they need to become productive, happy people. As you introduce your kids to the Internet, keep those two goals in mind and remember the following:

➤ Before you unleash your kids on the Internet, lay down the rules you want them to follow.

➤ The most essential rule kids must follow is to never give out any personal or sensitive information, including passwords, phone numbers, addresses, or credit card numbers.

➤ No censor program can replace the supervision of a loving, caring parent.

➤ If you cannot supervise your kids every minute they're on the Internet (what parent can?), install Cyber Patrol and learn how to use it.

➤ If a child is reluctant to explore the Internet, try starting the child out with some online games in Yahoo!'s Game Room. Go to **games.yahoo.com** and click the **Gameroom** link.

➤ To encourage a child to explore educational Web sites rather than just play on the Web, have the child check out the White House online at **www.whitehouse.gov**.

➤ Let your child's teacher know about **epals.com**. It's a great place for kids to learn about foreign cultures and people.

Chapter 29

Making a Family Photo Album

In This Chapter

➤ Storing your photos on CDs

➤ Scanning photos into your computer

➤ Adjusting the brightness, contrast, and colors

➤ Attaching photos to outgoing email messages

➤ Taking instant photos with a digital camera

Do you have shoeboxes packed with undated photos of people you don't even recognize? Do you frequently find rolls of film you forgot to drop off for developing? Do you find dusty photo envelopes behind cabinets and dressers? Do rodents commonly chew up your photos and use them for bedding?

If you answered "Yes" to any of these questions, consider changing the way you manage your photos. Instead of sticking with traditional negatives and prints, have your photos digitized and stored on a CD, or buy a digital camera and skip the film altogether! This chapter reveals your options and shows you how to use your computer to take control of your photos.

Getting a Kodak Picture CD

The easiest and cheapest way to go digital with your photos is to order a Kodak Picture CD when you drop off your next roll of film for developing. The developer does the standard negatives and prints but also converts the photos to a digital format and saves each photo as a separate file on a CD.

How Do I Change Screen Fonts?!

The Kodak Picture CD installation routine might indicate that Windows needs to be set up to use small fonts. Right-click the Windows desktop, click **Properties**, click the **Settings** tab, and click the **Advanced** button. On the **General** tab, open the **Font Size** list, and click **Small Fonts**. You might need to restart Windows.

The CD includes Kodak's digital image manager, a program that enables you to view your pictures onscreen; adjust the brightness, contrast, and colors; sharpen photos; remove the red-eye effect (if present); send photos via email; create your own photo albums; and print your photos.

When you get your Kodak Picture CD home, take the following steps to view your pictures on your computer:

1. Pop the Kodak Picture CD into the CD-ROM drive. The Kodak Picture CD installation routine should start. If it does not start, do the following:

   Double-click **My Computer**.

   Double-click the icon for your CD-ROM drive.

   Double-click the **Launch** icon.

2. Follow the onscreen instructions to install the Kodak Picture CD software. When the installation is complete, the Kodak Review magazine appears.

3. Click the arrow in the lower-right corner of the Kodak Review magazine cover to display the table of contents and thumbnail versions of your photos, as shown in Figure 29.1.

4. To view a photo, click its thumbnail version.

Figure 29.1

Kodak Picture CD displays your photos and the tasks you can perform.

Tasks you can perform

Thumbnail view of your photos

Click the arrows to navigate.

Click the dot between the arrows to display the master menu.

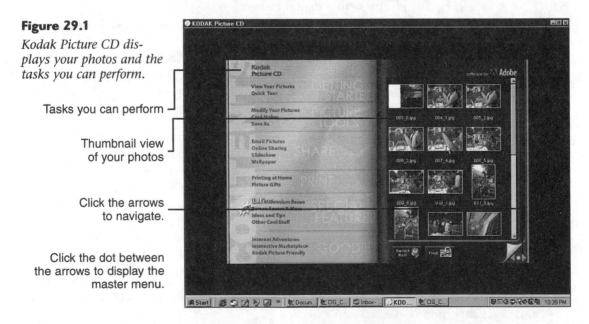

After you install the Kodak Picture CD software for the first time, you can run the program at any time by selecting it from the Start, Programs, Kodak Picture CD menu.

To view a full-screen slideshow of your photos, click **View Your Pictures**. The Kodak Photo CD flips one-by-one through the entire "roll." After familiarizing yourself with the basic functions, you can move on to use the Kodak Picture CD software to create a photo album, enhance and print photos, and attach digitized photos to outgoing email messages.

Adding Photos from Another Kodak Picture CD

When you get your next Kodak Picture CD, you should register the photos with the Kodak Picture CD program to add the photos to your catalogue. When the program catalogues your photos, it creates and stores a thumbnail version of the photo, which appears whether or not the CD is loaded. The program can then prompt you to insert the proper CD whenever you choose to view, enhance, print, or copy the photo.

To register a new Kodak Picture CD and catalogue its photos, take the following steps:

1. Click **Start**, **Programs**, **Kodak Picture CD**, **Volume # Issue #**, where # represents the Picture CD Volume and Issue number shown on the CD label.
2. Click the arrow in the lower-right corner of the Kodak Review magazine.
3. Click the **Switch Roll** button, just below the thumbnail preview window.
4. Insert the CD you want to register into your computer's CD-ROM drive.
5. Click **Get Kodak Picture CD**. Picture CD registers the new CD and creates thumbnail versions of all the photos on the CD. These appear in the thumbnail preview window.

To switch from one roll of pictures to another, click the **Switch Roll** button to view an entire list of Picture CDs you have registered. Click the name of the desired roll. Thumbnail versions of all photos stay on your hard drive, but if you try to display a photo full-size or edit a photo, the program prompts you to insert the appropriate CD.

Enhancing and Editing Photos

Are your photos too dark? Are some too light? Are they fuzzy and out of focus? Do your portraits all suffer from the red-eye effect? If so, you might be tempted to pitch that Photo CD and the accompanying prints right into the trash. Resist the temptation. With the Kodak Photo CD software, you can touch up your digitized photos—increase the brightness for dark photos, sharpen blurry images, and even remove the red-eye effect.

To edit and enhance your photos, run Kodak Picture CD, navigate to the menu, and click **Modify Your Pictures**. Click the desired image, click **Enhance**, and use the following tools to touch up the photo:

Instant Fix automatically adjusts the brightness, color, and contrast and sharpens out-of-focus photos. Instant fix does not remove the red-eye effect.

 Brightness Contrast enables you to brighten dull pictures and lighten dark pictures.

 Sharpen corrects for shots that are slightly out of focus. Don't get your hopes up; you can't do much to improve photos that are seriously blurry.

 Trim zooms in on the most important area of the photo and crops extraneous details from the borders. If you've ever taken a picture of your dog only to have it appear as a dot on the print, you'll love this feature.

 Remove Red Eye eliminates the red-eye effect that crops up in pictures of humans and animals. When all your subjects look like vampires, it's a good sign that you need to remove the red-eye effect.

 Remove All Changes returns the image to its original, mint condition. If you get carried away with your "enhancements," this button can be a lifesaver.

Done accepts your changes and returns you to the previous page, where you can select other options for modifying the photo lifesaver.

Stylize Photos with Special Effects

In addition to providing tools for improving picture quality, Picture CD features tools for applying special effects, such as making your photos look like colorful posters, transforming color photos into black-and-white, and animating photos. To access these special effects, click the **Done** button to go back to the previous page and click **Stylize**.

Typing Your Own Captions

The old adage "A picture's worth a thousand words" may be true, but a few select words (a caption) can enhance even the most detailed picture. A caption might specify the date and location, name the people in the photo, or even insert a witty remark. In addition to adding a little color to your photos, captions can make it easier to locate the photo later.

To add a caption to a photo in Kodak Picture CD, click **Modify Your Pictures**, click the picture below which you want to add a caption, and click the **Caption** button. Type the caption in the text box below the photo, as shown in Figure 29.2.

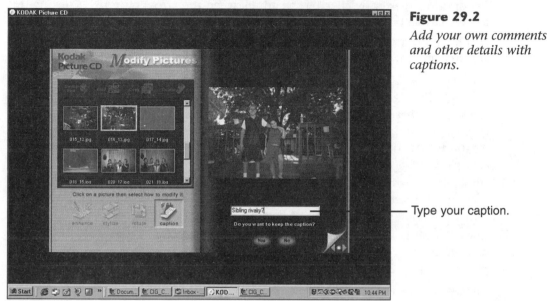

Figure 29.2
Add your own comments and other details with captions.

— Type your caption.

Printing Your Photos on Photo-Quality Paper

Digitized photos are great for sending via email and posting on the Web, but you might still want some old-fashioned prints. Of course, you can print your photos on standard inkjet or copy machine paper, but this cheaper paper stock tends to bleed, making photos and other graphics appear fuzzy.

For best results, purchase some photo-quality paper. This paper can be quite costly, but if you want photos that look like bona fide photo prints, don't go cheap. In addition, just before you give your final okay to start printing, double-check your print settings to be sure your printer is set for the highest-quality output. If you print photos in draft mode on photo-quality paper, your photos will come out dingy, no matter how good the paper is (not to mention wasting the expensive paper).

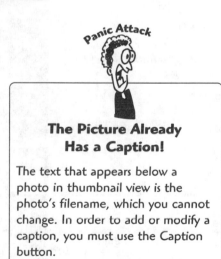

Panic Attack

The Picture Already Has a Caption!

The text that appears below a photo in thumbnail view is the photo's filename, which you cannot change. In order to add or modify a caption, you must use the Caption button.

When you're ready to print your photos from Kodak Picture CD, take the following steps:

1. Display the main menu by clicking the back-arrow button to flip back through the option pages or by clicking the dot between the arrow buttons. (Clicking the dot displays a pop-up menu with all available options.)

2. On the main menu, click **Printing at Home**. The Printing at Home page appears, as shown in Figure 29.3.

3. Click each photo you want to print. (To deselect a picture, click it again.) A yellow box appears around each picture you select, indicating that it will be printed.

4. Click the **Printer Settings** button and use the resulting dialog box to enter quality preferences for your printer. You might need to click the **Properties** button in the dialog box to access additional preferences. (The steps for entering printer settings vary from printer to printer.)

5. Under step 4 (onscreen), click **Custom Size and Quantity** and enter the desired print size and number of copies. (Check out the other two options under step 4 for some predesigned print layouts.)

6. Click **Preview and Print**. The Print Preview dialog box appears, showing the first photo.

7. Click the plus (+) and minus (–) buttons to flip through the photos, if desired.

8. Click **Print** to start printing.

Figure 29.3

With Kodak Picture CD, making additional prints is a snap.

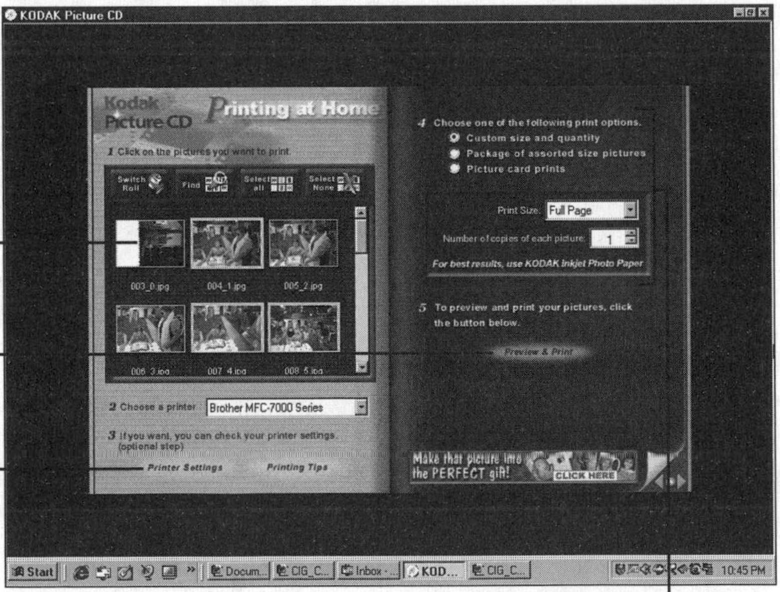

Click each picture you want to print.

Click **Preview** and **Print**.

Enter settings for your printer.

Specify the size and number of copies you want printed.

Sharing Photos via Email and Disk

You don't have to print your digitized photos in order to share them. Kodak Picture CD offers several tools enabling you to attach photos to outgoing email messages, make your own 3.5-inch Kodak Picture Disk, create an onscreen slideshow, and even order photo coffee mugs and other products.

To transmit your photos via email, display the main menu and click **Email Pictures**. The Email Pictures screen appears, as shown in Figure 29.4. Click each picture you want to send and then address and compose your message as you normally do. Click the **Send Pictures** button.

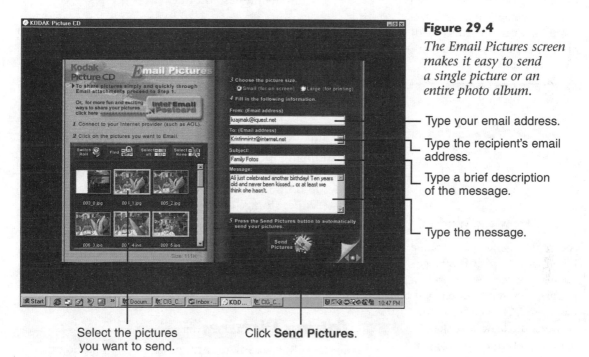

Figure 29.4

The Email Pictures screen makes it easy to send a single picture or an entire photo album.

Type your email address.

Type the recipient's email address.

Type a brief description of the message.

Type the message.

Select the pictures you want to send.

Click **Send Pictures**.

Avoiding the Middleman with a Digital Camera

Although digital cameras are one of the most popular computer toys around, they're not very practical. You can get a 35mm box camera at your local drugstore that's capable of taking better snapshots than a $200 digital camera. For another 80 bucks, you can get a 600-by-600dpi, 24-bit color scanner that produces better digitized images.

Pictures on T-Shirts, Mugs, and More

Several companies on the Web can transfer digital photos to T-shirts and make mugs, coasters, boxer shorts, and other products with your photos. Check out pix.com at **www.pix.com**.

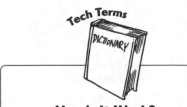

How's It Work?

A digital cameral, like a scanner, is built around a CCD (charge-coupled device). When you snap a picture, the shutter opens and bombards the CCD with light. The CCD converts the light into electrical impulses, which re then applied to a magnetic storage medium, such as a disk or PC card.

So, why are so many people running out and buying digital cameras? Several reasons come to mind:

➤ They're fun. Take a digital camera with an LCD viewfinder to a party, and you'll be the center of attention... or at least your camera will be.

➤ They provide instant gratification. With a digital camera, you don't even have to wait for one-hour service. You plug the camera in to your computer, download the images, and print as many copies as you like.

➤ They let you create digital photo albums that you can write to CDs or DVDs for easy storage and management.

➤ They save you money on film and developing.

➤ They make it easy to post pictures on Web pages and send photos via email.

Shopping for a digital camera is nearly as complicated as shopping for a computer. Prices range from $100 to over $1,000 and features vary widely. You need to consider resolution, color depth, memory, flash options, battery life, storage options, zoom features, and the method used for downloading photos to a computer. Special features, such as voice annotation and an LCD viewfinder, come at a premium price. As with any big-ticket item, try before you buy and read current reviews.

Taking Pictures

Because digital cameras are modeled from standard 35mm cameras, snapping a picture is easy. You just point and shoot. However, before you snap too many pictures, you should check the camera settings.

Most digital cameras have two buttons: one for changing modes (such as flash, image quality, timer, and audio) and another for changing the mode settings. You change to the desired mode (for instance, Flash) and then press the other button to change the setting (for instance, Auto Flash or Flash On). Check the following settings before taking a picture:

➤ **Resolution**—To fit more pictures in storage, crank down the resolution setting. For higher-quality pictures, choose a higher setting.

➤ **Flash**—In most cases, leave the flash setting on Auto. If you're taking all your pictures outside, turn off the flash. For backlit scenes, turn on the flash, if this option is available on your camera.

➤ **Audio**—If your camera supports audio input, turn on Audio, if desired. Keep in mind that audio recordings consume quite a bit of storage space.

Check the Remaining Storage

As you snap pictures, keep track of the amount of storage remaining. Most cameras have a small LCD display (not to be confused with the LCD viewfinder) that shows the number of pictures you've taken and the available storage.

Copying Pictures to Your Computer

Digital cameras come with their own software that transfers the image files from the camera to your computer. In addition, the camera should include a cable for connecting to one of the ports on your PC (typically the serial port, although USB connections are becoming more common). Some digital cameras require a PC card reader.

To transfer the images, connect the cable to your camera and to the specified port. Refer to the camera and software's documentation to run the photo transfer utility and enter the command to retrieve the images. The program retrieves the images from the camera and displays them onscreen. The program will then delete the images from the PC card or other storage area or give you the option to have the images deleted.

Scanning Photos

Now, about those boxes of photos stashed in the attic: How do you digitize those old photos? Get a scanner. With a high-quality scanner and the accompanying software, you can pull photos and other images off prints and store them on your hard drive.

If you have a *flatbed* scanner, first position the image face down on the glass as specified in the scanner's documentation. Run the scan program that came with your scanner and click the button for initiating the scanning operation. This typically calls up a dialog box enabling you to enter color settings, specify the resolution, and mark the area you want to scan (see Figure 29.5).

If the dialog box has a button for previewing the image, click the button so you can select the area you want to scan. Don't be shocked if the preview looks bad; the preview area typically shows a low-resolution version of the image. Enter your preferences and click the **Scan** button to start scanning. The scanner digitizes the image and typically displays a thumbnail view of the image onscreen.

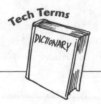

Scanner Types

Scanner types include handheld, which you drag over a picture manually; sheet-fed, in which you feed the photo into the scanner as you feed paper into a printer; and flatbed, which have a glass surface on which you lay the photo. Scanners' resolution, color depth, speed, connection type, and other features also vary. Shop carefully.

Choose the desired color setting.

Figure 29.5

Before you scan an image, select the area you want to scan and enter preferences for color and resolution.

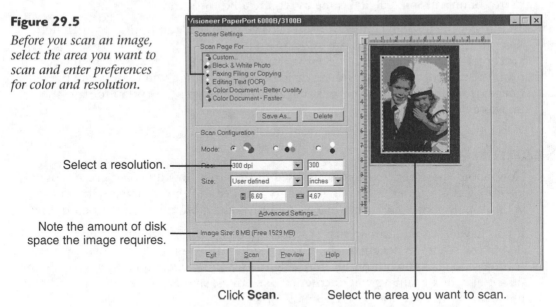

Select a resolution.

Note the amount of disk space the image requires.

Click **Scan**.　　　　Select the area you want to scan.

Some scan programs include tools for editing and enhancing the photos. If the program does not feature photo-editing tools or the tools are poorly designed, purchase a separate photo editor, such as Paint Shop Pro. You can download a shareware version of Paint Shop Pro from Jasc Software at `www.jasc.com/download.html`.

Computer Cheats

Scan at the Photo Shop

If you don't have a scanner, don't fret. You can take your photos to almost any photo shop or other store that develops film and scan them at the store. The scanner typically has a floppy drive or CD-RW, which can store the scanned images on a floppy disk or CD. Most of these photo scanners have built-in software for enhancing and editing the photos and a printer for creating high-quality prints.

Creating Your Own Digital Photo Album

Kodak Picture CD is a great tool for managing your *new* photos, but if you're scanning old prints, Picture CD offers little help. It doesn't allow you to import scanned images, enhance them, and combine them with Picture CD prints to create custom photo albums. To gain complete control over your photos, obtain a quality photo-management program, such as PhotoRecall.

With PhotoRecall, shown in Figure 29.6, you can create virtual photo albums and flip the pages onscreen. To pick up a free 30-day demonstration copy of PhotoRecall, go to **www.ga-imaging.com**.

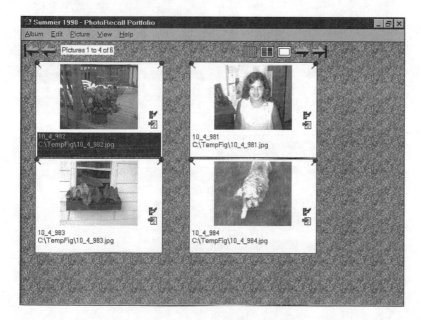

Figure 29.6

With PhotoRecall, you can create and print your own custom photo albums.

Changing Yourself and Others with Morphing

Are you feeling blue? Do you feel as though you need to do something drastic, like chop off your hair or run off with the UPS guy? Then, maybe you need a change. With a good morphing program, you can experience a complete body makeover without the risks of surgery. You simply take two pictures—before and after—and then tell the morphing program to morph the before picture into the after picture. You can then sit back and see your dumpy old self transformed into Brad Pitt or Cindy Crawford. Of course, you won't actually feel the change, but after you see the results, you might be happy just to be yourself.

Some photo-editing programs include morphing tools, but if you're looking for some professional results, try the following dedicated morphing programs:

➤ Elastic Reality by SoftImage (`www.softimage.com`) is one of the most powerful and precise morphing programs on the market. SoftImage's Web site offers a shareware version you can download.

➤ BitMorph by DC's Creation Software (`www.people.cornell.edu/pages/dmc27/`) is an easy-to-use morphing program that allows you to bend, stretch, and distort objects in an image, in addition to the standard morphing of one image into another. Get a shareware version of the program at DC's Web site.

➤ Morph Man by STOIK Software (`www.stoik.com`) not only morphs one image into another but can also morph an entire video clip into another video sequence. The shareware version, which you can download from STOIK's Web site, has the Save feature disabled, but it's fun to play with, anyway.

The Least You Need to Know

With your computer and the right add-ons, you can begin to organize your photo collection and use it in ways you never imagined you could. As you make the leap from negatives and prints to digitized images, keep the following in mind:

➤ When you drop off your next roll of film for developing, request a Kodak Picture CD.

➤ To run your Kodak Picture CD, pop it into your computer's CD-ROM drive and follow the onscreen instructions to install the software.

➤ To view a full-screen slideshow of your photos on a Kodak Picture CD, run the Picture CD software and click **View My Pictures**.

➤ You can use the Kodak Picture CD photo enhancement tools to adjust the brightness and contrast, sharpen the photo, trim extraneous areas of the photo, and eliminate the red-eye effect.

➤ A digital camera stores pictures on a memory card or disk instead of on film and enables you to copy the images to your computer.

➤ To digitize existing photo prints, scan the images using a color scanner and its accompanying software.

➤ To create and print custom photo albums, get a photo-management program, such as PhotoRecall.

Chapter 30

Drawing Your Family Tree

In This Chapter

➤ Buying the best genealogy program on the market

➤ Plugging in the information you know about your family

➤ Digging up more data from the CD-ROM collection

➤ Researching your roots on the Web

➤ Finding your long-lost relatives

➤ Getting help from other genealogy buffs

Although technology and industrialization have helped our society progress in many ways, they have weakened our family structure. We leave the towns and communities in which we grew up, dilute our cultures, and cut the ties that bind us to our closest relatives, all in the name of progress and independence. The nuclear family is set adrift, completely alienated from any sense of an extended family.

Sensing this loss, people increasingly have become more motivated to research their family history and trace their lineage. We want to know more about our parents, their siblings, and our parents' parents. We want to know what roles they played in human history. We're curious about how our ancestors lived and what they did. We crave to learn more about our heritage and better understand ourselves.

In the past, if you wanted a thorough report of your family's history, you needed to hire a professional genealogist to help. Now, with the assistance of a good genealogy program, you can perform the research yourself and reconstruct a detailed account of your family history for as far back as humans have been keeping records. This chapter shows you how to get started.

Picking a Good Genealogy Program

Not long ago, the genealogy software market consisted of one program—Family Tree Maker, which is still king of the hill. But is it still the best? That depends on what's most important to you: powerful research tools, ease of use, or low cost. When you look at those features, the choices become clear:

➤ **Family Tree Maker** offers the most robust collection of research tools and genealogy databases. This makes Family Tree Maker the top choice of serious genealogists. Because Family Tree Maker is the most popular genealogy program around, you can share data with a large population of users and work together to complete your tree. However, Family Tree Maker has a few drawbacks, including a poorly designed interface, poor handling of digitized photos, and additional expenses to access online genealogy services. Get more information at **www.broderbund.com**.

➤ **Generations Family Tree** is a user-friendly family tree program, providing simple tools for constructing and printing your family tree and incorporating photos. Family Tree's genealogy database is a little weak, however, making it more suiable for the weekend genealogist rather than professional researchers. Learn more about Generations Family Tree at **www.sierra.com/sierrahome/familytree/**.

Author MH

If the card absolutely refuses to go in its slot, it may be snagged on something else in your computer. Specifically, the backplane of the sound card may be snagging the back of the computer.

➤ **Ultimate Family Tree** is another powerful, yet user-friendly genealogy program that's excellent for laying out and printing a family tree. Ultimate Family Tree also makes great use of Internet tools to help you trace your lineage. Learn more about Ultimate Family Tree and pick up a free trial version at **www.uftree.com**.

➤ **Shareware programs**, such as My Family Tree (**huhnware.com/genealogy.htm**) and Fzip Family Tree (**www.ozemail.com.au**), are great if you have all the information you want to include in your family tree but need a tool to organize it.

Because Family Tree Maker is the most powerful and popular genealogy program on the market, this chapter uses it to illustrate the basic tasks you must perform to create your own family tree and map your family history.

Plugging In Names, Dates, and Relationships

The first step in creating a family tree is to enter data you already know. In most cases, you can safely enter your name, the names of your parents, and the names of your grandparents. Most genealogy programs can lead you through the process. Family Tree Maker, for instance, prompts you for some basic information the first timc you start the program. As shown in Figure 30.1, you must enter at least your own name to get started. Enter the requested information and click **Next**.

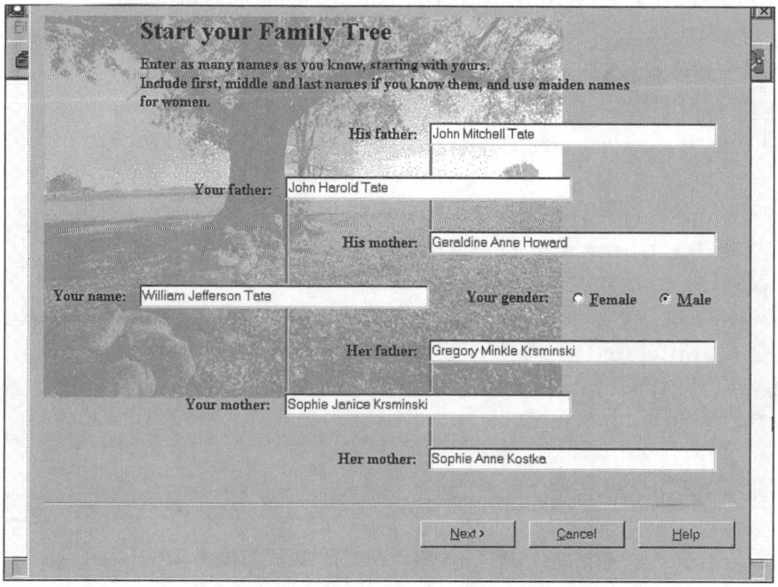

Figure 30.1

Start your family tree with a few simple entries and watch it grow.

After you enter a few names, click **Next** and Family Tree Maker prompts you to enter additional information about each person dangling from your tree, including each person's birth date and the geographical location in which they were born. You might be able to pick up some of this information by interviewing your living relatives, but if you can't find the information, don't worry—just fill in what you know. In the next few sections, you learn how to gather additional information.

Digging Up Your Roots with CD-ROM Databases

The top genealogy programs include 10 or more CDs packed with indexes, birth and death records, biographies, genealogies, military records, marriage indexes, immigration lists, land records, and even probate data. The Collector's Edition of Family Tree Maker comes with over 30 CDs! The first step in fleshing out your family tree is to search these CDs for information about the family members you have added to your family tree so far.

Of course, you can't shove the entire stack of CDs into your CD-ROM drive at one time. To make the stack of CDs more manageable, the first couple CDs include an index of everything on the CD collection. You pop in one of the index CDs, and enter the search command. The program uses the index to generate a catalog of pertinent information and prompts you to enter the other CDs in the collection as needed. Here's what you do in Family Tree Maker:

1. Click the **FamilyFinder Center** button in the Family Tree Maker toolbar. This displays the FamilyFinder page with links to several research tools.

2. Click **Run a FamilyFinder Search**. A FamilyFinder Cue Card appears, providing some tips on using FamilyFinder.

3. Read through the tips, if desired, and click **OK**. The Update FamilyFinder Report dialog box appears, asking whether you want to search online or search the FamilyFinder Index on CD (see Figure 30.2).

4. Click **CD FamilyFinder Index** and click **OK**. Family Tree Maker starts the search and prompts you to insert one of the index CDs.

5. Follow the onscreen instructions, inserting and swapping CDs as instructed. When you have fed Family Tree Maker all the CDs it asked for, the FamilyFinder Index returns a list of names that match the names you entered in your tree. (FamilyFinder ranks the matches with stars, a five-star match being the most promising.)

6. Click a name to view additional information.

Figure 30.2

FamilyFinder can search online or through the FamilyFinder Index.

Click **CD FamilyFinder Index**.

Click **OK**.

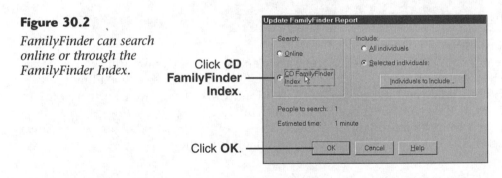

Researching Your Family Tree Online

Re-Search

After you have added for or five more people to your family tree, perform the FamilyFinder search again. The search is likely to return a list of additional matches.

Swapping 30 CDs in and out of your CD-ROM drive is no fun. Besides, by the time the company burns those CDs, they're already old and outdated. Where can you obtain the most comprehensive, up-to-date data? On the Web, of course. Many companies, including Broderbund and Sierra, have online databases to aid you in your search. In addition, many genealogy organizations and services maintain Web sites, bulletin boards, chat rooms, and other resources for genealogy buffs.

Searching Online with Family Tree Maker

The best way to search online is to go through your genealogy program. In most programs, you enter a single search instruction to search through multiple databases. In Family Tree, for instance, you take the following steps to perform a thorough Web search:

1. Click the **FamilyFinder Center** button in the Family Tree Maker toolbar. This displays the FamilyFinder page with links to several research tools.

2. Click **Run a FamilyFinder Search**. A FamilyFinder Cue Card appears, providing some tips on using FamilyFinder.

3. Read through the tips, if desired, and click **OK**. The Update FamilyFinder Report dialog box appears, asking whether you want to search online or search the FamilyFinder Index on CD.

4. Click **Online** and click **OK**. Family Tree Maker starts the search and might prompt you to establish an Internet connection. After connecting to the Internet, Family Tree Maker displays your browser window and then a dialog box showing the progress of the search. When the search is complete, the Search Results dialog box appears, displaying a summary of the results.

5. Click **OK** to close the Search Results dialog box and return to the main screen. If you performed a CD Index search earlier, the Internet search results are tacked onto the bottom of the report (see Figure 30.3).

6. Click the link to the far right of an entry to view information about the person. Family Tree Maker opens the corresponding page in your Web browser. (Most pages consist of information submitted from other Family Tree Maker users.)

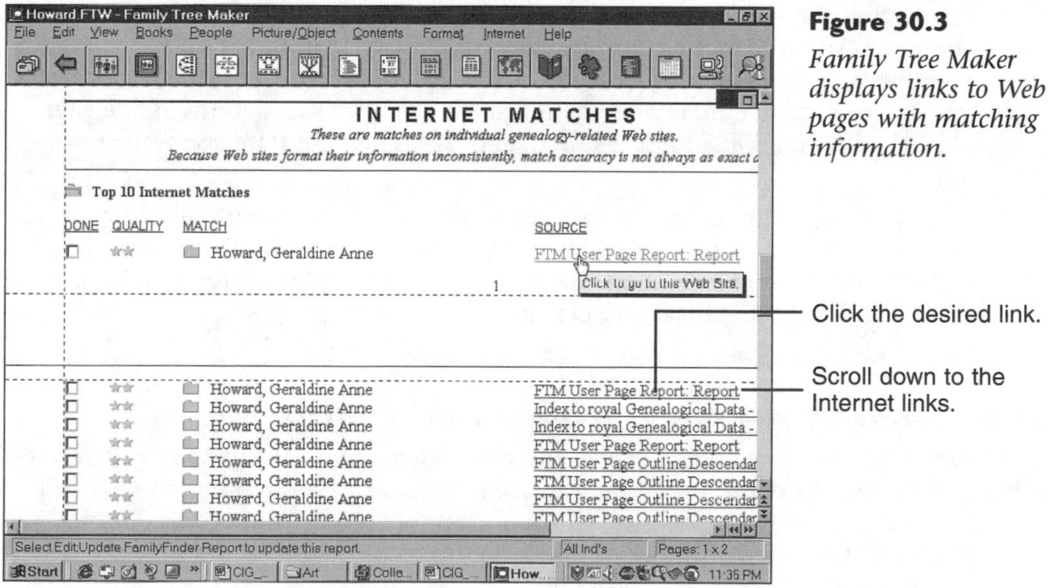

Figure 30.3

Family Tree Maker displays links to Web pages with matching information.

Click the desired link.

Scroll down to the Internet links.

Visiting Genealogy Web Sites

Even if you don't have a fancy family tree program, you can research your lineage on the Web. Many genealogy organizations and government agencies provide access to electronic databases that are publicly accessible. Some are even free. To take advantage of the Internet for family research, check out the following sites:

➤ Ancestry.com, at **www.ancestry.com**, is one of the best places to start your search. The home page greets you with a simple search form prompting you to enter a name. The search pulls up links to several free databases (such as a Social Security death index and telephone/address listings), as shown in Figure 30.4.

➤ Genealogy.com, at **www.genealogy.com**, is a great place for digging up information. Here, you can perform a search that sifts through several online databases and points you to the sources. This site also offers links to additional genealogy guides, tips, message boards, and other resources.

➤ Gensource.com, at **www.gensource.com**, provides another search tool that's a little less comprehensive, but returns a list of links that point you to other people on the Web who might be researching the same lineage. You might connect with someone who has already done much of your homework.

➤ FamilySearch, at **www.familysearch.org** (developed and maintained by the Church of Jesus Christ of Latter-day Saints), has the most interesting search form of the bunch, allowing you to type entries for an entire branch of your family tree. If the search returns no matches, try entering only a last name.

➤ GENDEX, at **www.gendex.com:8080**, is a genealogy site that indexes entries for numerous genealogy databases and makes the entries available via a single search. GENDEX offers free and member-only search options.

➤ GenExchange & Surname Registry, at **www.genexchange.com**, is one of the two or three largest, noncommercial genealogy database organizations on the Web. GenExchange is maintained and developed by volunteers to make genealogical data freely available to any and all researchers. After you reach the home page, click the link for performing a search, and then click the state you want to search.

➤ The Genealogy Home Page, at **www.genhomepage.com**, is a great place to go when you've hit a dead end or exhausted the resources listed here. This site features links to hundreds of helpful genealogy guides, mailing lists, search tools, organizations, maps, commercial services, and much more.

Getting Advice via Newsgroups and Email

A good genealogist is a good detective, and a good detective talks to people. If you're lucky, you'll find all the information you need by poking around on a few CDs and cruising genealogy sites on the Web. In most cases, however, you need to do some interviews and trace down people who have better records (and a better memory) than you have.

Figure 30.4

Ancestry.com can give you a good collection of leads.

Although the phone is still an excellent tool for contacting people directly, newsgroups (message boards) and email provide another avenue. As you research your family lineage, record email addresses you encounter and write to people who are researching the same surname or lineage. You should also check out the following newsgroups: `soc.genealogy.misc`, `soc.genealogy.methods`, `soc.genealogy.surnames.usa`, and `soc.genealogy.surnames.misc`. You can use Outlook Express, Netscape Messenger, or another newsreader to connect to these newsgroups.

Another great way to keep up on the latest information is to subscribe to Internet mailing lists. Go to The Genealogy Home Page at `www.genhomepage.com` for information on how to subscribe to hundreds of mailing lists. Many mailing lists are maintained by individuals who are searching for information about a particular surname (last name). If you're lucky, you'll find a mailing list devoted specifically to the family you're researching.

You can also learn more about genealogy and make some contacts through chat rooms and online clubs. America Online and other commercial online services host chat rooms devoted to genealogy topics. Yahoo! hosts more than 1,000 genealogy clubs at `clubs.yahoo.com/Family___Home/Genealogy/`. Also, check out the chat rooms at GenForum (`chat.genforum.com`). To find additional chat sites, use your favorite Web search tool to look for "genealogy chat."

Inside Tip

Message Boards on the Web

If you don't want to mess with a newsreader, check out some message boards on the Web at `genforum.genealogy.com`. One of the best genealogy message boards I've found is Genchat (`chat.genealogy.org`).

Tracking Down Lost Relatives

When you lose contact with your relatives, through divorce, adoption, or just plain lack of trying, you might need to start doing a little good old-fashioned detective work. Keep in mind that most telephone books are accessible on the Internet. If you have a unique last name, go to **people.yahoo.com** or another people search page on the Web and search email and phone book listings for your last name. Try contacting prospective relatives individually. You might just find someone who knows your family! (See Chapter 20, "Poking Around on the Web," for more information.)

If you're having little luck on your own, get some professional help. Private eyes and genealogy researchers abound on the Internet. For about 40 bucks, you can hire a firm such as Find People Fast (**www.fpf.com**) or (**www.1800ussearch.com**) to do an individual or family name search for you.

Growing Your Family Tree

As you gather data and shake a few more individuals out of your family tree, you can start expanding your tree. Your genealogy program has the tools you need to add entries. In Family Tree Maker, for instance, you take the following steps to add entries to your family tree:

1. Click the **Family Page** button, as shown in Figure 30.5. A tabbed "book" appears, displaying the names of the people already entered in your family tree.

Whoa!

Back Up Your File First

Before you append or merge family trees, back up your original file using the **File, Backup Family File** command. Grafting a branch to another family tree has been known to cause problems.

2. Click a person's name to display the page of information about that person. The person's information page appears, and a "Parents of" tab appears for entering information about the parents of the selected individual. This tab appears regardless of whether or not you entered information about the person's parents.

3. To enter additional information about the selected individual, type the information in the appropriate text boxes.

4. To add information about the parents of the individual, click the **Parents of...** tab, and type the information you have obtained. (This enables you to add people to the tree.)

As you research your family history, you might meet someone who has a branch of your family tree that feeds into your own tree. In such a case, you can graft (append) that branch to your tree—assuming you can get the person to send you his or her Family Tree Maker file.

To append a branch, open your family file, and then choose the **File, Append/Merge Family File** command. This displays a dialog box prompting you to select the file. Change to the disk and folder in which the file is stored and double-click its name. Follow the onscreen instructions to complete the process.

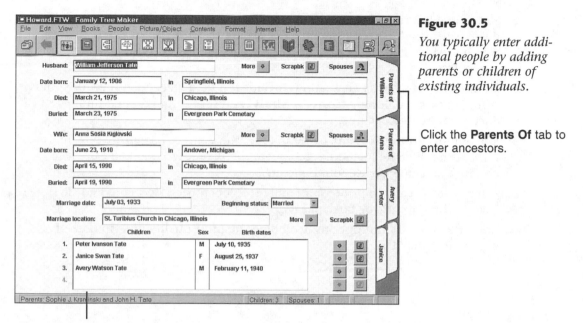

Figure 30.5

You typically enter additional people by adding parents or children of existing individuals.

Click the **Parents Of** tab to enter ancestors.

Enter direct descendants (children) here.

Printing Your Family Tree

At some point in the process, you will want to print your family tree to frame it, pass it along to interested relatives, or file it for your own records. Because family trees can be so complex, not to mention enormous, the printing operation is critical and contains several options for fitting the tree on paper. In Family Tree Maker, for instance, you must pick a tree type and then enter the Print command:

1. Open the **View** menu and click the desired family tree type:

   All-in-one Tree displays you and all of your relatives in one continuous tree.

   Ancestor Tree shows the pedigree of the selected individual (the person's parents, grandparents, great-grandparents, and so on, omitting brothers, sisters, uncles, and aunts) .

   Descendant Tree shows the selected individual's children, grandchildren, great-grandchildren, and so on.

   Hourglass Tree shows the upward and downward lineage of the selected individual. In other words, the selected individual appears in the center with parents, grandparents, and so on branching out from the top and children, grandchildren, and so on branching out from the bottom.

Outline Descendant Tree is a space-saving descendant tree. Instead of displaying a box for each person, the tree displays offspring in text-only outline view.

2. To include information other than each person's name, birth date, and date of death, open the **Contents** menu, click **Items to Include in Each Box**, and use the resulting dialog box to specify the data you want to include in your family tree.

3. To limit the number of generations included in your tree, open the **Contents** menu, click **# of Generations to Show**, and specify the desired number of ancestors and descendants.

4. Use options on the **Format** menu to enter the desired formatting preferences for your family tree, including the font and box border type. You can even choose to include a background picture.

5. When you're ready to print your family tree, open the **File** menu and click **Print**. The Print dialog box appears.

6. Enter the desired print options, including the print quality and number of copies, and click **OK**.

Printing Bigger Trees

Cramming a large family tree on 8.5-by-11-inch sheets of paper is like growing an oak tree in a glass house. To make your family tree fit, consider printing it as a banner or taking your file to a professional printer to have it rendered by a plotter. If you choose to print on a banner, you must change the print settings for your printer. To access your printer settings, choose **Start**, **Settings**, **Printers**, right-click the icon for your printer, and choose **Properties**.

The Least You Need to Know

When you start shaking your family tree, you never know who's going to fall out of it, and that's half the fun of doing research. As you set out on a quest to discover your roots, don't lose sight of the basics:

➤ Get yourself a good genealogy program, such as Family Tree Maker, and learn how to use it.

➤ When you first start Family Tree Maker, it leads you through the process of recording information about a few of your closest relatives.

➤ Use the search tools in your genealogy program to search through the database CDs included with most programs.

➤ Use the Internet search commands in your genealogy program to perform more thorough searches of up-to-date databases.

➤ Even if you don't have a fancy genealogy program, you can explore your roots at such sites as www.ancestry.com.

➤ If you're having trouble tracking down long-lost relatives, try a professional service such as www.1800ussearch.com.

➤ Before you print your family tree in Family Tree Maker, check out the options on the View, Contents, and Format menus for options on laying out your family tree.

Part 7

Maintaining Your Investment

You don't need to be a mechanic to use a computer, but you should perform some basic maintenance tasks on a regular basis to keep your computer in tip-top condition.

This part acts as your computer maintenance manual. Here you learn how to clean your monitor, keyboard, mouse, printer, and system unit and give your computer a regular tune-up to keep it running at top speed.

Chapter 31

Keeping Your Computer Clean

In This Chapter

➤ Sucking the dust from your computer

➤ Squeegeeing your monitor

➤ Picking hair and other gunk out of your mouse

➤ Keeping your printer shiny and new

➤ Spin-cleaning your disk drives

I live in an old and dusty house. Cobwebs hang from the ceiling, and dust bunnies scurry across the hardwood floors. Fortunately, I have one of the best clean-air machines on the market—a computer. The cooling fan in my computer constantly sucks in the dusty air and filters out the dust. My monitor acts like a dust magnet, pulling in any airborne particles unfortunate enough to get close to it. And my keyboard and mouse are great for picking up crumbs and other debris that happens to accumulate on my desk.

Unfortunately, in keeping my work environment clean, my computer risks its own health. The dust and smoke that my computer filters out eventually deposits itself on the mechanical and electrical components inside of it. The dust on the monitor makes my screen look gray, and the dust on my printer (mixed with a little lubricant) creates a sludge that gunks up its innards. And as my mouse and keyboard collect hair and crumbs, they start to stick and behave erratically.

To keep your computer in tip-top condition, clean it regularly. This chapter shows you just what to do.

Tools of the Trade

Before you start cleaning, turn off your computer and any attached devices, and gather the following cleaning equipment:

➤ **Screwdriver** or **wrench** for taking the cover off of your system unit. (If you don't feel comfortable going inside the system unit, take your computer to a qualified technician for a thorough annual cleaning. It really does get dusty in there.)

➤ **Computer vacuum**. Yes, they have vacuum cleaners especially designed for computers.

➤ **Can of compressed air**. You can get this at a computer or electronics store. If you decide to forego the vacuum cleaner, you can use the compressed air to blow dust out of the system unit.

➤ **Soft brush** (a clean paintbrush with soft bristles will do). Use the brush to dislodge any stubborn dust that the vacuum won't pick up.

➤ **Toothpicks** (the only tool you need to clean your mouse).

➤ **Cotton swabs**.

➤ **Paper towel**.

➤ **Alcohol** (not the drinking kind, save that for when you're done).

➤ **Distilled water**. (You can get special wipes for your monitor, but paper towels and water do the trick.)

➤ **Radio or CD player**. (When you're cleaning, you need music.)

Don't run out and buy a floppy disk or CD-ROM cleaning kit. If your drive is having trouble reading disks, then clean it. If it's running smoothly, let it be.

Vacuuming and Dusting Your Computer

Work from the top down and from the outside in. Start with the monitor. (You can use your regular vacuum cleaner for this part; if you have a brush attachment, use it.) Get your vacuum hose and run it up and down all the slots at the top and sides of the monitor. This is where most of the dust settles. Work down to the tilt-swivel base and vacuum that (you might need a narrow hose extension to reach in there). Now, vacuum your printer, speakers, and any other devices. If the dust is stuck to a device, wipe it off with a damp (not soaking wet) paper towel.

Now for the system unit. When vacuuming, be sure that you vacuum all the ventilation holes, including the floppy disk drive, power button, CD-ROM drive, open drive bays, and so on. If you have a CD-ROM drive, open it and gently vacuum the tray.

Now for the tough part—inside the system unit. Before you poke your vacuum hose in there, you should be aware of the following precautions:

➤ Shut down your computer, turn it off, and unplug the system unit, monitor, printer, and other devices.

➤ Use only a vacuum designed for computers or use a can of compressed air to blow out the dust. Don't use a Dust Buster, your regular vacuum cleaner, or your ShopVac. These can suck components off your circuit boards and can emit enough static electricity to fry a component. A computer vacuum is gentle and grounded.

➤ Be careful around circuit boards. A strong vacuum can suck components and jumpers right off the boards. Also be careful not to suck up any loose screws.

➤ Touch a metal part of the case to discharge any static electricity from your body, and keep your fingers away from the circuit boards.

Cheap Air Filter

Some PCs have a fan that pulls air from the outside and pushes it through the ventilation holes. If the system unit case has openings near the fan, cut a square of sheer hosiery fabric, stretch it over the openings, and tape it in place with duct tape, keeping the tape away from the openings. Check the filter regularly and replace it whenever dust builds up.

Now, take the cover off the system unit and vacuum any dusty areas. Dust likes to collect around the fan, ventilation holes, and disk drives. Try to vacuum the fan blades, too. If you can't get the tip of the vacuum between the blades, gently wipe them off with a cotton swab. Some fans have a filter where the fan is mounted. If you're really ambitious, remove the fan (careful with the wires) and clean the filter.

WASH ME: Cleaning Your Monitor

If you can write "WASH ME" on your monitor with your fingertip, the monitor needs cleaning. Check the documentation that came with your computer or monitor to see whether it's okay to use window cleaner on it—the monitor might have an antiglare coating that can be damaged by alcohol- or ammonia-based cleaning solutions. (If it's not okay, use water.) Spray the window cleaner (or water) on a paper towel, just enough to make it damp, and then wipe the screen. DON'T spray window cleaner or any other liquid directly on the monitor; you don't want moisture to seep in. You can purchase special antistatic wipes for your monitor. These not only clean your monitor safely, but they also discharge the static electricity to prevent future dust buildup.

Shaking the Crumbs Out of Your Keyboard

Your keyboard is like a big placemat, catching all the cookie crumbs and other debris that fall off your fingers while you're working. The trouble is that, unlike a placemat, the keyboard isn't flat; it's full of crannies that are impossible to reach. And the suction from a typical vacuum cleaner just isn't strong enough to pull up the dust (although you can try it).

The easiest way I've found to clean a keyboard is to turn it upside-down and shake it gently. Repeat two or three times to get any particles that fall behind the backs of the keys when you flip it over. If you don't like that idea, get your handy-dandy can of compressed air and blow between the keys.

For a more thorough cleaning, shut down your computer, and disconnect the keyboard. Dampen a cotton swab with rubbing alcohol and gently scrub the keys. Wait for the alcohol to evaporate before reconnecting the keyboard and turning on the power.

Cheap Trick

If you don't want to waste your money on antistatic wipes, wipe your monitor with a used dryer sheet. (A new dryer sheet might smudge the screen with fabric softener.)

Thrills and Spills

If you spill a drink on your keyboard, try to save your work and shut down the computer fast, but properly. Flip the keyboard over and turn off your computer. If you spilled water, just let the keyboard dry out thoroughly. If you spilled something sticky, give your keyboard a bath or shower with lukewarm water. Take the back off the keyboard, but do not flip the keyboard over with the back off or parts will scurry across your desktop. Let it dry for a couple of days (don't use a blow-dryer), and put it back together. If some of the keys are still sticky, clean around them with a cotton swab dipped in rubbing alcohol. If you still have problems, buy a new keyboard; they're relatively inexpensive.

Making Your Mouse Cough Up Hairballs

If you can't get your mouse pointer to move where you want it to, you can usually fix the problem by cleaning the mouse. Flip the mouse over and look for hair or other debris on the mouse ball or on your desk or mouse pad. Removing the hair or wiping off your mouse pad fixes the problem ninety percent of the time.

If that doesn't work, remove the mouse ball cover (typically, you press down on the cover and turn counterclockwise). Wipe the ball thoroughly with a moistened paper towel. Now for the fun part. Look inside the mouse (where the ball was). You should see three rollers, each with a tiny ring around its middle. The ring is not supposed to be there. The easiest way I've found to remove these rings is to gently scrape them off with a toothpick. You have to spin the rollers to remove the entire ring. You can also try rubbing the rings off with a cotton swab dipped in rubbing alcohol, but these rings are pretty stubborn. When you're done, turn the mouse back over and shake it to remove the loose crumbs. Reassemble the mouse.

Cleaning Your Printer (When It Needs It)

Printer maintenance varies widely from one printer to another. If you have a laser printer, you need to vacuum or wipe up toner dust and clean the little print wires with cotton swabs dipped in rubbing alcohol. For an inkjet printer, you might have to remove the print cartridge and wipe the print heads with a damp cotton swab. If you have a combination scanner/printer, you might have to wipe the glass on which you place your original. Be sure to check the documentation that came with your printer for cleaning and maintenance suggestions.

You also need to be careful about the cleaning solution you use. Most printer manufacturers tell you to use only water on the inside parts—print rollers, print heads, and so on. In other cases, you can use a mild cleaning solution. Some manufacturers recommend rubbing alcohol on some, not all, parts.

Even with these variables, there are a few things the average user can do to keep the printer in peak condition and ensure high-quality output:

➤ When turning off the printer, always use the power button on the printer (don't use the power button on your power strip) or press the Online button to take the printer offline. This ensures that the print head is moved to its rest position. On inkjet printers, this prevents the print head from drying out.

➤ Vacuum inside the printer. Open any doors or covers to get inside.

➤ If the ink starts to streak on your printouts (or you have frequent paper jams in a laser printer), get special printer-cleaner paper from an office supply store and follow the instructions to run the sheet through your printer a few times.

➤ Using a damp cotton ball, wipe paper dust and any ink off the paper feed rollers. Do not use alcohol. Do not use a paper towel; fibers from the paper towel could stick to the wheels.

> ### Rubbing Alcohol Rule of Thumb
>
> Rubbing alcohol is an excellent cleaning solution for most electronic devices, because it cleans well and dries quickly. Use it for your keyboard, plastics, and most glass surfaces (except for some monitors). Avoid using it on rubber (for example, your mouse ball), because it tends to dry out the rubber and make it crack.

What About the Disk Drives?

Don't bother cleaning your floppy or CD-ROM drives unless they're giving you trouble. If your CD-ROM drive is having trouble reading a disc, the disc is usually the cause of the problem. Clean the disc and check the bottom of the disc for scratches. If the drive has problems reading every CD you insert, then try cleaning the drive using a special CD-ROM drive cleaning kit. The kit usually consists of a CD with some cleaning solution; you squirt the cleaning solution on the CD, insert it, remove it, and your job is done.

If you have a floppy disk drive that has trouble reading any disk you insert, you can purchase a special cleaning kit that works like the CD-ROM cleaning kit. Although cleaning the disk drive might solve the problem, the problem can also be caused by a poorly aligned read/write head inside the drive, which no cleaning kit can correct.

The Least You Need to Know

Now that you know all about computer maintenance, you can save yourself 50 bucks on the maintenance agreement. Just be sure you do the following maintenance regularly:

➤ Vacuum your system, especially around its ventilation holes.

➤ Wipe the dust off your screen using a paper towel and the cleaning solution recommended by the manufacturer.

➤ Blow the crumbs out of your keyboard with compressed air.

➤ Remove those nasty mouse rings with a toothpick.

➤ Vacuum any ink dust that accumulates inside your printer.

➤ Clean your floppy or CD-ROM drive if it is having trouble reading disks.

Chapter 32

Giving Your Computer a Tune-Up

In This Chapter

➤ Clear useless files off your hard disk

➤ Streamline the Windows startup

➤ Repair hard disk storage problems with ScanDisk

➤ Double your disk space without installing a new drive

➤ Get more memory without installing more RAM

Over time, you will notice that your computer has slowed down. Windows takes a little longer to start up. Programs that used to snap into action now seem to crawl. Scrolling becomes choppy. Your computer locks up almost every day. You might begin to think that you need a new processor, more RAM, a larger hard disk drive, or a whole new computer altogether.

Before you take such drastic action, work through this chapter to give your computer a tune-up. By clearing useless files from your disk drive, reorganizing files, and reclaiming some of your computer's existing memory, you can boost your computer's performance and save a lot of money at the same time.

One-Stop Optimization with the Maintenance Wizard

The Windows Maintenance Wizard (included with Windows 98) can help you keep your computer in tip-top condition. It automatically performs a series of tests and corrections at a scheduled time to check for problems on your hard disk, defragment files, delete temporary files, remove programs from the StartUp menu, and optimize your hard disk.

With the Windows Maintenance Wizard, you rarely have to go behind-the-scenes with Windows to perform these tasks manually, as explained later in this chapter.

To run the Wizard, take the following steps:

1. Click the **Start** button, point to **Programs, Accessories, System Tools**, and click **Maintenance Wizard**.

2. Click **Express** and click **Next**. Express tells the Wizard to delete temporary files and Web files from your hard disk, optimize your hard disk, and check it for errors, but Express does not tell the wizard to remove programs from the StartUp menu.

3. Click the desired time (a time when you normally have your computer on but are not using it) and click **Next**.

4. The Wizard displays a list of optimization activities it performs at the scheduled time(s). To have the Wizard perform these activities now, choose **When I Click Finish...**.

5. Click the **Finish** button, as shown in Figure 32.1. Be sure to leave your computer on at the scheduled time so that Windows can perform the optimization activities at the scheduled time(s).

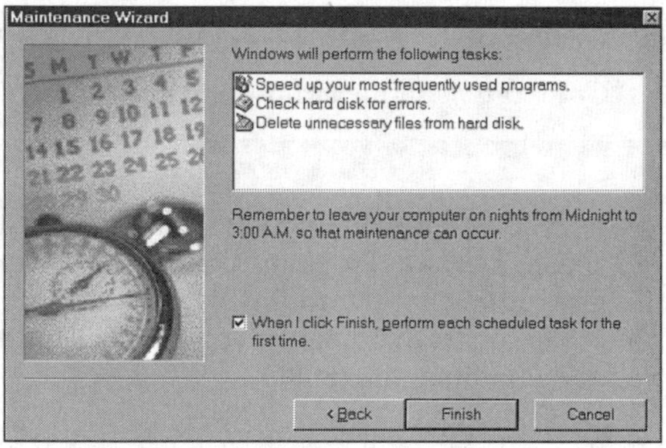

Figure 32.1

The Windows Maintenance Wizard optimizes your system on schedule.

Clearing Useless Files from Your Hard Disk

Your hard disk probably contains temporary and backup files that your programs create without telling you. These files can quickly clutter your hard disk drive, taking room that you need for new programs or new data files that you create. You can easily delete most of these files yourself.

The first candidates for removal are temporary (TMP) files. These are files that your programs create but often forget to delete. You can safely delete all temporary files from your hard drive. Click the Windows **Start** button, point to **Find**, and click **Files or Folders**. Type ***.tmp** and press **Enter**. Press **Ctrl+A** to select all the files, and then press **Shift+Delete**. Gone! You should now have an extra megabyte or more of disk space. (Windows might not be able to delete some TMP files that it is currently using.)

Deleting Backup Files

When you save a file that you created, most programs create a backup file that contains the previous version of the file. These files typically have the BAK extension. If you mess up a file, you can open the backup file instead. Before deleting backup files, be sure you don't want the previous versions of your files.

To remove temporary files that your Web browser saves, clear the disk cache in your browser. To clear the disk cache in Internet Explorer, open the **View** or **Tools** menu and click **Internet Options**. Under Temporary Internet Files, click the **Delete Files** button. In Navigator, open the **Edit** menu, click **Preferences**, click the plus sign next to **Advanced**, click **Cache**, and click the **Clear Disk Cache** button.

While you're at it, open your email program and delete any email messages you no longer need. When you delete email messages, some email programs, such as Outlook Express, stick the deleted messages in a separate folder (called Deleted Items in Outlook Express); be sure to delete the messages from that folder, as well.

Now, most of the stuff you deleted is sitting in the Recycle Bin, where it is still hogging disk space. First, open the Recycle Bin, and scroll down the list of deleted files to be sure you will never ever again need anything in the Bin. If you find a file that you might need, drag it onto the Windows desktop for safekeeping. Now, open the **File** menu and click **Empty Recycle Bin**.

Checking for and Repairing Damaged Files and Folders

Windows comes with a utility called ScanDisk that can test a disk (hard or floppy), repair most problems on a disk, and refresh the disk, if needed. What kind of problems? ScanDisk can find defective areas on a disk and block them out to prevent your computer from using defective storage areas. ScanDisk can also find and delete misplaced (usually useless) file fragments that might be causing your computer to crash.

You should run ScanDisk regularly (at least once every month) and whenever your computer seems to be acting up (crashing for no apparent reason). Also, if you have a floppy disk that your computer cannot read, ScanDisk might be able to repair the disk and recover any data from it. To run ScanDisk, take the following steps:

1. Open the **Start** menu, point to **Programs**, **Accessories**, and **System Tools**, and then click **ScanDisk**. The ScanDisk window appears.

2. Click the letter of the drive you want ScanDisk to check, as shown in Figure 32.2.

3. To check for and repair only file and folder errors, click the **Standard** option; to check the disk for defects (in addition to file and folder errors), click **Thorough**. (Thorough can take hours; select it only if you're on your way to bed.)

4. If you want ScanDisk to fix any errors without asking for your confirmation, be sure that **Automatically Fix Errors** is checked. (I always choose this option and have never encountered problems with ScanDisk doing something it was not supposed to do.)

5. Click the **Start** button.

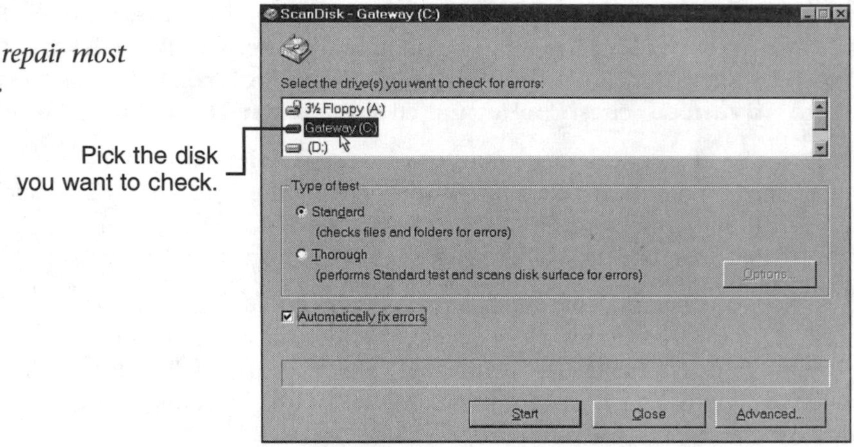

Figure 32.2

ScanDisk can repair most disk problems.

Pick the disk you want to check.

Defragmenting Files on Your Hard Disk

Whenever you delete a file from your hard disk, you leave a space where another file can be stored. When you save a file, your computer stores as much of the file as possible in that empty space, and the rest of the file in other empty spaces. The file is then said to be *fragmented*, because its parts are stored in different locations on the disk. This slows down your disk drive and makes it more likely that your computer will lose track of a portion of the file or the entire file.

ScanDisk Is Running on Startup!

If Windows shuts down improperly (if you press the power button on your system unit before Windows is ready, the power goes out, or Windows locks up), Windows might run ScanDisk automatically when you restart your computer. It reminds you to shut down properly next time, even though it's usually not your fault.

Every month or so, you should run a defragmentation program to determine the fragmentation percent and to defragment your files, if necessary. If you ran the Maintenance Wizard, as explained earlier in this chapter, Windows Disk Defragmenter automatically performs the operation at the scheduled time. If you did not run the Maintenance Wizard, you can run Disk Defragmenter yourself.

To have Disk Defragmenter defragment your files, take the following steps:

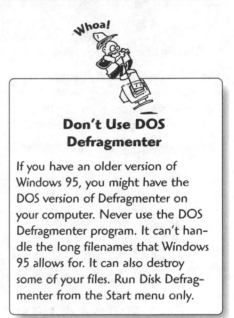

Don't Use DOS Defragmenter

If you have an older version of Windows 95, you might have the DOS version of Defragmenter on your computer. Never use the DOS Defragmenter program. It can't handle the long filenames that Windows 95 allows for. It can also destroy some of your files. Run Disk Defragmenter from the Start menu only.

1. Open the **Start** menu, point to **Programs**, **Accessories**, **System Tools**, and click **Disk Defragmenter**. A dialog box appears, asking which disk drive you want to defragment.

2. Open the **Which Drive Do You Want to Defragment?** drop-down list, and click the desired disk. You can defragment all your disks by clicking **All Hard Drives**, as shown in Figure 32.3. (You don't need to defragment floppy disks.)

3. Click **OK**. Another dialog box appears, indicating both the percent of file fragmentation on the disk and whether or not you need to defragment the disk.

4. Click the **Start** button. Defragmenter starts to defragment the files on the disk.

5. Wait until the defragmentation is complete. It's best to leave your computer alone during the process, because this might change a file and cause Defragmenter to start over. Don't run any programs or play any computer games.

Figure 32.3

You can defragment any or all of your disks.

Click the disk you want to defragment, or click **All Hard Drives**.

Select Drive

Which drive do you want to defragment?

💾 Drive C	Physical drive
💾 Drive D	Physical drive
💾 Drive E	Physical drive
💾 Drive F	Physical drive
💾 All Hard Drives	

Intel Application Launch Accelerator

intel Optimizers

| OK | Exit | Settings... |

Inside Tip

Configure Defragmenter

The Advanced or Settings button in the opening Disk Defragmenter dialog box enables you to specify how you want Defragmenter to proceed.

Making Windows Start Faster

Windows is a slow starter, even on a quick machine. If you have some power-saving features on your computer, you can make Windows start a lot faster. Instead of turning your PC off and on, use the **Power** or **Power Management** icon in the Control Panel to have Windows put your PC in sleep mode when you're not using it. Then, you can quickly restart by pressing **Enter** or rolling the mouse around.

If your computer has advanced power-saving features, you might also be able to shut down your computer by placing it in Standby mode. When you're done for the day, click the **Start** button and click **Shut Down**. In the Shut Down dialog box, click **Stand By** and click **OK**. To restart your computer, press the **Shift** key.

If you need to turn your computer completely off, or you just like to, try the following to reduce the startup time:

➤ To prevent Windows from running programs on the StartUp menu, hold down the **Shift** key right after you log on to Windows. If you don't log on to Windows, press and hold **Shift** when you see the Windows splash screen (the screen that appears before you get to the desktop).

➤ To remove programs from the StartUp menu, right-click the taskbar, click **Properties**, click the **Start Menu Programs** tab, click the **Remove** button, and click the plus sign next to **StartUp**. Click the program you want to remove and click the **Remove** button. (Careful, if you have an antivirus program that runs on startup, you might want to keep it on the StartUp menu.)

➤ To quickly restart Windows without restarting your computer, click **Start**, **Shut Down**, and click **Restart**. Hold down the **Shift** key while clicking **Yes** or **OK**.

If you have Internet Explorer on your computer, and you have your Windows desktop displayed as a Web page, the active desktop components can add a lot of time to the Windows startup. If you don't use the desktop components, turn them off.

Right-click a blank area of the desktop, point to **Active Desktop**, and choose **Customize My Desktop**. Remove the check mark next to every desktop component and click **OK**. Also, consider turning off View As Web Page; right-click the desktop, point to **Active Desktop**, and, if **View As Web Page** is checked, click the option to remove the check mark.

Change Your BIOS Settings

Every computer comes with a set of startup instructions, called the BIOS (Basic Input/Output System). These instructions include boot settings that can make your computer start faster. For instance, you can enter a setting to have your computer start directly from drive C (instead of checking drive A first). Check the startup screen or your computer's manual for instructions on accessing the BIOS settings, but don't change any settings you are unsure of.

Boosting Performance with Shareware Utilities

Does your 56Kbps modem seem slow? Does Windows frequently lock up or display the insufficient memory message, even though your computer has over 64MB of RAM and plenty of free disk space? Has your computer's performance become so degraded that you just can't stand using your computer for another day? Then, it's time to bring out the big guns—utility programs designed to optimize your computer automatically.

Following is a list of shareware programs along with information on where to find out more about them and where to go to download the latest version:

➤ **MemTurbo** is a memory (RAM) optimizer. When you exit some programs, they fail to free up the memory they were using, reducing the amount of free memory available to other programs. MemTurbo reclaims this memory, as shown in Figure 32.4, to make programs run faster and prevent Windows from locking up. Find out more about MemTurbo and download a trial version at `www.memturbo.com`.

➤ **WinOptimizer** is designed to pick up where the Windows Maintenance Wizard leaves off. It clears redundant, duplicate files from your system and streamlines the Windows Registry to boost overall system performance. Learn more about WinOptimizer and pick up a shareware version of the program at `www.ashampoo.com`.

➤ **TweakDUN** is an Internet connection optimizer for Windows. It automatically adjusts the Windows Dial-Up Networking settings to make Windows transfer data more efficiently over a modem connection. If you're using a 56Kbps modem and aren't ready to move up to an ISDN or DSL connection, TweakDUN can improve your current connection speed. Check it out at **www.pattersondesigns.com/tweakdun**. (You should also check out Download Accelerator at **www.speedbit.com**.)

➤ **SiSoft Sandra** is a system information utility that provides a complete inventory of your system's resources. Sandra shows you the type and speed of the processor, the amount of memory, the amount of free storage space, the monitor make and model, and descriptions of all installed peripherals. When you want to know more about your computer, check out Sandra at **www.sisoftware.demon. co.uk/sandra/**.

Figure 32.4

MemTurbo reclaims memory from selfish programs.

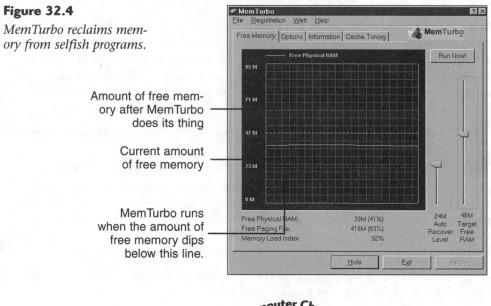

Amount of free memory after MemTurbo does its thing

Current amount of free memory

MemTurbo runs when the amount of free memory dips below this line.

Computer Cheats

Reclaim Memory for Free

If you don't have a utility for reclaiming memory, shut down Windows and restart your computer. You might need to do this every day or two to keep your computer running smoothly.

The Least You Need to Know

As you can see, you can do a lot to keep your computer tuned; however, if you like to do as little as necessary to keep your computer in shape, be sure you do the following regularly:

➤ If you have Windows 98, use the Windows Maintenance Wizard to schedule regular tune-ups.

➤ Clear temporary files, old email messages, and temporary Internet files from your hard disk, and don't forget to dump the Recycle Bin.

➤ To avoid system crashes and lost files, run ScanDisk and Disk Defragmenter at least once every month.

➤ Defragment files on your hard disk, if needed.

➤ If you have an older computer that you're not ready to upgrade or replace, obtain a set of utilities for optimizing performance.

➤ If your computer seems to be running slowly, exit all programs and restart Windows to clear your computer's memory.

Speak Like a Geek

When you flip through computer documentation, books, and magazines, you might begin to feel as though you just stepped into the tomb of King Tut. How do you interpret the hieroglyphics stamped on your computer? How do you make sense of all the cryptic terms? Where can you get translations for the most common acronyms?

Well, you've come to the right place. Although this limited glossary can't possibly cover all the gobbledygook you'll encounter, it does define enough basic terms to get you through your next job interview.

application   Also known as *program,* a set of instructions that enable a computer to perform a specific task, such as word processing or data management. An application can also be a collection of programs, called a suite.

ASCII file   A file containing characters that any program on any computer can use. Sometimes called a text file or an ASCII text file. (ASCII is pronounced "ASK-key.")

attachment   A file that's tacked on to an email message. Attachments enable users to exchange files without having to use disks.

BIOS (basic input/output system)   The BIOS, pronounced "BUY-ose," is the built-in set of instructions that tell the computer how to control the disk drives, keyboard, printer port, and other components that make up your computer.

bit   The basic unit of data in a computer. A computer's alphabet consists of two characters—1 and 0. 1 stands for on, and 0 stands for off. Bits are combined in sets of eight to form real characters, such as A, B, C, and D. See also *byte*.

bits per second   A unit for measuring the speed of data transmission. Remember that it takes 8 bits to make a byte (the equivalent of a single character). Modems have common bps ratings of 28,800 to 56,600.

boot To start a computer and load its operating system software (usually Windows).

bps See *bits per second*.

bus A superhighway that carries information electronically from one part of the computer to another. The wider and faster (speed is measured in MHz) the bus, the faster your computer. The old ISA bus could carry 16 bits of data at a time; the newer PCI bus can carry 32 bits or 64 bits.

byte A group of eight bits that usually represents a character or a digit. For example, the byte 01000001 represents the letter A.

cable modem A modem that supports high-speed connections to the Internet via a TV cable connection. (To use a cable modem, you must have a cable company that offers Internet service.) See also *modem*.

cache Pronounced "cash," is a temporary storage area in memory or on disk that computer components and various programs use to quickly access data.

CD-ROM (Compact Disc Read-Only Memory) A storage technology that uses the same kind of discs you play in an audio CD player for mass storage of computer data. A single disk can store more than 600MB of information. Pronounced "see-dee-rahm."

cell The box formed by the intersection of a row (1,2,3...) and column (A,B,C...) in a spreadsheet. Each cell has an *address* (such as B12) that defines its column and row. A cell might contain text, a numeric value, or a formula.

chat To talk to another person by typing at your computer. What you type appears on the other person's screen, and what the other person types appears on your screen. You can chat on the Internet or an online service, such as America Online.

click To move the mouse pointer over an object or icon and press and release the mouse button once without moving the mouse.

client Of two computers, the computer that's being served. On the Internet or on a network, your computer is the client, and the computer to which you're connected is the *server*.

Clipboard A temporary storage area that holds text and graphics. The Cut and Copy commands put text or graphics on the Clipboard, replacing the Clipboard's previous contents. The Paste command copies Clipboard data to a document.

COM port Short for COMmunications port. A receptacle, usually at the back of the computer, into which you can plug a serial device, such as a modem, mouse, or serial printer.

command An order that tells the computer what to do. In command-driven programs, you have to press a specific key or type the command to execute it. With menu-driven programs, you select the command from a menu.

computer   Any machine that accepts input (from a user), processes the input, and produces output in some form.

cookie   An electronic identification "badge" that many Web sites store on your computer to help identify you when you return to the site or to record items you buy as you shop online.

CPU (central processing unit)   The computer's brain. See also *microprocessor*.

crash   Failure of a system or program. Usually, you realize that your system has crashed when you can't move the mouse pointer or type anything. The term *crash* is also used to refer to a disk crash (or head crash). A disk crash occurs when the read/write head in the disk drive falls on the disk, possibly destroying data.

cursor   A horizontal line that appears below characters. A cursor acts like the tip of your pencil; anything that you type appears at the cursor. See also *insertion point*.

data   The facts and figures that you enter into the computer and that are stored and used by the computer.

database   A type of computer program used for storing, organizing, and retrieving information. Popular database programs include Access, Approach, and Paradox.

density   A measure of the amount of data that can be stored per square inch of storage area on a disk.

desktop   The main work area in Windows. The desktop displays several icons for running programs and accessing common Windows tools.

desktop publishing (DTP)   A program that enables you to combine text and graphics on the same page and manipulate the text and graphics onscreen. Desktop publishing programs are commonly used to create newsletters, brochures, flyers, résumés, and business cards.

dialog box   An onscreen box that enables you to enter your preferences or supply additional information. You use the dialog box to carry on a "conversation" with the program.

digital camera   A device for taking photographs and storing them as files rather than on film.

directory   A division of a disk or CD, which contains a group of related files. Think of your disk as a filing cabinet and think of each directory as a drawer in the cabinet. Directories are more commonly called *folders*.

disk   A round, flat, magnetic storage medium. A disk works like a cassette tape, storing files permanently so that you can play them back later. The disk itself is typically sealed inside a plastic case, so you rarely see the disk itself. See *floppy disk* and *hard disk*.

disk drive   A device that writes data to a magnetic disk and reads data from the disk. Think of a disk drive as a cassette recorder/player for a computer.

DOS (disk operating system)   DOS, which rhymes with "boss," is an old program that used to provide the necessary instructions for the computer's parts (keyboard, disk drive, central processing unit, display screen, printer, and so on) to function as a unit. Although Windows makes DOS nearly obsolete, you still see its name floating around in Windows.

DOS prompt   An onscreen prompt that indicates DOS is ready to accept a command but provides no clue as to what command you should type. It looks something like C> or C:\.

download   To copy files from another computer to your computer, usually through a modem. See also *upload*.

drag   To hold down the mouse button while moving the mouse. You commonly drag an object to move it or drag over text to select it.

DSL   Short for *digital subscriber line*, DSL uses standard phone lines to achieve data transfer rates of up to 1.5Mbps (9Mbps if you're within two miles of an ADSL connection center). Phone companies hope that advances in DSL technology and availability will help them compete with cable companies for Internet access and entertainment.

DVD (digital versatile disc or digital video disc)   Discs that can store more than seven times as much data as a CD, making them useful for storing full-length movies and complete, multimedia encyclopedias. DVD drives are designed to handle the discs of the future, but are also designed to play discs of the past (CDs).

email   Short for electronic mail, email is a system that enables people to send and receive messages from computer to computer. Email is available on networks, online information services, and the Internet.

emoticon   A text-only symbol commonly used in email messages and chat rooms to quickly express an emotion or physical gesture. :), for instance, represents a smile.

executable file   A program file that can run the program. Executable files end in .BAT, .COM, or .EXE.

expansion slot   An opening on the motherboard (inside the system unit) that enables you to add devices to the system unit, such as an internal modem, sound card, video accelerator, or other enhancement.

extension   The portion of a file's name that comes after the period. Every filename consists of two parts—the base name (before the period) and an extension (after the period). The filename can be up to eight characters in DOS and Windows 3.x (up to 255 characters in Windows 95 and later). The extension (which is optional) can be up to three characters.

family tree program   See *genealogy program*.

field   A blank in a database record, into which you can enter a piece of information (for example, a telephone number, ZIP code, or a person's last name).

file   A collection of information stored as a single unit on a floppy or hard disk. Files always have a filename to identify them.

File Transfer Protocol (FTP)   A set of rules that govern the exchange of files between two computers on the Internet.

fixed disk drive   A disk drive that has a nonremovable disk, as opposed to floppy drives, in which you can insert and remove disks.

floppy disk   A wafer encased in plastic that stores magnetic data (the facts and figures you enter and save). Floppy disks are the disks that you insert in your computer's floppy disk drive (located on the front of the computer).

folder   The Windows name for a directory, a division of a hard disk or CD that stores a group of related files. See also *directory*.

font   Any set of characters of the same *typeface* (design) and *type size* (measured in points). For example, Times New Roman 12-point is a font, Times New Roman is the typeface, and 12-point is the size. (There are 72 points in an inch.)

format (disk)   To prepare a disk for storing data. Formatting creates a map on the disk that tells the operating system how the disk is structured. The operating system uses this map to keep track of where files are stored.

format (document)   To establish the physical layout of a document, including page size, margins, running heads, line spacing, text alignment, graphics placement, and so on.

FTP   See *File Transfer Protocol*.

function keys   The 10 or 12 F keys on the left side of the keyboard, or 12 F keys at the top of the keyboard (some keyboards have both). F keys are numbered F1, F2, F3, and so on, and you can use them to enter specified commands in a program.

geek   1. An overly obsessive computer user, who sacrifices food, sleep, and other pleasantries of life to spend more time at the keyboard. 2. A carnival performer whose act usually includes biting off the head of a live snake or chicken.

genealogy program   Software that helps you lay out and print a family tree. Most commercial genealogy programs provide additional tools for researching your lineage.

gigabyte   A thousand megabytes. See also *megabyte*.

handle   A square that appears on the border of a picture, text box, or other object when the object is selected. You drag a handle to resize an object.

hard disk   A disk drive that comes complete with a nonremovable disk. It acts as a giant floppy disk drive and usually sits inside your computer.

Hayes-compatible   Used to describe a modem that uses the Hayes command set for communicating with other modems over the phone lines. Hayes-compatible modems usually are preferred over other modems because most modems and telecommunications software are designed to be Hayes-compatible.

347

history list   A list of the names and addresses of Web sites and pages you accessed with your Web browser. Your Web browser keeps a history list, so you can quickly return to sites even if you've forgotten a site's address.

HTML   Short for Hypertext Markup Language, the code used to create documents for the World Wide Web. These codes tell the Web browser how to display the text (titles, headings, lists, and so on), insert anchors that link this document to other documents, and control character formatting (by making it bold or italic).

icon   A graphic image onscreen that represents another object, such as a file on a disk.

IM   Short for "Instant Message," a private message that reaches the recipient almost immediately after a user sends it. IMs are commonly used on America Online to communicate privately with other users.

insertion point   A blinking vertical line used in most Windows word processors to indicate the place where any characters that you type are inserted. An insertion point is the equivalent of a cursor.

integrated program   A program that combines the features of several programs, such as a word processor, spreadsheet, database, and communications program.

interface   A link between two objects, such as a computer and a modem. The link between a computer and a person is called a user interface, and refers to the way a person communicates with the computer or a program.

Internet   A group of computers all over the world that are connected to one another. Using your computer and a modem, you can connect to these other computers and tap their resources. You can view pictures, listen to sounds, watch video clips, play games, chat with other people, and even shop.

Internet service provider   The company that you pay in order to connect to their computer and get on the Internet.

IRC   Short for Internet Relay Chat, this is the most popular way to chat with others on the Internet. With an IRC client (chat program), you connect to an IRC server, where you are presented with a list of available chat rooms. You can enter a room and then start exchanging messages with others in the room.

ISDN (Integrated Services Digital Network)   ISDN is a system that enables your computer, using a special ISDN modem, to perform digital data transfers over special phone lines. Non-ISDN modems use analog signals, which are designed to carry voices, not data. ISDN connections can transfer data at a rate of up to 128Kbs, compared to about 56Kbps for the fastest analog modems.

ISP   See *Internet service provider*.

keyboard   The main input device for most computers. You use the keyboard to type and to enter commands.

kilobyte (K)   A unit for measuring the amount of data. A kilobyte is equivalent to 1,024 bytes (each byte is a character).

laptop   A small computer that's light enough to carry. Notebook computers and subnotebooks are even lighter.

load   To read data or program instructions from disk and place them in the computer's memory, where the computer can use the data or instructions.

mail merge   A feature of most word processing programs that allows you to link an address book with a form letter or mailing label document to generate a set of personalized form letters and/or mailing labels.

megabyte   A standard unit used to measure the storage capacity of a disk and the amount of computer memory. A megabyte is 1,048,576 bytes (1,000 kilobytes). This is roughly equivalent to 500 pages of double-spaced text. Megabyte is commonly abbreviated as M, MB, or Mbyte.

memory   An electronic storage area inside the computer, used to temporarily store data or program instructions when the computer is using them. Also referred to as RAM.

menu   A list of commands or instructions displayed onscreen. Menus organize commands and make a program easier to use.

microprocessor   Sometimes called the central processing unit (CPU) or processor, this chip is the computer's brain; it does all the calculations for the computer.

modem   An acronym for MOdulator/DEModulator. A modem is a piece of hardware that converts incoming signals (from a phone line, cable service, or other source) into signals that a PC can understand and converts outgoing signals from the PC into a form that can be transmitted.

monitor   A television-like screen on which the computer displays information.

morph   To gradually transform one image into another or distort an original image in a creative manner.

mouse   A handheld device that you move across the desktop to move an arrow, called a mouse pointer, across the screen. Used instead of the keyboard to select and move items (such as text or graphics), execute commands, and perform other tasks.

MS-DOS (Microsoft Disk Operating System)   See *DOS*.

multitasking   The process of performing two computer tasks at the same time. For example, you might be printing a document from your word processor while checking your email in Prodigy.

newsgroup   An Internet bulletin board for users who share common interests. There are thousands of newsgroups ranging from body art to pets (to body art with pets). Newsgroups let you post messages and read messages from other users.

notebook   A portable computer that weighs between four and eight pounds.

online   Connected, turned on, and ready to accept information. Used most often in reference to a printer or modem.

online service   A network that allows members to obtain information, communicate, and get files via a modem connection. Common online services include America Online, Prodigy, and CompuServe.

pane   A portion of a window. Most programs display panes, so you can view two different parts of a document at the same time.

parallel port   A connector used to plug a device, usually a printer, into the computer.

partition   A section of a disk drive that's assigned a letter. A hard disk drive can be divided (or partitioned) into one or more drives, which your computer refers to as drive C, drive D, drive E, and so on. The actual hard disk drive is called the physical drive, and each partition is called a logical drive; however, these terms don't matter much—the drives still look like letters to you.

patch   A set of program instructions designed to fix a programming bug or add capabilities to a program. On the Internet, you can often download patches for programs to update the program.

path   The route that the computer travels from the root directory to any subdirectories when locating a file.

PC card   An expansion card that's about the size of a credit card, though thicker, and slides into a slot on the side of the notebook computer. PC cards enable you to quickly install RAM or a hard disk drive, modem, CD-ROM drive, network card, or game port, without having to open the notebook computer.

peripheral   A device that's attached to the computer but is not essential for the basic operation of the computer. The system unit is the central part of the computer. Any devices attached to the system unit are considered *peripheral*, including a printer, modem, or joystick. Some manufacturers consider the monitor and keyboard to be peripheral, too.

personal finance program   Software that helps you write checks, reconcile your accounts, track investments, calculate loan payments, budget, and perform other money management tasks.

pixel   A dot of light that appears on the computer screen. A collection of pixels forms characters and images on the screen.

PnP   Short for plug-and-play, PnP enables you to install expansion cards in your computer without having to set special switches. You plug it in, and it works.

port replicator   A slimmed-down version of a docking station.

ports The receptacles at the back of the computer. They get their name from the ports where ships pick up and deliver cargo. In this case, the ports enable information to enter and leave the system unit.

PPP Short for Point-to-Point Protocol, a language that computers use to talk to one another. What's important is that when you choose an Internet service provider, you get the right connection—SLIP or PPP.

program A group of instructions that tells the computer what to do. Typical programs are word processors, spreadsheets, databases, and games.

prompt A computer's way of asking for more information. The computer basically looks at you and says, "Tell me something." In other words, the computer is *prompting* you or prodding you for information or a command.

protocol A group of communications settings that control the transfer of data between two computers.

pull-down menu A menu that appears at the top of the screen, listing various options. The menu is not visible until you select it from the menu bar. The menu then drops down, covering a small part of the screen.

Quick Launch Toolbar A toolbar that's nested in the Windows taskbar and provides convenient access to the programs you use most often. Microsoft introduced the Quick Launch toolbar in later versions of Windows 95 and kept it as a standard feature in Windows 98. See also *toolbar*.

random-access memory (RAM) A collection of chips your computer uses to store data and programs temporarily. RAM is measured in kilobytes and megabytes. In general, more RAM means that you can run more powerful programs and more programs at once. Also called *memory*.

record Used by databases to denote a unit of related information contained in one or more fields, such as an individual's name, address, and phone number.

Recycle Bin A virtual trash can into which Windows places files and folders when you choose to delete them. The Recycle Bin is a temporary storage area that acts as a safety net for deleted files. If you delete a file or folder by mistake, you can usually retrieve it from the Recycle Bin.

ROM BIOS See *BIOS*.

scanner A device that converts images, such as photographs or printed text, into an electronic format that a computer can use. Many stores use a special type of scanner to read bar code labels into the cash register.

screen saver A program that displays a moving picture on your computer screen when the computer is inactive. Screen savers are typically used as decorative novelties and to prevent passersby from snooping.

Screen Tip See *tooltip*.

scroll   To move text up and down or right and left on a computer screen.

server   Of two computers, the computer that's serving the other computer. On the Internet or on a network, your computer is the *client*, and the computer to which you're connected is the *server*.

shareware   Computer programs that you can use for free, and then pay for if you decide to continue using them. Many programmers start marketing their programs as shareware, relying on the honesty and goodwill of computer users for their income. That's why most of these programmers have day jobs.

shortcut   A cloned version of an icon that points to a document or program on your computer. Shortcuts enable you to place programs and documents in more than one convenient location on your computer.

software   Any instructions that tell your computer (the hardware) what to do. There are two types of software: operating system software and application software. *Operating system software* (such as Windows) gets your computer up and running. *Application software* enables you to do something useful, such as type a letter or chase lemmings.

spreadsheet   A program used for keeping schedules and calculating numeric results. Common spreadsheets include Lotus 1-2-3, Microsoft Excel, and Quattro Pro.

Start button   The button in the lower-right corner of the opening Windows screen, which provides access to all the programs on your computer.

status bar   The area at the bottom of a program window that shows you what's going on as you work. A status bar might show the page and line number where the insertion point is positioned and indicate whether you are typing in overstrike or insert mode.

style   A collection of specifications for formatting text. A style might include information for the font, size, style, margins, and spacing. Applying a style to text automatically formats the text according to the style's specifications.

system tray   The area on the right end of the taskbar that displays the current time and icons for programs that are running in the background.

table   A feature in most word processing programs that helps you align text in rows and columns.

taskbar   A fancy name for the button bar at the bottom of the Windows desktop. The taskbar includes the *Start button* (on the left) and *system tray* (on the right).

TCP/IP (Transmission Control Protocol/Internet Protocol)   A set of rules that govern the transfer of data over the Internet.

toolbar   A strip of buttons typically displayed near the top of a program window, below the menu bar. The toolbar contains buttons that you can click to enter common commands, enabling you to bypass the menu system.

tooltip   A small text box that displays the name of a button when you rest the mouse pointer on the button. Tooltips help you figure out what a button does, when you cannot figure it out from the picture. Also known as a *Screen Tip*.

undo   A feature in most programs that enables you to reverse one or more actions. For example, if you delete a paragraph by mistake, you can enter the Undo command to get it back.

uninterruptible power supply (UPS)   A battery-powered device that protects against power spikes and power outages. If the power goes out, the UPS continues supplying power to the computer so that you can continue working or safely turn off your computer without losing data.

upload   To send data to another computer, usually through a modem and a telephone line or over a network connection.

URL (Uniform Resource Locator)   An address for an Internet site.

USB (Universal Serial Bus)   The ultimate in Plug-and-Play technology, USB enables you to install devices without turning off your computer or using a screwdriver. USB enables you to connect up to 127 devices to a single port.

utility   A program designed to optimize, protect, or maintain a computer rather than perform a task for the user. Utilities include backup programs, antivirus software, and memory optimizers.

virtual   Not real. Virtual worlds on the Internet are three-dimensional computer-generated areas that you can navigate but never physically enter... unless, of course, you're Keanu Reeves or Sandra Bullock.

virtual memory   Disk storage used as RAM (memory).

virus   A program that attaches itself to other files on a floppy or hard disk, duplicates itself without the user's knowledge, and might cause the computer to do strange and sometimes destructive things, such as formatting your hard drive.

wallpaper   A graphic design that appears as the background for the Windows desktop.

Web   See *World Wide Web*.

Web browser   A program that enables you to navigate the World Wide Web (the most popular feature of the Internet). See also *World Wide Web*.

windows   A way of displaying information in different parts of the screen. Often used as a nickname for Microsoft Windows.

word processor   A program that enables you to enter, edit, format, and print text.

word wrap   A feature that automatically moves a word to the next line if the word won't fit at the end of the current line.

World Wide Web A part of the Internet that consists of multimedia documents that are interconnected by links. To move from one document to another, you click a link, which might appear as highlighted text or as a small picture or icon. The Web contains text, sound and video clips, pictures, catalogs, and much, much more. See also *Web browser*.

Index

375